THE BOXERS OF WALES
Volume 7:
North, Mid and West Wales

GARETH JONES

ST DAVID'S PRESS
Cardiff

Published in Wales by St. David's Press, an imprint of

Ashley Drake Publishing Ltd
PO Box 733
Cardiff
CF14 7ZY

www.st-davids-press.wales

First Impression – 2021

ISBN
Paperback 978-1-902719-79-7
eBook 978-1-902719-98-6

© Ashley Drake Publishing Ltd 2021
Text © Gareth Jones 2021

The right of Gareth Jones to be identified as the author of this work has been asserted in accordance with the Copyright Design and Patents Act of 1988.

Every effort has been made to contact copyright holders.However, the publishers will be glad to rectify in future editions any inadvertent omissions brought to their attention.

Ashley Drake Publishing Ltd hereby exclude all liability to the extent permitted by law for any errors or omissions in this book and for any loss, damage or expense (whether direct or indirect) suffered by a third party relying on any information contained in this book.

All rights reserved. No part of this publication may be reproduced, stored in a retrieval system, or transmitted, in any form or by any means without the prior permission of the publishers.

British Library Cataloguing-in-Publication Data.
A CIP catalogue for this book is available from the British Library.

Typeset by Prepress Plus, India (www.prepressplus.in)
Cover Designed by Welsh Books Council, Aberystwyth

CONTENTS

Acknowledgements   iv
Introduction   v

Jake ANTHONY	1	Alan JONES	99
Jim CRAWFORD	4	Dai 'Farmer' JONES	102
Nipper Pat DALY	7	Emrys JONES	105
Dave DAVIES	14	Henry JONES	108
John DAVIES	18	Ivor JONES	111
Ocky DAVIES	22	Mike JONES	114
Steve DAVIES	26	Stanley JONES	116
Tommy DAVIES	29	Chris LAWSON	119
Zack DAVIES	32	Dudley LEWIS	122
Phil DICKS	35	Eddie LLOYD	126
Tom DORAN	37	Willie LLOYD	129
Angelo DRAGONE	41	Terry MAGEE	133
Paul ECONOMIDES	44	Mickey McDONAGH	136
Tiger ELLIS	48	Iorrie MORRIS	139
Dale EVANS	52	Robert PEEL	141
Danny EVANS	57	Bryn PHILLIPS	144
Kevin EVANS	60	Dennis POWELL	147
Mark EVANS	63	James PROBERT	152
Rocky FELICIELLO	65	Billy QUINLAN	154
Bob FIELDING	68	Reg QUINLAN	158
George FIELDING	72	Tim REDMAN	161
Leon FINDLAY	74	Archie RULE	163
Scott GAMMER	76	Ned TURNER	166
Carl GIZZI	81	Allan WILKINS	169
Ray HOOD	87	Johnny WILLIAMS	172
Chris JENKINS	89	Craig WINTER	177
Kevin JENKINS	97		

Supporting Cast   180
Bibliography   184

ACKNOWLEDGEMENTS

There is one group of people who deserve particular thanks for their contribution to this book and its predecessors in the *Boxers of Wales* collection: the fighters themselves. Not only have their efforts, achievements and disappointments provided the content, but their ready accessibility and unvarnished honesty stand in stark contrast to so many modern athletes, guarded by an army of PR bouncers and conditioned to regurgitate tired clichés and bland sound-bites.

I have appreciated the co-operation and, indeed, friendship of so many across nearly half a century covering the sport and it has been heartening that those from the early years have been so welcoming when contacted decades later.

Of course, many older warriors have heard the final bell, while even more lived and died before I saw my first punches thrown. Invariably, their families and friends have stepped up to the plate to slake my thirst for knowledge. To them, too, I tip my metaphorical hat.

A nod also goes to the hard-working officers and staff at the British Boxing Board of Control and its Welsh Area Council, along with those at the Welsh Amateur Boxing Association.

Members of online local history groups have supplied information and, often, introductions to old-timers' relatives. And individuals like Wynford Jones, Cyril Thomas, Paul Boyce, Dave Furnish, Graham Brockway, Gwyndaf Evans, Darren Wilson, Nick Hodges, Hywel 'Cass' Davies and record-compiler extraordinaire Harold Alderman MBE have all done their bit.

Most photos included came from the boxers and those close to them, but I should acknowledge the professional snappers who have let me use their work: Huw Evans Picture Agency (www.huwevansimages.com), Wayne Hankins, Kris Agland, Lawrence Lustig/Matchroom, Philip Sharkey and the late Peter Westall.

My publisher, Ashley Drake, who first suggested this project over coffee at the National Eisteddfod in Cardiff in 2008, has given constant support.

Finally, to mark the completion of the series I must proclaim my heartfelt gratitude to the anonymous donor of the kidney I received almost 18 years ago. Without that selfless generosity and the skill and dedication of the transplant surgeons and their team at the University Hospital of Wales, it is unlikely any of these books would have been written.

INTRODUCTION

Some might wonder why such a wide and disparate area is shoe-horned into one book, while comparatively small geographic regions have their individual volumes. The answer lies in a single word: population.

Not only do two-thirds of the people in modern Wales live within the confines of the old Glamorgan and Monmouthshire, they are crammed together in the sort of industrial conurbations that have produced most of our boxers.

There may well have been just as much talent in the countryside, but the opportunities to display it were lacking. Brawny farm workers might have matched the miners and steelworkers for physical prowess, but few would have had the means or the dedication to travel long distances to the nearest gym. And, even today, those facilities available are unlikely to provide the variety of sparring and regular competition taken for granted in their urban equivalents.

It is no coincidence that the Amman Valley, similar in make-up to its coal-rich cousins to the east, provides a disproportionate number of the practitioners profiled between these covers. But there have been a significant number of champions from the more isolated parts as well and they will be found here: some household names, others whose achievements might come as something of a surprise to the younger members of their own families.

Boxing (or prizefighting) was hardly unknown to rural Wales. Brecon, Knighton and Wrexham were among the race tracks which staged fisticuffs as a bonus attraction for those who followed the horses. And there is a long tradition of bareknuckle battles among travellers in the area, with such luminaries as Jack Hearn, Chasey Price 'The Blackbird' and Black Bob Evans, while Bartley Gorman, widely renowned as 'King of the Gypsies', was brought up near Welshpool.

As well as chronicling their ring prowess, let me introduce you to the fighter who gave his name to a character in *Under Milk Wood*, as well as the old-timer who used his pet dogs to teach road safety to generations of schoolchildren. And the teenage sensation whose Welsh origins were unsuspected by most of those who cheered him to a world ranking at just 16. I hope their stories give you as much pleasure in the reading as they gave me in writing about them.

GARETH JONES
September 2021

THE BOXERS OF WALES

Johnny Vaughan, boxer, manager and promoter, was the force of nature behind the success of the sport in the Amman Valley between the wars. He is seen here with four of his Welsh champions (clockwise from bottom left): Ginger Jones, Danny Evans, Randy Jones and Billy Quinlan.

JAKE ANTHONY
(1998-)

Welsh Super-Middleweight Challenger 2019

The lad from Ammanford took up boxing after watching Joe Calzaghe on television. Seeing him hand out a masterclass to Jeff Lacy piqued the boy's interest; when the Newbridge man triumphed in a thrilling collision with Mikkel Kessler the die was cast. Nine-year-old Jake Anthony wanted to try for himself.

So his father, Nigel, took him to the Towy ABC gym, just five minutes from their home at Saron. He learned the basics from Paul Davies, father of Welsh light-heavy champion Shon, and his talent was soon clear, with Welsh titles at both schools and junior level; there might have been more had he not repeatedly run into outstanding Rhymney Valley southpaw Kyran Jones.

The ring ran parallel with rugby for a while until a broken nose while playing flanker for Amman United Youth meant missing a bout the following week. A choice had to be made: the oval ball was binned and boxing stood alone at centre stage.

As a senior Anthony, now trained by former pro Stanley Jones, reached the national semi-finals only to be beaten by the experienced Jamie Evans, from Merthyr, and when he lost a controversial verdict on a North Wales club show, he decided to abandon the amateur game and earn a few bob to supplement his wages as a heating engineer. He signed up with solicitor Richie Garner as manager; by now he was being trained by his father, who, despite never having boxed, had learned the ropes alongside his son – another parallel with hero Calzaghe!

Jake's introduction to this new world was pretty standard, with a series of unthreatening journeymen lined up to provide the education needed. Yet it was not as straightforward as that sounds. The record books show that

Jake Anthony

Jake (left) and Somerset's Liam Hunt get together after the best victory of the Welshman's career to date

Italian-born debut foe Victor Edagha had lost all 21 bouts before facing Anthony at Swansea's LC2. Those same sources describe him as "orthodox"; in fact, the ungainly Edagha is one of the most stylistically eccentric performers on the British scene, but Jake managed to solve the conundrum.

His next two opponents were less problematic, but then, before his first six-rounder, a late pull-out left him facing an unexpected challenge in the shape of Weston-super-Mare's Liam Hunt, who had won seven of his 10 contests. No matter: Anthony produced his best performance to date, dropping Hunt with body punches and dominating for a wide points win.

A couple more four-round decisions kept the ball rolling until he was handed a shot at the vacant Welsh super-middleweight throne on a Chris Sanigar promotion broadcast live on Welsh-language channel S4C on September 13, 2019. Two-time national amateur champion Morgan Jones was in the other corner.

It all began so well at a packed LC2. Jones, having suffered upset losses in his previous two outings, lacked belief and Jake went in hooking from the off. His all-out aggression paid in the second when a series of blows to the head, culminating in a thumping right hook, dropped Morgan in a neutral corner. He rose uncertainly, his low left hand offering a target, but the West Walian was unable to capitalise in the limited time remaining in the session.

The third continued Anthony's supremacy, but Jones gradually started to settle. By the fifth, his left lead, while carrying little power, was paying regular visits to Jake's face and interrupting his flow.

That proved the template for the remainder of the fight. Anthony kept seeking to destroy, but was rarely able to land cleanly as Jones kept on the move. A gash over the Aberdare man's left eye in the fifth needed medical clearance, but never really affected its now confident owner.

Jake produced a cluster of solid shots in the sixth, but Morgan took them without blinking, underlining the new order of things. Not until the bout's final 15 seconds, as Anthony hurled punches in desperation, did Jones look troubled.

Referee Martin Williams, hardly seen during a clean and technically skilled contest, had Jones two points clear at the end. The announcement, naturally, went down badly with Jake's backers: one well lubricated fan even berated ringside co-commentator Enzo Maccarinelli, demanding to know how much the former world champion had been paid for the decision. Enzo, who actually had Jake in front, showed commendable restraint.

Anthony floors Morgan Jones, but it was not enough

The anger inside the ropes, though unfuelled by drink, was equally palpable and similarly unfounded. Manager Garner, already infuriated – with much more justification – by an earlier decision against Angelo Dragone, lambasted the third man, Mr Williams having previous with a disputed ruling against another of Garner's charges, Newport's Craig Woodruff.

In truth, there was little between the two warriors; whoever had his arm raised, the loser would have been aggrieved. And, at 21, Jake had time on his side. The arrival of Covid-19, of course, ate into that reservoir of opportunity and it was two years before he had the chance to box again.

On the first post-pandemic promotion in Wales, Anthony announced his return with a third-round stoppage of dangerous Hungarian veteran Norbert Szekeres. The show is back on the road.

JIM CRAWFORD
(1910-1971)

- Welsh Featherweight Challenger 1930
- British Bantamweight Contender 1931

Jim Crawford

The miner's son from Pentre Broughton was too good for his own good. His combative skills pulled in the punters and had promoters salivating over the cash they handed over. That's when a boxer needs a good manager.

Unfortunately, the people guiding James Henry Crawford were equally dazzled by the possibilities of regular paydays and ignored advice – from the legendary Jimmy Wilde, among others – to put a foot on the brake from time to time.

Young Jim was still at school when he first laced up the gloves on Bert Hughes's booth, but his exploits had made him something of a celebrity in the Wrexham area even before his first appearance as a 16-year-old at the Liverpool Stadium. He drew with more experienced fellow-Welshman Ben Doyle, from Shotton, in the iconic Pudsey Street arena that became his second home.

There were early setbacks: a disputed decision loss to ringwise Sheffielder Dickie Inkles, before future world flyweight ruler Jackie Brown stopped him with body shots – although Crawford lasted the course in two further meetings with the talented Mancunian. But the defeats were hugely outnumbered by victories as the Welshman built a reputation among the knowledgeable Scouse fight followers.

Naturally, the growing number of North Walians heading across the Mersey to cheer him on were keen to see their young idol on home ground, so Coedpoeth businessman Stan Owens began staging shows at Wrexham's Drill Hall. Across the border there were similar stirrings in Oswestry and Shrewsbury. And they all added to the teenager's workload.

Twice in three weeks Crawford fought 15-rounders (a draw and a loss) against Abercrave-born phenomenon Nipper Pat Daly, even younger and also in danger of burn-out. But the treadmill ground on. Crawford was invited to London to show his wares, comprehensively outpointing Frenchman Georges Gourdy on a National Sporting Club promotion at Holborn Stadium.

It was after this contest that former world flyweight champion Wilde, while impressed, was shocked to discover that Jim, still only 18, had already had nearly 50 fights and warned not to push him too quickly. As with Wilde's similar comments regarding Daly, the advice was ignored. Big brother Tom, a fixture in the Crawford corner despite losing a leg in a childhood accident, was among those caught up in the excitement.

Jim in retirement – and still smiling

Six weeks (and four fights) later the Wrexham teenager was back in The Smoke - at the shortest of notice. When former world bantam king Teddy Baldock cried off sick on the afternoon of his bout with Parisian import Robert Tassin at London's Olympia, the call was made to North Wales. Crawford jumped into the first available train and arrived at the hall with the show already underway. Despite the rush, he outpointed Tassin, the French featherweight champion, over 15 rounds. It was his 28th and final action of 1929.

Yet he was back in the ring on New Year's Day, halting George Mainwaring, from Llysfaen, in two at Wrexham Drill Hall and claiming the North Wales featherweight title. Thoughts of greater glory were born. The reigning national champion was Brynmor Jones, a Rhondda-born, Ammanford-based campaigner known to one and all as 'Ginger'. And he was enticed to Liverpool to face Crawford in a clash made at 9st 2lb, a couple of pounds above the divisional limit.

But Jones came in three-and-a-half pounds over the target weight; Jim agreed to go through with the bout, but was conceding five pounds as well as age and top-level experience. From early on Crawford's face was a mask of blood and in the fourth Ginger's ring smarts brought further anguish, a low blow – ignored by the referee – had Jim in trouble and Jones stormed in to floor him. An uppercut in the eighth sent the tiring Northerner back to the canvas and a repeat in the following session brought the towel floating to the rescue.

Crawford's manager, Tom Felton, was not deterred by this disaster and persuaded the Welsh authorities that his charge had been competitive enough to merit a shot at the title, where at least the weight discrepancy would not be so great. Jim restored some self-belief with a second-round demolition of two-weight German champion

Karl Schulze, before tackling Jones again on home ground at the Racecourse on August 4, 1930.

Much to the satisfaction of Liverpool Stadium boss Johnny Best, who promoted the event, a Bank Holiday crowd in the thousands turned up to cheer the local hero. It made no difference. Crawford, looking nervous, was dropped for two lengthy counts in the third and another in the next, only courage and grit enabling him to survive. Jim began to score with his left lead in the middle sessions, but lacked the power to take control, while Ginger was frequently able to manoeuvre the challenger so that he had the sun in his eyes. Jones's points victory was never in doubt.

Crawford dropped to bantamweight and enjoyed a run of success against men his own size, yet even then was allowed to go ahead with a 12-rounder against Benny Sharkey in Leeds despite the Newcastle-based Scot weighing half a stone more. Jim used his speed to keep out of serious trouble, but lost a clear decision.

Apart from that blemish, he did well enough to be included in a tournament to find the next British title challenger at 8st 6lb and Best returned to the Racecourse for a Northern section semi-final against Wheatley Hill's Pat Gorman. Jim quickly established control with a succession of two-fisted assaults, but the Durham miner was merely a slow starter and the second saw him spear his left into Jim's face with regularity, increasing his pace in the third. In the fourth Crawford became more and more erratic and when the bell rang he threw a couple of extra punches, which brought an immediate disqualification.

Crawford stopped Gorman in a rematch in Leeds, but his wider title dreams were over. Domestically, however, he rebounded from a points defeat to former Welsh bantam boss Stan Jehu with a thrilling victory over Jehu's conqueror, Terence Morgan, though the bout was over 12 rounds rather than 15, so not recognised as for the belt. But when Jim avenged the Jehu loss, Wrexham promoter Matt Knight agreed terms for Morgan to defend in Wrexham the following month. It never happened.

In fact, the Pentre Broughton man's ring story was nearing its end. He was hammered in four rounds by Mottee 'Kid' Singh, a visitor from British Guiana, and then faced local rival George Fielding, billed for the North Wales feather crown. Fielding knocked him out in 12 and, with doctors warning that eye damage meant he would risk his sight by continuing, Crawford heeded their counsel and called it a day.

NIPPER PAT DALY
(1913-1988)

There are no honours listed at the top of this chapter. No surprise, that, as Pat Daly never even contested a title. In addition, he never once laced up a glove in a Welsh ring. But he was nonetheless a Welshman and his incredible tale demands his inclusion in this book.

Back in September 1929, before the alphabet boys and their politically skewed ratings, *Ring* magazine listed Daly as the 10th best bantamweight in the world. He was just 16. By his 18th birthday, his career was over.

The story begins in Ireland. Denis Daley and his wife, Honorah, followed so many in leaving their poor and hungry homeland for a better life, in their case to London. It was in the Marylebone area of the city that son Patsy was born, growing up in the slums behind the Edgware Road. As a teenager, he worked as a road sweeper and had a stint in the Army before he and brother Dinny sought a new life in West Wales.

They found jobs in a local pit, while lodging with miner and Boer War veteran Will Evans in Abercrave. Will's two daughters helped make the Cockney boys feel at home and, in due course, there were two weddings. Patsy and his bride, May, went to live at Brookland Terrace, where their first child was born. He was christened Patrick, after his father, but known in the family by his middle name, Clifford. The wider world would soon call him 'Nipper'.

With the outbreak of World War I, Patsy, as a reservist, was quickly called back into uniform, although his service in the trenches was curtailed by a shoulder wound which saw him discharged. Still able to cope at the colliery, he went home to his wife and son. But in 1918, with May expecting a second baby, they moved to join the rest of the Daley clan in Marylebone.

The new addition, Con, tragically died shortly after his first birthday. His parents, perhaps seeking to escape the memories, headed for Canada and the small Alberta mining town of Wayne, where May at least

Nipper Pat Daly

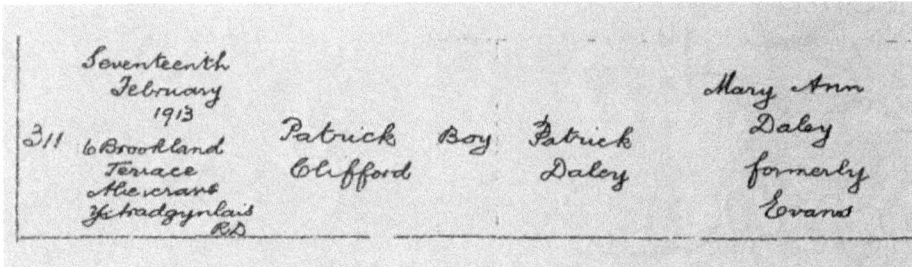

Pat's birth certificate

had familiar Welsh-speaking company in the hundreds of emigrants who had gone before them in the search for employment.

Young Cliff was enthralled by the "bunkhouse fights" his father helped stage and began to imagine the day when he might be personally involved. But the Depression was hitting the coal industry and Patsy – now with two more sons, Bob and Kenneth, to provide for – began to look elsewhere for the family's future.

A trip Down Under convinced him that neither Australia nor New Zealand held the answer and the Daley crew set sail once more. They arrived back in London and, after a period with Patsy's sister, settled in a house on Hatton Street, not far from their old haunts. It was also a short stroll from the Empire School of Arms, run by the self-styled 'Professor' Andrew Newton.

Once Cliff heard about its existence, he began to beg his father to take him there. Eventually, Patsy gave in and his nine-year-old son was immediately hooked by the atmosphere of the barn-like edifice, full of punchbags and shelves stacked with boxing gloves and medicine balls, with men hard at it sparring, doing floor work and swinging Indian clubs, all observed by the likes of Jack Dempsey, Jack Johnson and Ted 'Kid' Lewis, via their pictures on the walls.

The proprietor peered over his thick moustache at the new arrival as he swapped blows with a couple of the regular inhabitants. What he saw convinced the 'Professor' that he had someone special on his hands. And neither he nor the boy intended to waste any time in earning some money.

Within months Pat, as he was called outside the family, had won his first contest, staged at the gym itself, and he gradually became a familiar figure in London rings. But it was an exhibition he boxed at an event in Hertfordshire, topped by former world bantam king Joe Bowker, which earned him a wider audience. John Murray, the editor of *Boxing*, was referee for the night; he and renowned trainer Jack Goodwin were amazed at what they witnessed.

"The kid appeared to know pretty nearly everything there is to be known about the boxing game," wrote Murray later, recalling that he and Goodwin had agreed that this was the cleverest young boxer they had ever seen. At the time, Pat was still nine days short of his 11th birthday.

The North of England had its own prodigy in Johnny Summers, from Leeds, and a showdown was inevitable. They met three times in two days, in London and Kent, and Nipper Pat Daly – mentor Newton had begun to bill him thus, losing the 'e' from

Daley in the process – won all three six-rounders. It was the sort of insane schedule which was to bedevil his career. The exploitation was all the more obvious when the 'Professor' handed him 13s for his efforts; Pat later discovered his trainer had been paid almost £10.

When he made his big-time bow at the popular Premierland arena in Whitechapel, Daly, now 12, learned another lesson. Despite giving away a chunk of weight, he floored and outboxed East End prospect Billy Boulger, only to see his rival's hand raised at the end. Boulger was, after all, managed by Joe Morris, the man who made the matches at Premierland!

His next two setbacks came in the same hall, one via disqualification for an alleged low blow and the other because of a cut eye. In each case, Pat was clearly ahead at the time. But they were exceptions. He enjoyed regular success there, becoming a firm favourite. His displays were impressing the experts, too: *Boxing* predicted that "we shall not have to look elsewhere when we are seeking world champions some four or five years hence." In fact, by then Daly would have hung up the gloves for good.

When Pat left school at 14, he wanted to continue his education, but that was vetoed by Newton, who insisted that the ring must come first. He invariably found himself up against bigger opponents and there were already warnings about the dangers of overworking a body still not fully developed. The 'Professor' derided them and Patsy and May, glad of the regular supplements to the family income, were happy to go along with him.

The wonder boy's growing reputation meant that provincial promoters wanted a piece of the action and Nipper showed off his skills as far afield as Nottingham and Leeds. And he kept on winning.

His first appearance at the legendary Liverpool Stadium saw him cheered to the echo as he took all 15 rounds against popular local Lud Abella and he charmed Brummie sportsmen by outclassing future British flyweight king Bert Kirby, now trained in London by Cardiff's famous 'Singing Boxer', Fred Dyer. There were even a couple of triumphant visits to Germany.

When still well short of his 15th birthday, Daly sparred with Mickey Walker, in town to defend his world middleweight crown against Scot Tommy Milligan. After their exchanges, the American told his manager – Jack 'Doc' Kearns, the brains behind Jack Dempsey – that

Nipper with mother May

Nipper Pat with his controversial mentor, 'Professor' Andrew Newton

the kid had landed more punches in their brief encounter than many had managed in a 15-round fight.

For all his travels, London was still Pat's (and Newton's) main source of revenue. There were outings at the Alcazar, a fake Moorish palace in Edmonton, in front of the toffs at the National Sporting Club's premises at Covent Garden and, of course, at his beloved Premierland, where he began to top the bill. That meant boxing a round for each year of his 15-year-old life, and, while these lasted two minutes rather than three, it was still a big ask for an adolescent, especially as it occurred three or four times a month.

Boxing editor Murray, so impressed with the 10-year-old Daly, was now becoming worried by the boy's workload. Repeating his frequent assertion that Pat was the country's best prospect for years, Murray said it would be "a crime and a national disaster if he is allowed to be cut to pieces before he has even approached his prime."

The journalist's plea was lost in the clamour to cash in on the teenage marvel and, as Pat kept on winning, Murray changed his views completely and apologised to the 'Professor' for the implied criticism. In retrospect, he was right the first time.

The Albert Hall saw Daly widely outpoint Nicolas Petit-Biquet, a Belgian who had beaten some of Britain's best and went on to reign twice as European bantam champion. It prompted further acclaim from the ringside press, though Swansea-born Trevor Wignall asked in the *Daily Express*, "Is it wise to work him as he is being worked?"

Another Welsh columnist handing out praise was Jimmy Wilde, in the *News of the World*, calling him "an exceptional youngster". Some were beginning to compare Daly with Wilde himself, although Pat lacked the power that earned the Rhondda man the unforgettable nickname of 'The Ghost with a Hammer in his Hand'.

Nipper was now going in with the best. He outpointed once-beaten Dubliner Packey McFarland and East Ender Dick Corbett, later to enjoy two reigns over the bantamweights of Britain and the Empire. But the growing lad found that by the time he had decent claims to contest a Lonsdale Belt he would be struggling to make the weight.

It happened at flyweight, and then again at bantam, but not before the mouthwatering possibility of a fight in the land of his birth, where his precocious achievements were being closely monitored. Newton, aided and abetted by Bill Allen, of the *South Wales Echo*, issued a challenge to reigning Welsh 8st 6lb ruler Danny Dando, of Merthyr. But no Welsh promoters took the bait; they seemed to feel they couldn't afford the sort of purse needed to put on the teenager who was packing them in in London.

Instead, it was back to Premierland for Daly, who climbed off the deck to outpoint Alf 'Kid' Pattenden, a Londoner who had been British bantam boss until losing to the great Teddy Baldock two months earlier. His appearance in the *Ring* rankings, supported by the accounts of witnesses like Jack Kearns, prompted the offer of a trip to the US, with Tom O'Rourke, the New Yorker who had promoted Wilde's final showdown with Pancho Villa, offering £1,000 to buy Pat's contract. The 'Professor' turned it down, along with interest from Australia and South Africa.

But there were lucrative possibilities at home and the youngster was lined up to tackle British featherweight champion Johnny Cuthbert in a non-title clash – the newly created Board of Control had ruled that nobody under 21 could contest a national belt.

Nipper (left) faces Ludwig Minow in Germany

There was still a prize for the winner: former world fly ruler Fidel La Barba, now also a nine-stoner, was in Paris and Europe-based American promoter Jeff Dickson was ready to pay Pat a four-figure sum to face him at the Albert Hall. Victory over the outstanding, but fading Californian would open all sorts of doors.

First he had to deal with Cuthbert – and the scales. Daly had struggled to make 9st 4lb for a fight six days earlier and now had to lose a further three pounds to meet the contracted weight for the Sheffielder. He wore five sweaters and a sheepskin jacket as he worked out and somehow shed the surplus, but it took its toll.

Nevertheless Pat, with a height and reach advantage, controlled the first seven rounds at Holborn Stadium on October 10, 1929, but in the eighth his concentration faltered and the champion pounced, landing a big right which sent his tormentor crashing, his head thudding into the boards. He tried to rise, but could not beat the count of top referee Eugene Corri and had to be helped from the ring.

Only in his dressing-room did Daly fully come around, in time to hear Jimmy Wilde offer his sympathy and tell him he could still rule the world. But when the visitor urged Newton not to rush his pupil, the angry 'Professor' told Britain's greatest-ever fighter to mind his own business. Perhaps he felt a pang of conscience: in the 12 months leading up to the bout, Pat had boxed 34 times, 24 of them scheduled for 15 rounds. And this was a lad of just 16.

Wilde's opinion was widely shared. The following morning's fight reports, while praising Daly's brilliance over the first seven sessions, repeated the warnings against overworking the young man. And Jimmy's fellow-countryman, Wignall, at the time the top sportswriter in Fleet Street, again pleaded that he should be given time to rest and then to grow normally.

"If this is not done," he told his *Express* readers, "his life as a fighter will end long before he is 20." But Nipper was to box six more times in the next seven weeks.

He was back in action a fortnight later, winning in five, but was then halted in the third by East Ender Jim Ashley. A mere six days more – no mandatory suspensions then – and the treadmill ground on. Pat was winning again, but lacked sparkle and even the stubborn Newton decided he should have six weeks off.

The break seemed to work and 1930 began with a series of victories before the wheels abruptly came off the bandwagon with three defeats in a row.

In his keenness for a payday, it seemed the 'Professor' cared little about his charge's increasing problems making weight, happily accepting contracts which forced Pat to shed pounds. One example involved a Geordie called Seaman Tommy Watson, a future British champion and world title challenger; having sweated his way down to 9st 6lb, Pat was floored twice in the second and saved by the bell, before battling back to take control. But he was exhausted by the end of the tenth and the next session saw him floored four times and stopped by the referee as a panic-stricken Patsy clambered over ringsiders in a bid to reach the corner and surrender for his son.

For five weeks the teenager could barely walk in a straight line, his father having to go out with him to stop him stumbling into traffic. When he returned to the gym, Newton, who had made no attempt to contact his boxer, promptly booked him to meet Donald Jones, from Penygraig, at the Alcazar, only for a doctor to veto it on the night, insisting that Pat was still suffering from concussion. Yet two weeks later he was back at Premierland, facing another Rhondda boy, Nobby Baker.

The 22-year-old from Trealaw was decent enough – he challenged three times for Welsh titles, after all – but not in Nipper's league. Yet the wonder boy was making mistakes, notably staying within range after his own attacks. He was caught and floored three times before referee Jack Hart stepped in during the 13th. Daly protested, insisting he had not been hurt, but later thanked the official.

"That fight might have killed me," he wrote. "I realised afterwards that I'd had concussion ever since the Cuthbert fight."

Struggling with the thought that his dream might be over – and he was still only 17 – Pat fell into depression, even contemplating suicide. Instead, he decided to leave the 'Professor'. It wasn't easy, as Newton went to court to prevent his cash cow making a comeback on a Jeff Dickson card at the Albert Hall; the judge rejected his claim for an injunction and ruled that the contract Pat had signed in his early teens was null and void. The way was clear for a new start.

But, even after months on the sidelines, this was not the old Nipper and his much-hyped return saw him lack sharpness and accuracy, somehow managing to lose a six-round decision to a hand-picked Brummie called Tom Banks.

Pat vowed to take two years out to build up his strength, yet was persuaded back a month later, having to survive a knockdown to earn a draw against veteran Fred Green. Having already agreed to a contest five days on, Daly went through with it – and a third-round knockout victory revived his spirits.

Even without Newton in the driving seat, Pat went back to the hectic non-stop schedule he was used to, with four bouts in December 1930 and another couple the following month. All were won, five of them inside the distance, but he was now a welterweight and the former brilliance was seen only in flashes.

Hit by flu before facing Londoner Harry Jenkins, he struggled in a bout which ended when Jenkins retired with a broken nose. His "world champion" dream now in tatters, Daly – with the backing of promoter Fred Austin – decided to go through with his planned two-year break. He never boxed again. The brilliant meteor that had lit up the sporting sky had burned out, three weeks before he turned 18.

He was not lost to boxing entirely, training kid brother Bobby during a brief amateur career, and actually returned to the ring a few years later – as a wrestler! The grapple game was becoming popular across Britain and earned Pat, now a muscular 13st, a few quid for a couple of years. It also brought him a wife, having met Mary Newrick at a show where she was working behind the bar.

They had three sons, while Daly worked during the war years at the Handley Page aircraft factory. He had his own gym for a while and then ran a dance hall. When that folded there were a succession of jobs until he finally settled as a cleaner at the *Daily Mirror* offices, staying there until retirement.

He lived to the age of 75, although his final years were marred by Alzheimer's disease. His own memory may have become impaired, but his story should never be forgotten by those who follow a sport that is sometimes a long way from the lauded 'Noble Art'.

DAVE DAVIES
(1948-)

- Commonwealth Games Silver Medallist 1970

- Welsh Light-Middleweight Champion 1974-77

The Bangor bricklayer was not the first sporting hero in the family. His grandfather, Reg Meek, was renowned as a rugby player. Dave himself preferred the round ball and was good enough to reach a final trial for the Wales youth side. But the ring always had a special attraction.

The three Davies boys – Les and Steve also wore the gloves – began as kids with Bangor YMCA, though Dave spent a couple of seasons travelling along the A55 to represent Liverpool's famous Golden Gloves club. Although two years younger, it was Les, twice a losing finalist in the Welsh ABAs, who turned pro first – under the management of world champion Terry Downes, who was also keen to sign his big brother.

Dave was less enthusiastic about moving to London. Besides, he was enjoying too much success in the vest. Four years running he proved himself the best amateur in Wales and if his first crack at the British came a cropper at the talented hands of future world titleholder John H. Stracey, he saw off all-comers in 1970 and 1971. The first season, of course, led into the Commonwealth Games in Edinburgh and suddenly Davies found fame beyond hardcore boxing fans.

Dave Davies

The North Walian scraped through his first contest at light-welterweight, his aggression winning the support of three of the five judges against Stephen Baraza, a tall prison warder from Kenya. There was a similar 3-2 split in his favour next time out, despite being floored in each round by Nigerian Anthony Andeh, a gold medallist at lightweight four years earlier. Andeh's team manager, the legendary Hogan Bassey, angrily lodged a protest, but was overruled.

There was no controversy over the semi-final, in which a relentless Davies outpunched Zambian Paul Mulenga to gain an overwhelming unanimous decision, but his luck ran out dramatically when he met Mohammed Muruli, an Olympic quarter-finalist and one of five Ugandans to reach the last stage. By his own admission, Dave lost the opener, but seemed to take the second and dominated a one-sided third session, scoring heavily with right crosses as his rival faded. The 3-2 vote for Muruli brought a prolonged chorus of boos from the packed Murrayfield Ice Hall.

Welsh team leader John Llewellyn railed against the make-up of the arbiters – two Africans and a Fijian sided with Muruli, while a Canadian and an Ulsterman scored for Davies – but accusations of racial bias ignored the fact that Dave's earlier contentious wins saw black observers favour him while white judges disagreed. Nonetheless, Dave had to fight off tears of frustration as he collected his silver medal.

Turning down suggestions that he should cash in on his success, Davies, now up at welter and eyeing an Olympic place, represented Wales at the 1971 Europeans, only to be drawn against Hungarian ace János Kajdi in his first contest. The experienced Kajdi won on points and went on to take the gold, before beating Briton Maurice Hope on the way to a silver in the big one in Munich the following year. That could easily have been a rematch with the Welshman: hampered by a hand injury, Davies was outscored by Hope in a box-off for the GB Olympic spot.

Having missed out on the Games, Dave, with more than 200 amateur contests behind him, finally opted to get paid for his punching. But he snubbed offers from more established managers – and that man Downes was still interested – to become the first signing of the newly licensed Alan Rudkin, recently retired from a stellar career in which he challenged three times for world titles.

Training was in the hands of Tommy Bache, a man with whom Davies could empathise. A dozen years before Dave's own Commonwealth experience, the Scouser had also struck silver when the Games were staged in Cardiff. Under Bache's watchful eye, the Bangor man made his bow in September 1972, five months after brother Les had the last outing of a 25-bout career.

Rudkin had enough pull to get Dave on a major show at Wembley Pool and, if Chris Finnegan came up short against world ruler Bob Foster in the main event, Davies had no problems, knocking out Cardiffian Ray Thorogood in two rounds. But he was soon touching gloves with an old rival.

Davies's last British ABA bid had seen a hotly disputed loss to Trevor Francis, from Basingstoke, although the Bangor man soon turned the tables on a club show. Now they were at it again, with similarly mixed results. This time Dave won the first clash, with Francis claiming revenge a few weeks later. It demonstrated that nothing was guaranteed in the pro ranks.

Davies in his Welsh vest

Dave signed up as the first pro managed by Corwen-born Alan Rudkin

The Welshman opted to step up to middle, returning at Liverpool Stadium eight months later to knock out Ronnie Hough and end the local man's career. But the answer to his weight quandary was in sight: the Board of Control had finally caught up with the rest of the planet and introduced a light-middleweight class, with an 11st limit. The Welsh Area took their cue and matched Dave with namesake Colin Davies to contest their inaugural title in the new division.

They met at the Club Double Diamond, in Caerphilly, on March 26, 1974. Colin kept his southpaw lead in Dave's face for three rounds, but then the tide began to turn and by the sixth the colliery welder from Aberfan was barely able to see out of his right eye. The Bangor Davies took full advantage, piling on the pressure to floor his southern foe three times with body shots and prompt referee Jim Brimmell to leap to the rescue late in the eighth.

A British title eliminator beckoned, but tackling amateur conqueror Hope just six weeks later was too big a task. The Antigua-born Londoner dominated their showdown in a Mayfair hotel, making an early statement with a second-round left to the jaw which dropped Dave for a count of six. Courage alone enabled the Welshman to stay with him until the eighth, when referee Harry Gibbs decided enough was enough. Hope went on to dethrone inaugural champion Larry Paul and continue to the WBC belt; Davies lost seven of his next nine.

Future British ruler Jimmy Batten outpointed him, while unbeaten Italian Angelo Jacopucci won in four rounds in Rome as he moved towards European honours and a tragic death four years later following a hammering by Alan Minter. Dave boxed only once in the next 19 months, claiming an increasingly rare victory and setting up a Welsh title defence against Cardiffian Pat Thomas at Liverpool Stadium on March 5, 1977.

Davies can do little to prevent Pat Thomas taking his Welsh crown

Thomas, for some time struggling with the scales, had just moved up a division after losing his British welter crown. He had dropped the acid-tongued and unsympathetic Les Roberts for Kettering-based Welshman Clive Hall, while Dave was also under new management, having swapped one Scouser for another and linked up with Charles Atkinson.

Pat looked comfortable at his new weight and dominated from the start. While Davies showed his customary aggression, he walked on to shots and found himself on the deck in the second and third rounds – not to mention another knockdown between the sessions when the pair ignored the bell. He battled on gamely, but the eighth saw him drop to a knee on two occasions to avoid the constant punishment. With blood oozing from above his left eye, Dave now had little to offer and referee Brimmell waved an end to the bout – and to the Bangor man's reign.

Lowering his sights a little and campaigning almost exclusively on Merseyside, Davies went on a decent run, though a trip across the Pennines brought a cuts stoppage by future British champion Prince Rodney, before new handler Atkinson enabled Davies to fulfil a lifetime ambition by staging a show at the Plaza Cinema in his home town. Dave did his bit by stopping Brummie Clifton Wallace in six and, although bad weather kept the attendance down, the venture still raised a few bob for Bangor City AFC.

A couple more fights at Liverpool Stadium – he had exactly half his 30 pro bouts there – and that was that.

Brother Les stayed in touch with the sport, as a trainer with his old amateur club and with Wales, before serving as a referee and judge. For Dave, however, retirement meant a clean break. Recent years have seen him struggle with ill-health. But he is deservedly ranked among the best fighters ever produced by the north.

The 'Bangor Bricklayer' in later life

JOHN DAVIES
(1964-)

Welsh Welterweight Champion 1990-92

The fight had been close. The crowd at Dudley Town Hall held its collective breath. With victory came the vacant WBC International light-middleweight belt and, back in the early days of such second-tier titles, a ranking which made the holder eligible to challenge WBC champion Terry Norris, the man who had ended the career of the great Sugar Ray Leonard.

Andy Till, a milkman from Northolt, was a hard man of limited subtlety, whose constant pressure wore down opponents; Ammanford's John Davies, on the other hand, had no shortage of skill, but lacked dedication. On the night there was little between them. It was one of those contests that depended on personal preference – which did you like more, Davies's cleaner punching or Till's higher workrate?

John Davies

Judges John Coyle and Paul Thomas each scored 116-112, Coyle favouring the Welshman and Thomas his rival, while referee Micky Vann, who had the pair level with a round to go, rewarded Andy for his non-stop final session.

And as the decision sank in and the Londoner celebrated, the expression on the loser's face was one of sheer relief. Prior to the bout, Till's manager, Harry Holland, had insisted that the winner should be drug-tested afterwards. Davies knew he would fail. It summed up the conflict between his love for the ring and a laissez-faire lifestyle beyond the ropes.

Born in Mancot, he moved to Cross Hands when he was five and went to school in Cefneithin, but spent long periods in Flintshire with his mother. Yet it was in the south that his father, also John, first took him to the Towy ABC gym as a nine-year-old; he was stopped by a more experienced rival in his first bout,

Davies (left) seems happy as Andy Till celebrates

something never repeated as he became one of the best juniors Wales had ever seen, representing his Dad's newly established Blaenau club.

Davies collected five Welsh schoolboy titles, three times going on to win the British as well. At 18 he turned pro with Colin Breen, while John, Sr, continued to look after his training.

There were a couple of minor setbacks – a points loss in Liverpool to Rhyl's Rocky Feliciello and a draw with Brummie Ian 'Kid' Murray, whom he halted in a rematch just five days later – but things were going according to plan. Yet after six fights in eight weeks he abruptly disappeared from the gym.

His father did not discover the real reason until he emerged from one of several periods behind bars: his son had drifted into the twilight world of heroin addiction. The older man travelled north to confront him and a month later the boy was back in training.

Four years had passed before the younger Davies returned to action, but after four victories in seven months there was another break, this time lasting nearly two years.

Back with Breen, while Dave Roberts took over training duties, the comeback kid's renewed enthusiasm was demonstrated with a punishing eight-round decision over Liverpool journeyman John Smith. Smith, now a respected trainer, considered Davies the hardest hitter he had met in 92 pro fights: "To look at me the next day, you would have thought a lorry had run over me."

John with his father, John, Sr

A three-round stoppage of David Andrews, from Trelewis, was followed by a trip to Capetown, where Davies established his top-class credentials by clearly outpointing future South African champion Linda Nondzaba.

Next up, on April 26, 1990, at Merthyr's Rhydycar Sports Centre, John was to claim his own national crown. In the other corner was Kelvin Mortimer, a stocky slugger from Trebanog. Davies prepared for the fight by sparring Kirkland Laing, about as unlike the Rhondda man as is possible to imagine.

Not that it did John any harm: cool and accurate, the West Walian dismantled his crude, swinging opponent in less than five minutes. He picked off Mortimer with ease, cut him in the opener and decked him early in the second. With Kelvin under heavy pressure, referee Wynford Jones stepped in midway through the round.

By now John had bought a house at Landore, which he shared with British champion Robert Dickie, while working as a glasscutter for Dickie's brother-in-law, though he soon quit the job, fearing possible damage to his hands. As it was, those fists were in perfect working order when he returned to South Africa and dropped former national ruler Phumzile Madikane three times in the ninth, ending matters in the tenth and final round.

The Welshman was becoming a man to avoid and it was 11 months before he was back in action in that fateful encounter with Till. Afterwards, Breen said Davies would move back to welter and seek a shot at the British title, marking time with a fifth-round stoppage of dreadlocked Leicester switch-hitter Trevor Ambrose. Once more, John was on the verge of something big. Yet he never again climbed through the ropes.

There was a planned bid for Gary Jacobs's Lonsdale Belt in July 1993, but Davies damaged a rib cartilage and cried off. When the Scot relinquished, John was matched with former WBO challenger Pat Barrett for the vacant throne, with home advantage at the STAR Centre in Cardiff; six weeks before the proposed date, he claimed his ribs were still painful and pulled out.

Within days he had flown to Goa to follow the hippy lifestyle which had always battled with boxing for his affections.

OCKY DAVIES
(1908-1983)

Welsh Middleweight Challenger 1934

Most Welsh people have heard of 'Ocky Milkman', the character in *Under Milk Wood* who dreamed of pouring all his wares into the river, "regardless of expense". But how many know that he was named after a boxer from Pembrokeshire?

Dylan Thomas began his working life as a reporter on the Swansea newspaper, the *South Wales Evening Post*, and covered sport as part of his brief. At the time, Ocky Davies, dubbed the 'Fighting Milkman', was a popular figure on the local scene; the pair became friends and remained in touch for the rest of the poet's life.

The original Ocky was born William David Davies at Lower Rickeston, a dairy farm on the outskirts of Milford Haven. It belonged to his father, Octavius, and the lad became known by his dad's name as a means of differentiating him from all the other Willie Davieses around.

Ocky Davies

The youngster was always good with his fists and it led to him being expelled from school when he was 14. His mother said he would have to work on the farm – the family had moved to West Hill, Steynton – but that did not appeal, so it was eventually agreed he would be given a pony and trap to set up a round to deliver milk to customers who had previously needed to come to the farm and collect it. It remained his job until he retired at 65 – and he never had a day off, even travelling through the night after fights to make sure his clients had something to put in their breakfast tea.

He first donned boxing gloves – he and his mates clubbed together to buy a pair – in a makeshift ring in local woodland, where they ran a rope around four trees. The Davies boy was clearly the best of the gang and when Taylor's booth came to town, his friends urged him to take up the challenge of lasting

'The Fighting Milkman' from the cows' point of view

six rounds with one of the occupants. Ocky flattened the man in the third and was promptly invited to accompany the showmen for the rest of the summer, which brought experience as well as a few quid.

There were other scraps too, often in the back rooms of pubs, where civic dignitaries would watch him take on crewmen from foreign trawlers. With Stanley and Toddy Williams now training him at Merlins Bridge, it was time to enter a more regulated world.

He officially turned pro in the summer of 1927 and by the end of the year had shown his potential with a draw against future Welsh middleweight king Glen Moody, from the Pontypridd fighting family, and a points win over Swansea's useful Arthur Davies. Yet it was Arthur who handed out his namesake's first defeat three months later at Bridgend, in a bout considered by some as for the lightweight championship of West Wales. The Pembrokeshire man was caught in the opener by a right cross "that would have dropped 19 boxers out of 20" and was under fire throughout the early rounds. His exceptional stamina allowed him to cut the deficit and finish the stronger, but referee Fred Yeates still had Arthur in front at the end of 15 rounds.

As he met a higher class of opponent, Ocky found things harder, losing decisions to former champions Billy Moore and Billy Fry and drawing with reigning lightweight boss Gordon Cook in a non-title bout. He also lost again to that other Davies, Arthur, this time via disqualification – something which became an all-too-frequent occurrence as enthusiasm overcame self-control.

Such carelessness spoiled his London debut, against Jarrow southpaw Jim Shippen at the famous Blackfriars Ring. Though floored in the second, Ocky repeatedly landed his low-held right and finally decked the Tynesider with a body shot in the tenth.

When he rose, the Welshman charged in wildly and his head caught Shippen on the jaw, prompting referee Jim Kenrick to turf him out.

Despite the outcome, Davies impressed enough to be invited back to the Ring a few weeks later to face Archie Sexton. The Bethnal Green man, father of future Manchester United and Chelsea manager Dave, had trouble coming to terms with Ocky's unorthodox style, but gradually took control and won a clear decision. Davies's stubborn courage earned him a huge ovation as he left the ring.

At the end of the month, Ocky was back at the famous old venue, but this time had to be rescued after 12 hard rounds against Chelsea bus conductor Billy Bird. Again the West Walian gained the respect of the fans, but decided to focus on home.

He was moving through the weights, eventually reaching middleweight, where he outscored former champion Jerry Daley before thrilling the Rhondda punters at Judge's Hall, Trealaw, with a toe-to-toe draw against Caerau's Ivor Pickens in which neither paid much heed to the idea of self-protection.

Ocky was rewarded with inclusion – ahead of a couple of former champions, somewhat controversially – in a series of eliminators for the Welsh crown. He had home advantage at Haverfordwest Market Hall – local promoter P.G. Male having put in the highest bid – against Bunny Eddington, from Pontycymer, and suppressed his usual impetuosity to edge a close verdict in a battle of the straight lefts.

This meant another trip to the Rhondda to face Albert Donovan. Despite the Cardiffian's amateur pedigree – he won three Welsh ABA titles, once beating a teenage Jack Petersen – there was little science on display. Albert's best work was in defence, but Davies kept his nose in front to take the decision, much to the approval of the Trealaw crowd.

It was back west for the crunch. Glen Moody – later to run the Globe Inn, Fishguard, for 29 years, while British champion brother Frank was mine host at the Royal Hotel in Milford – having been stripped after rejecting the purse on offer for a third meeting with Billy Thomas, the Welsh middle throne needed an occupant. Ocky was matched with Thomas and they met in Haverfordwest on January 24, 1934. But despite home advantage, Davies could not match the Deri man's experience and ringcraft.

For all Davies's energy and determination to make the fight, he found it difficult to land cleanly on the elusive Thomas, while constantly having to absorb the straight lefts coming his way. Ocky was more restrained than usual, without the wild rushes that sometimes marred his work. Indeed, many regular observers considered he had never boxed better. It still wasn't enough.

Cut over the left eye in the third, Davies was given a breather when one of his gloves split in the fifth and the bout was delayed while new pairs were found for both combatants. There was some success when Billy's left eyebrow was badly gashed in the 11th, but it was too late to change things. The more fervent Pembrokeshire supporters booed the verdict in Thomas's favour, but it looked fair enough.

There was nevertheless a call for a rematch, with the West Walians tempting Billy back to Haverfordwest on October 31, 1934, to give their man another shot. Thomas was below par, relying more on spoiling tactics than before, but Ocky, for all his forward movement, rarely found an end product. Once again Billy went home with the belt.

It was nearly the end. One retirement announcement was followed (as they so often are) by a comeback, with victory over Thomas's successor as Welsh ruler, Dai

Ocky v steak at The George's Inn, Haverfordwest

'Farmer' Jones, spawning hopes that he might yet reach the summit. But when the Ammanford man won a return, 'Ocky Milkman' hung up the gloves.

He might have made more money from boxing had it not been for his innate generosity. Frequently, when told that an opponent was enduring hard times, he shared his purse with his rival. It was a trait that continued into later life, when he regularly put on variety shows to raise money for good causes.

Ocky was also generous with his advice to wannabe fighters, famously warning them never to spar with a cow! Like former British middle king Tom Thomas, born at Glynarthen in Ceredigion but brought up on a Rhondda farm, he kept in trim by training with a bull. "When bulls charge," he explained, "they come at you with their heads down and their eyes shut. You can sidestep them easily. But cows keep their heads up and their eyes open. Leave them well alone!"

Long after his ring days were over, the 'Fighting Milkman' was still up for a challenge. He was holding court in a Pembrokeshire hostelry when someone mentioned that Rocky Marciano, at the time heavyweight champion of the world, could eat a five-pound steak. "I can do that," insisted Davies.

Bets were laid and the stage was set. The steak was cut into 19 inch-thick pieces. "Eating the first nine will give me an appetite for the last 10," claimed the ex-boxer.

It took him an hour and 20 minutes, but he managed it and celebrated with a glass of champagne, admitting, "I've had a lot easier fights than that".

STEVE DAVIES
(1958-)

- Welsh Light-Middleweight Champion 1986-87
- Welsh Middleweight Challenger 1987

The builder's mate from Pembroke was never supposed to be a Welsh champion. Sure, he had been a good amateur, even representing his country in the European championships, but his record after turning pro in 1980 was patchy, to say the least.

He had been in the away corner on bills all over Britain, with top prospects like Jimmy Cable and Nick Wilshire on the other stool, and even bouts on home soil did not guarantee success, with Terry Matthews needing just 45 seconds to beat him at Swansea's Top Rank Suite.

Steve Davies with his Welsh belt

But he was still chosen to contest the vacant Welsh light-middle throne against Swansea's John McGlynn. When McGlynn withdrew with hand problems, in came Frank McCord, a man who had twice tried in vain to claim a national belt at welter. They met at Swansea Leisure Centre on March 26, 1986, on the first show staged by Teresa Breen, wife of Colin, who – like several other wives and daughters across the UK – had taken out a licence to get around a new Board rule limiting the number of a promoter's own boxers he could use.

Many thought this was Frank's chance, but it was southpaw Davies who took control from the start, partly inspired by watching a *Rocky* film in the cinema that afternoon. A right cross in the first rocked McCord – "I knew then that the title was mine," claimed Steve – and a series of head shots in the fourth sent him to the canvas. When he rose at three, bravado overcoming common sense, he was still groggy and Davies floored him again. This time the victim's head crashed on to the bottom rope and the fight was over.

Steve Davies (left) takes on Frank McCord for the vacant title

A fit-again McGlynn was granted his opportunity in the Patti Pavilion on November 18, 1986, but the Pembrokeshire man was on top throughout their brief encounter. The Swansea challenger had split with Breen shortly before and the disgruntled ex-manager encouraged Steve to hurt him straightaway, suggesting that John would lose heart, whereas if allowed to settle he would be a tough opponent.

Davies, himself guided by Breen as a new pro while waiting for mentor Roy Witts – "the beat trainer in the world" – to acquire a managerial licence, took the advice. McGlynn was staggered early and was further discouraged when his troublesome hand went again in the second. Steve pounded him throughout the third and when John reeled backwards towards a neutral corner, the towel floated in.

The victor was rewarded with a pre-Christmas payday at London's National Sporting Club against male model Gary Stretch, who fitted his fights between dates with some of the city's most desirable women. The Merseysider was focussed enough to halt Davies in four as he continued his progress towards a British title, an unsuccessful challenge to WBO boss Chris Eubank and an eventual film career in Hollywood.

Denys Cronin may have lacked Stretch's glamour, but the Senghenydd man had pedigree as a former British ABA champion who had stopped all four foes after losing his pro debut. Silver-tongued promoter Eddie Thomas persuaded Steve to step up to middleweight and face him for the vacant Welsh crown, stressing the opportunity to make history as a two-weight champion. Those at the Newport Centre on January 20, 1987 soon realised this was not going to happen.

Cronin, one of eight children born to an Irish father, floored Davies in the opener – he actually stunned him with a left hook, Steve stepping back and dropping to one knee for a few seconds' relief – and was catching him at will by the bell. The West Walian lacked the power to earn the bigger man's respect: even when he landed five punches in a row in the second, Denys simply walked through them to hurl a right which lifted Davies off his feet before he hit the deck. When he clambered up at nine referee Ivor Bassett took a long look before letting him continue.

Bravely, Steve tried to step up the pace, but a left hook put him flat on his back. Once again he managed to scramble up, but this time Mr Bassett had seen enough.

At least he still had his light-middle honour – but not for long. He gave that up when he saw the pittance offered for his next projected defence.

There was just one more ring adventure to come. Shaven-headed Brummie Kid Milo had beaten former British light-middle king Jimmy Cable last time out, but had not boxed for nine months and Davies was expected to give him a decent test. It did not turn out that way. Rights to the head dropped Steve twice in the opener and there were three more knockdowns in the second – one, admittedly, from a low blow, referee Bassett allowing him time to recover, while warning Milo – before Hywel Davies, by now in charge in the corner, tossed in the towel that ended the 29-year-old's career.

Still in love with the sport, Davies spent a few months sparring around the gyms before finally accepting his boxing days were over. There was a brief flirtation with rugby, but these days he gets his kicks fishing from the harbour in his new home town of Tenby.

TOMMY DAVIES
(1920-1998)

● Welsh Middleweight Champion 1943-1952

Tommy Davies

They called him "the Welsh Joe Louis". Some thought the Cwmgors youngster had a facial resemblance to the man who had recently ascended the world heavyweight throne. Certainly Tommy studied the films of the 'Brown Bomber' in action and made a conscious attempt to mimic the American's style.

But Louis never had to work down the pit to supplement his ring income. Thomas Glanville Davies, one of 12 children, headed underground as soon as he left school and remained a miner throughout his 13-year pro career.

He never boxed as an amateur, making his debut shortly after his 18th birthday under the management of Ammanford-based Johnny Vaughan and trained by Archie Rule, whose brother, Crad, handed him a points loss in his second outing. But there were few setbacks from then on as Tommy learned his trade.

When he halted former Welsh welter king Ivor Pickens, observers began to tout him as a coming star, especially as he had run future British and Empire king Dick Turpin close over 10 rounds. Davies was indeed nominated to challenge the current domestic boss at 10st 7lb, Taffy Williams, but the Swansea fighter relinquished the crown to move up in weight.

Across the border Tommy enjoyed mixed fortunes, British welter ruler Ernie Roderick flooring him several times en route to a points verdict. But three weeks later, on July 31, 1943, he won the vacant Welsh middleweight title, halting Merthyr's Tommy Smith in the sixth in front of an appreciative crowd at St Helen's.

Tommy receives a Boxing News cerificate of merit from Welsh Area Council chairman Jim Evans

Smith, lacking in confidence following a series of losses in England, spent much of the fight behind a crab-like guard and it took Davies a good three rounds to break through. But once his punches began to land consistently, victory was a matter of 'when' rather than 'if'. Smith was down four times in the fifth and when he paid two more trips to the canvas in the sixth the referee called a halt.

When Tommy, recently married, faced Roderick again in London it was considered an unofficial eliminator for the British middle belt. Ernie, in his 13th year of paid combat, dropped Davies in the first and did so twice more in the seventh, but had to settle for a decision after 10 rounds. The Welshman had torn a ligament in his left elbow and the injury was partly responsible for two defeats by Hampshire hard man Vince Hawkins before he finally revealed it to manager Vaughan and was sternly ordered to rest.

With long-time champion Jock McAvoy having handed back his belt, it was the worst time for an ambitious young middleweight to be sidelined, but when Tommy returned after five months little joy awaited him. Despite nearly a stone advantage on the scales, he could not prevent the wily Roderick completing a hat-trick at his expense.

Davies came near to claiming the scalp of veteran McAvoy on a rainswept day at the Vetch Field. Floored early on, Tommy decked Jock in the last of the eight scheduled rounds and the 'Rochdale Thunderbolt' was on unsteady legs as he lurched to the corner at the final bell. He took Eugene Henderson's points decision, but, at 38, was never to box again.

There could be no question marks after Tommy visited Paris the following month. The phenomenal Marcel Cerdan, beaten only twice – each time by disqualification – in 89 bouts, demolished him inside a round with a left hook which parted its recipient from his senses for a full minute. The French idol went on to win the world middleweight crown; Davies, after a seven-month break, had to content himself with proving himself the best on his own patch.

The aforementioned Taffy Williams, who started his career as a soldier in Scotland, had claimed a draw when they met the previous year and was finally given his title chance. Both he and Davies were coming off losses to Pentre boy Tommy Jones, but as Northern Area titleholder the Derby-based Jones was not eligible to rule his native country.

Perhaps something of the lustre was thus taken off the meeting of the two losers at Swansea's Ravenhill Garage on June 11, 1946, but there was no lack of ferocity in the exchanges. Davies took the opener, a right hand rocking Williams, but it was a head clash in the second that meant the challenger was fighting on borrowed time as he bled profusely from a gash below his left eye. Tommy made the injury his target and by the end of the fourth it was obvious that Williams could no longer continue.

Across Offa's Dyke there were further setbacks, however, with losses to a brace of Turpins. Future world middleweight king Randy collected his ninth straight success since turning pro with a second-round knockout at Harringay Arena, while big brother Dick won in the fifth in Liverpool when Davies tore a muscle in his left arm and could not continue. It kept him out for six months before he returned to defend his belt with a comfortable decision over former conqueror Johnny Houlston, from Cardiff, at Neath's Gwyn Hall.

The next to try his luck was Ron Cooper, from Pyle, who faced Davies at the Gnoll rugby ground in Neath, where punters had to sit through a downpour before Tommy emerged victorious in a fairly one-sided contest. The wild-swinging Cooper managed to drop him in the third and the 12th, but these were aberrations and after the holder stepped up the pace referee C.B. Thomas waved it off at the end of the 14th.

When Tommy flattened Welsh light-heavy champion Jack Farr inside a round, it prompted thoughts of targeting the Abertillery man's belt. But instead of giving him a title rematch, the Welsh Area Council insisted that he first face fast-rising Dennis Powell in a final eliminator. It proved a disaster, Tommy being floored three times and cut over both eyes before he was pulled out after 12 rounds. The Mid-Wales man had the shot at Farr and duly despatched him in 62 seconds; Davies turned his attention back to his middleweight fiefdom.

Just three weeks after the Powell setback, on June 23, 1949, Tommy defended against Tredegar's Des Jones at Neath. Promoter Bob Teesdale staged it in a marquee on the town's fairground and 4,000 turned up for a scrap booked for live commentary on the BBC's Welsh Home Service. The programme was due to start at 8 p.m., but the first bell rang five minutes earlier – can you imagine today's broadcasters allowing that? – and Tommy almost finished matters before the radio men had switched on their microphones.

Twice he landed rights to the jaw, sending Jones staggering to the ropes, but – no doubt to the relief of the boys from the Beeb – the challenger saw out the opener and proceed to spoil his way through the next few sessions. Matters livened up in the sixth and Des, now fully recovered, dropped the champion with a body punch. Tommy bounced back to close Jones's left eye, while bringing up a large swelling on his left ear. It was one-way from here on, with Davies comfortably retaining his crown.

Defeats by former British welter ruler Henry Hall and South African Doug Miller were followed by bouts of ill-health which prompted Tommy to walk away after nearly nine years in charge. There was no turning his back on boxing, however. Tommy opened a gym and its popularity spawned others in neighbouring villages.

ZACK DAVIES
(1992-)

- Commonwealth Youth Silver Medallist 2008

That old saying about one door closing and another opening was particularly significant for the young man from Pontyberem. When a recurrent problem with his left wrist meant a premature end to a promising professional career, the opportunity arose to move into coaching with the Welsh Amateur Boxing Association. It was an appropriate destination, given that his finest achievements had come while wearing the Welsh vest.

With grandfather, father and brother Luke all boxers – indeed, grandad Alan had his own gym in the village – it was fairly inevitable that Zack Davies would lace up the gloves. He first did so at 11 in Ammanford, though it was only after moving to Cwmgors ABC and the keen eyes of coach Ronnie Morris that he began to show what he was capable of. Welsh honours were accompanied by British titles at cadet and youth level, while he reached the light-flyweight final of the Commonwealth Youth championships in India.

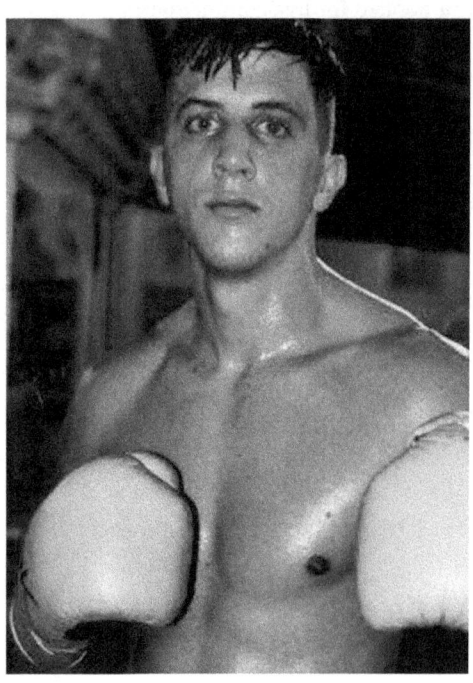

Zack Davies

Lesotho's Rorisang Motopi was dismissed inside a round, while Guyanese Orlando Allicock was durable, but outclassed by a 22-3 margin on the computer scoring system. The semi-final was even more one-sided, with the Welshman racking up a 33-0 scoreline over Samoan Lalomauga Sinopapa Sanele, far and away the biggest margin in the whole tournament.

But the ease of his progress did little to prepare him for the title-deciding clash with the host nation's Nanao Singh and the Pune crowd cheered their Sikh warrior to a 25-10 verdict and the first of three Indian golds. Two weeks later Singh was celebrating another place on top of the podium at the world youth championships.

Davies (left) faces Scotland's Josh Taylor, now an undisputed world pro champion

Davies, after moving up to bantam, had his own crack at the following year's global tournament in Baku. An impressive opener saw him clearly outscore former world junior gold medallist Ivan Baranchyk, from Belarus, although there were only two points in it when he saw off Tadjikistan's Oraz Afzolshoyev. Then came disaster – and controversy.

In a hard-fought quarter-final against Romanian Alexandru Marin, Zack was docked two points and ended up a 9-7 loser. The Welsh camp appealed and the penalty was annulled, but, bizarrely, the result was allowed to stand. The last four were to qualify for the inaugural Youth Olympics and AIBA, as if acknowledging the injustice of what had happened, said Davies could go anyway.

The only British competitor in Singapore, Zack was outpointed by classy Indian Shiva Thapa, but the somewhat strange tournament rules still allowed him to contest third place, only to lose another decision to Pole Dawid Michelus.

Moving into the senior ranks, Davies dominated the Welsh scene, with four consecutive national titles – two at lightweight, two up at light-welter – while picking up further experience internationally. The nearest he came to a significant medal was at the 2014 Commonwealth Games in Glasgow, where victories over foes from Swaziland and Nigeria merely brought him up against the home country's Josh Taylor, whose quarter-final win helped him towards a popular gold medal.

Josh and Zack both turned pro, the Welshman with trainer Gary Lockett, but while the Scot stormed to the rare status of undisputed world champion, Davies had

Zack Davies flies the flag for Wales

constant injury problems. He did fit in a trip to Moscow, where he climbed off the floor to halt a veteran Russian on the same bill that saw Swansea's Enzo Maccarinelli demolish faded legend Roy Jones, Jr.

But, after one loss in nine outings, Zack had to step away from the action and focus on helping national coach Colin Jones develop the next generation of Welsh boxing talent.

PHIL DICKS
(1967-)

- Welsh Flyweight Challenger 1989

The young southpaw from the Amman Valley had only half a dozen pro fights. He won just one of them. But he will be remembered for his part in one of the greatest battles for a Welsh title in living memory.

It took place in Swansea's Patti Pavilion on February 6, 1989. A fairly ramshackle building near the sea front, it was named for renowned opera star Adelina Patti and looked as if one of the soprano's high notes might have brought it tumbling down. Yet somehow it withstood the ceaseless tumult as the fans cheered an unforgettable encounter.

It was never expected to be thus. Dicks had met his opponent, David Afan-Jones, more than a year earlier and the Port Talbot man had halted him in five rounds. Most thought their rematch would go the same way. At the start it looked as though Afan-Jones agreed, immediately targeting the body in the manner that had produced his first victory.

But Phil was superbly fit on this occasion and survived the onslaught to respond with two-fisted attacks of his own. His supporters were in a frenzy as he hooked repeatedly to the head, while Afan-Jones showed his wider repertoire by including jabs and occasional uppercuts in his replies.

David, also in the pink of condition, constantly drove the Penybanc plumber back to the ropes, but Phil would invariably wait for the storm to blow itself out before hurling himself at his tormentor and forcing him on to the back foot. There was little difference in the pattern, but Afan-Jones gradually imposed himself and, in the sixth, there was a spell when Dicks looked desperately tired.

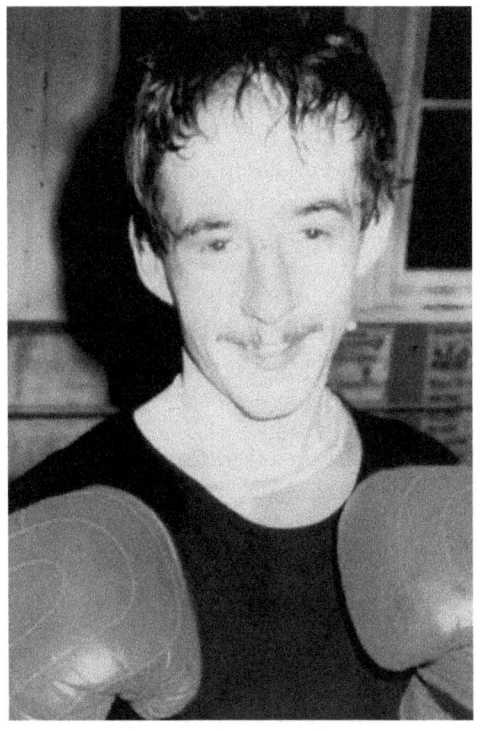

Phil Dicks

Dicks blocks a lead by the taller Afan-Jones

Yet he dug deep, found further fuel within, and threw himself back into the fray. A left sent David reeling across the canvas and encouraged further chanting from Phil's backing choir, but the taller man kept matters at long range throughout the ninth.

Realising that he needed a knockout, Dicks went for broke in the last. It was magnificent, but in vain. At the final bell, referee Wynford Jones crowned Afan-Jones as the new Welsh flyweight champion by a six-round margin; it reflected the winner's greater technical skill, but did nothing to recognise the other man's contribution to a true war.

Phil had begun boxing with Towy ABC, picking up a Welsh youth title and reaching three senior finals, before turning pro with Hywel Davies. Most of the stable found themselves travelling to find employment and in Dicks's case it was to Nottingham, where he floored local boy John Hales twice before referee Terry O'Connor ended it late in the second.

There followed the body-punch stoppage by Afan-Jones before Dicks headed for Glasgow and a draw with unbeaten fellow-southpaw Wull Strike. But fellow-Welshman Kerry Webber widely outpointed him on neutral ground in Northampton and future WBO title challenger Danny Porter halted him in four.

Porter had done exactly the same to Afan-Jones in his previous bout, so it did not derail plans for the pair to meet for a Welsh crown uncontested for 37 years. The match was postponed when Dicks needed an operation to remove a troublesome wisdom tooth.

But it was worth waiting for. And for Phil, it was a great way to bow out.

TOM DORAN
(1987-)

- British Middleweight Challenger 2016
- WBC International Middleweight Champion 2016

Ask Tom Doran why he took up boxing at the precocious age of six and he is stumped for an answer. There was no family connection with the square ring, no local hero to inspire him. He was not being bullied at school, nor was he a hyperactive child needing a focus for his excess energy.

"I can't remember why," he admits, "but my parents tell me I used to pester them all the time about letting me try it."

Their agreement had immediate and long-lasting consequences. His arrival at Shotton ABC, along the road from their home at Connah's Quay, brought an introduction to club coach Shane Thomas, who was to be in Tom's corner for the rest of his career. His father, Clive Doran, soon mutated from an ordinary fight fan to become a trainer himself, who still helps out at the club while Tom's mother, Diane, serves as secretary.

Their lad's aptitude for the game was clear from the start. At 11 Tom claimed his first Welsh schoolboy title and a decade later matched it with national honours at a senior level.

The idea of seeking a Commonwealth Games place the following year did not appeal – like many Northerners, Doran felt undervalued by the Cardiff-based Welsh ABA, while squad sessions would have involved long trips to the capital – and, by the time his successor as middle champion, Kieron Harding,

Tom Doran parades the Prizefighter Trophy

earned a bronze in Delhi, 'Dazzlin' Doran had accumulated half a dozen contests as a pro, all won without losing a round.

Thomas and Dad Clive took out licences to work his corner, while Oliver Harrison was his first manager and promoter. Four bouts in, Harrison and partner Neil Marsh encouraged the young prospect to link up with another Mancunian, former world champion Ricky Hatton, whose shows offered TV exposure.

Suddenly Tom revealed previously hidden power, three of his next four victims being dismissed inside a round. He despatched former amateur ace Terry Adams and unbeaten Jamie Boness – there was a closer-than-usual decision over Dee Mitchell in between – before facing Max Maxwell in the short, but thrilling encounter that introduced him to a wider audience.

The clash at Deeside Leisure Centre was scheduled for 10 rounds and billed as a Commonwealth light-middleweight eliminator, but any questions over the Welshman's stamina – he had never been beyond six – went unanswered. An early right from the Jamaican-born Brummie dropped an off-balance Doran, but Tom came back blasting. With seconds left in the opener, a succession of rights had 'Mad Max' draped over the ropes, prompting top referee Howard Foster to jump in. The Maxwell camp were irate; Doran's fans raised the roof with their celebration.

Yet he never cashed in on his new-found fame. While Maxwell challenged for the British crown 10 months later, his conqueror did not box for three years. A damaged hand sidelined him initially, while there were also work commitments, with 12-hour shifts as an aircraft electrician at Hawker Beechcraft in Hawarden. But he was also becoming disillusioned with the business.

However, the itch was still there and, after a couple of unlicensed bouts failed to scratch it, Doran returned to the mainstream with Sheffield-based manager Dave Coldwell, who was enthusiastic enough about his new charge to promote a show at Queensferry to mark his reappearance. Yorkshireman Harry Matthews was outscored – though Tom was floored in the last – before the opportunity arrived to compete in one of Matchroom's Prizefighter tournaments.

The draw for the middleweight competition was far from favourable, but no matter. Midlands Area champion Craig Cunningham, who had won all 11 fights (the same as Doran), was outpointed; an identical fate befell another unbeaten rival, Luke Keeler, in the semi-final. Peterborough banger Cello Renda was then demolished by s perfect left hook in the third to give the Deesider a £2,000 bonus to add to the £32,000 prize money.

His exciting victory endeared Tom to Matchroom boss Eddie Hearn as well as the general public and he was rewarded with a British title eliminator against Midlander Rod Smith at Liverpool's Echo Arena. Then Doran came in nearly half a stone over the middleweight limit. His wedding and honeymoon weeks earlier had impacted on his preparation and although he starved himself to pass an official check-weigh in fight week, it left him so weak that the need to rehydrate meant he failed the scales when it mattered.

Smith, after taking six weeks off work to prepare, opted to go through with the fight to get paid, but with such a massive handicap found himself counted out from a body shot in the third. The Board fined the Welshman, who duly added a nutritionist to his team; it proved a wise move and he made 11st 6lb comfortably for his next

Doran completes a repeat victory over Luke Keeler to claim the WBC International belt

outing, a clash with Prizefighter victim Keeler for the vacant WBC International belt, also at the Echo Arena, on April 2, 2016.

The Dubliner started like a train, hurting Tom with a left and dropping him with a right. But the Welshman dragged himself upright and, as his Irish foe charged in for the kill, landed a thunderous left which scrambled Luke's legs. A follow-up right sent him staggering backwards, unsuccessfully trying to regain his balance.

The second round saw Keeler walk on to another left and go down again. He rose, but Doran piled on the pressure. As Luke crumpled to the canvas once more, referee Ian John-Lewis jumped in and cornerman Paschal Collins hurled in the towel. After four and a half minutes of frenetic action, Tom had his first title.

The success – and the victor's obvious vulnerability – meant those behind British champion Chris Eubank, Jr, decided Doran would be an ideal choice for a first defence. It was the Brighton youngster's first ring appearance since the near-tragic ending to his title-winning contest with Cardiff-trained Nick Blackwell, but Junior never seemed to suffer the doubts harboured by his father, Chris, Sr, after his similarly traumatic bout with Michael Watson.

The legendary two-weight world champion was already badgering promoter Hearn for his boy to face world No 1 Gennady Golovkin and Tom was seen as a perfect no-risk candidate to keep the bandwagon rolling at the O2 Arena on June 25, 2016.

The challenger, naturally, was annoyed at all the pre-fight talk of 'Triple G', warning that Eubank should focus on the business at hand. In the event, however, the holder's confidence proved well-founded. After the pair were introduced by American MC Michael Buffer, the first bell saw Eubank indicating that his opponent would soon be lying on the canvas at his feet, a gesture which brought an immediate ticking-off from referee Marcus McDonnell.

Although that prophecy was never actually fulfilled, Tom was to visit the deck on four occasions, each time on hands and knees. The first two sessions saw the Welshman land a few decent rights with no discernible effect and once Eubank stepped up a gear in the third, the die was cast. An uppercut dropped Doran late in the session and more solid punches in the fourth saw him down a further three times before Mr McDonnell called a halt.

Eubank has yet to meet Golovkin, but went on to world honours up at super-middleweight. For Doran, the usual recovery time stretched into months and, eventually, years. There has been no formal retirement announcement, but a comeback appears less likely with each passing day.

ANGELO DRAGONE
(1990-)

🥊 Welsh Super-Featherweight Challenger 2019

The Welsh strand of the Italian diaspora has produced an impressive number of top fighters. World champions Joe Calzaghe and Enzo Maccarinelli lead the way, of course, but there have been four others who have reigned over their adopted land. A bearded dairyman from Carmarthen should have made it five.

Grandfather Felice Dragone was the first of the clan to settle in Wales, arriving as a young refugee from his wartorn homeland. Known in Carmarthen as Mario, he married a local girl and set up a taxi firm, as well as running the Butcher's Arms pub for a spell. Two of his sons, Anthony – later to appear as a centre for Llanelli RFC – and Simon, boxed as amateurs, although their brother Nigel, Angelo's father, went into the milk business.

His *son* used to help out on the rounds before school and at weekends and when the recession put an end to a planned career as a plasterer he joined Nigel's Dairy full-time. By then he had taken his first steps in the ring. Uncle Simon's son, Luca, was making an impression at Swansea's Premier ABC – he was to win Welsh titles at junior and youth level – and 16-year-old Angelo joined them. There were three defeats in his first three bouts, but he kept going.

His attendance was somewhat sporadic, however, with only a couple of dozen bouts over the next 11 years and his solitary crack at the Welsh ABAs saw him lose a lightweight semi-final to the eventual champion, Pembroke boy Nico Morrison, the son of former pro Mike. (Nico's brother Kyle also won Welsh amateur honours.)

Like many others, Dragone became disillusioned with the scene in Wales and decided to earn a few quid for his efforts. Initially that involved responding to an

Angelo Dragone

advert and appearing on a couple of unlicensed shows in London. His second contest was seen on YouTube by Richie Garner, who got in touch to ask if he was interested in "going legit" with the Board of Control

Angelo agreed, taking on Garner as his manager, while training with Jason Hughes. Given his spotty amateur record it was no surprise to see him matched with a series of journeymen as he found his feet in the paid ranks.

Debut foe Ibrar Riyaz brought the experience of more than 160 fights to the Academy of Sport at Llandarcy and the first-timer had to work to claim the decision. But win he did – and the same applied to his next four outings, in which the ever-improving Carmarthen man, who had dropped a session to Riyaz, took every round, including against Cardiffian Rhys Saunders, which Angelo calls his "coming-out fight".

When a Welsh title chance arose, it meant a change of focus. Getting up at the crack of dawn to deliver milk was not the best preparation for a 10-round fight and Dragone left the family firm to concentrate on boxing, while becoming a personal trainer to ensure a regular income.

Some thought a crack at the belt was premature. But the throne was vacant and his rival, Kristian Touze, was similarly placed. A former soldier, deservedly lauded for giving half his purse money to local children battling cancer, '2ZEE' was also unbeaten, but his 10 opponents had suffered 304 defeats between them, while winning just 28 – and two of them had held the Swansea hairdresser to a draw. Dragone was a clear favourite.

The early rounds reinforced the bookies' opinion. Able to demonstrate decent boxing skills when allowed to dictate his own pace, Kristian found himself forced on to the back foot as Dragone maintained a high workrate, ending the opener with a crunching right which brought blood from the recipient's nose.

Head clashes caused a cut above Touze's left eye, while frequent close-quarter exchanges led to Angelo picking up matching injuries on each cheek. When permitted, Touze showed ability, but as the bout developed he fell into a pattern, tossing two or three blows before stepping inside to claim his man.

Referee Reece Carter cast a forgiving eye on the repeated holding, but it still seemed that Dragone was scoring more often. Touze, ringsiders agreed, had enhanced his reputation, but when the West Wales contingent began chanting their hero's name in the interval before the last session, the Swansea clan were muted in response.

At the final bell, mentor Garner lifted Angelo on his shoulders and paraded the ring. Again, the Touze faction looked resigned to defeat. When MC Ricky Wright announced the score – 97-94 – some thought it a little close, but acknowledging Kristian's heart and defiance.

Then came the bombshell: it was in favour of the local fighter. Anguish crossed Dragone's features, while Touze dropped to his knees in joy; behind him, his stunned manager, Chris Sanigar, seemed to take several seconds to absorb the fact that he had another champion in his stable. Angelo, hugging his two children during S4C's post-bout interview, showed class in his acceptance of the verdict, showering praise on his rival; inside, he must have been fuming.

As the dust settled, the prospect of a rematch seemed enticing. But once coronavirus brought a total shutdown of the sport in Wales, a contest of mainly local interest went on the back-burner. With only the big promoters staging shows, jobs had to be

Dragone has Touze on the ropes

taken when offered and, after 15 months' idleness, Dragone accepted a short-notice invitation to face unbeaten hotshot Donte Dixon on the undercard of a defence by his manager, world super-middle champion Billy Joe Saunders, behind closed doors at Wembley Arena.

Unknown to most, there had been a query over Angelo's brain scan and it was only two days before fight night that he was cleared for action. Despite the stressful build-up, Dragone, who had slimmed down to featherweight, started on the front foot and forced Dixon back in the first three rounds, but the Sheffield switch-hitter remained cool and began to use his mobility to outbox the tiring Welshman.

The sixth and last saw Angelo suffer a broken jaw and he did well to get through an uncomfortable final minute. The 58-56 scoreline in Donte's favour was an accurate reflection of what went before, but the Carmarthen man's gutsy display earned him respect beyond Offa's Dyke. And Matchroom boss Eddie Hearn rewarded him by covering the £2,000 bill from the neurologist whose approval had enabled the scrap to go ahead.

PAUL ECONOMIDES
(1986-)

- WBC International Super-Bantamweight Challenger 2016
- Central Area Super-Bantamweight Champion 2017-18
- Welsh Super-Bantamweight Challenger 2011
- Welsh Featherweight Challenger 2012

There have been many boxers in Wales – including two world champions – whose names proclaim their Italian heritage. Paul Economides stands alone, however. He is the only Welsh fighter with Greek blood to reach title status.

His parents arrived in Britain from Cyprus. Electrician father Andreas and mother Eleni were born on the Mediterranean island, but met each other in London and were married there. They went into the fish-and-chip trade, moving in due course to Deeside to open a shop at Queensferry and then Connah's Quay.

Paul, the youngest of three children, took his first breath over the border in Chester, the nearest maternity unit to home. Given the family business, it was no surprise that he became a chubby youngster and his father took him along to Shotton ABC to shed a few pounds.

But he proved useful at his new sport and claimed Welsh titles at schoolboy and youth level, yet after losing a Welsh senior semi-final to skilful Andy Davis, he was inactive – though a regular in the gym – for a couple of years before opting to let his talent earn a few quid to supplement his income as a personal trainer.

He linked up with Chester-based Steve Goodwin and made his debut – labelled 'The Spartan' in a nod to his background – in Stoke on St David's Day 2008, edging out fellow first-timer Duane Cumberbatch, from Manchester, to begin a run of seven straight points successes. But (Cumberbatch apart) all his victims had

Paul Economides

losing records. When Ricky Hatton, then setting out as a promoter, came to town with a show topped by brother Matthew, Economides was put in with undefeated Scottish southpaw Stephen Russell and was beaten in just over two minutes – on Friday the 13th, too!

But, after two wins over Yorkshireman Shaun Doherty, Paul was called up to contest the Welsh super-bantam throne with Robbie Turley, a Cefn Fforest lad who had already challenged in vain for the featherweight title. They met in front of Turley's chanting supporters at the Newport Centre on February 5, 2011.

The blond Turley, pacing himself after chicken pox had interrupted his preparation, baffled the shorter Northerner with his movement and unusual angles, although rarely able to penetrate the Economides guard with anything substantial. Paul landed occasional rights of his own, but lacked the power to trouble his rival and referee Wynford Jones's 99-92 margin, while too wide, meant Robbie became the nation's first champion in the division.

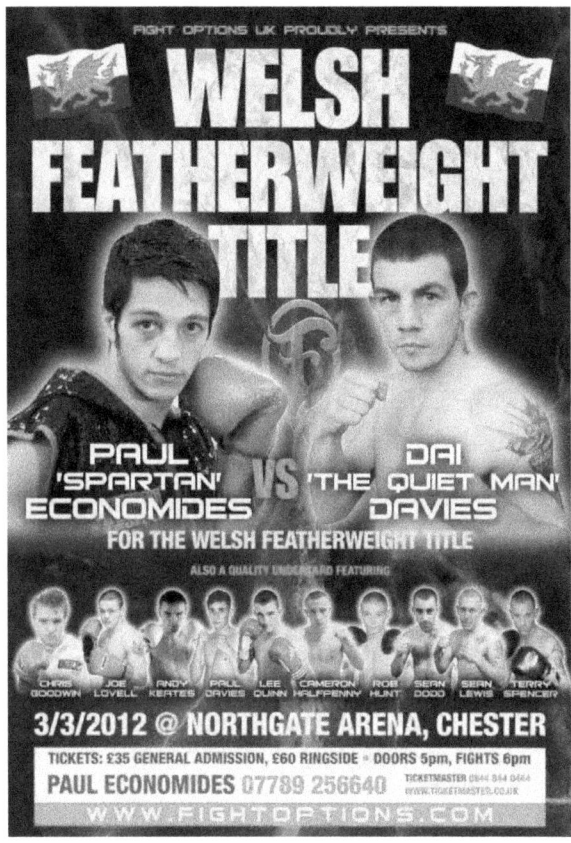

The poster for Paul's second Welsh title shot, with former holder Dai Davies visiting Chester

Three more victories before the end of the year included the acquisition of so-called Masters belts at both super-bantam and feather before Paul was handed another shot at a proper title, this time the vacant Welsh 9st crown. Talented former holder Dai Davies was in the other corner on March 3, 2012, but Economides had territorial advantage just over the border at Chester's Northgate Arena.

It made no difference. The experienced Merthyr man, with three world champions among the names on his CV, was simply too good. Paul enjoyed some success in the middle rounds, but the third man – again Wynford Jones – voted 99-91 for Davies.

The Deesider faced a future world ruler of his own when he was outpointed by Yorkshireman Gavin McDonnell, but by the end of 2013 he and the rest of the Goodwin stable were tempted to leave the Board's jurisdiction with the promise of more regular action – a decision he now regrets.

While in the sport's netherworld he picked up two "titles" belonging to the discredited World Boxing Federation. It was a strange scenario, even for them: twice Hungarian journeyman David Kanalas visited Chester, twice Economides halted him in the second. The first victory brought him the organisation's vacant International super-bantam title, but the repeat performance four months later saw him given the WBF's Inter-Continental strap, with no mention of the other "honour".

He had spent two whole years in the wilderness and was toying with retirement when a friend persuaded him to go to the second Anthony Crolla-Darleys Pérez fight in Manchester. In a bar afterwards he met trainer Dave Coldwell, who invited him to spar with Jamie McDonnell. Paul impressed in his work with the WBA bantam boss and Coldwell promptly signed him up, sorted out his return to the Board's good books and arranged a couple of outings on major shows, where he outpointed a brace of Spanish-based Nicaraguans.

The second was on the undercard of Tony Bellew's WBC cruiser defence against American B.J. Flores. And his appearance meant he was fresh in Matchroom minds when Commonwealth super-fly king Gamal Yafai pulled out of the following week's event at Birmingham's Barclaycard Arena with an ankle injury. They duly called in the Welshman to face Yafai's proposed challenger, the unbeaten Sean Davis, and quickly obtained WBC sanction for their International belt to be at stake.

Torrid early exchanges saw repeated head clashes and by the fifth both were bleeding, Davis by the right eye and above the hairline and Economides along the left eyebrow. Straight punches were a rarity as the pair went toe-to-toe.

Sean, whose parents lived just down the road from the venue, looked ahead at halfway – though he, strangely, felt otherwise – but 'The Spartan' enjoyed a successful seventh and eighth, forcing his rival on to the back foot. The Brummie responded with a complete tactical change, using fine footwork and neat boxing to skate the ninth and a last-round effort by the Welshman was not enough to save the day, all three judges favouring Davis by 96-94.

Like many North Walians, Economides was actually licensed via the Central Area – the trip to Manchester is rather more convenient than travelling to Cardiff – and, on October 6, 2017, he contested their vacant super-bantamweight title at the Metrodome in Barnsley. The other stool held Artif Ali, an Accrington lad crossing the Pennines for the first time, whose only defeat in a dozen outings had come against future Commonwealth king Bobby Jenkinson.

Economides was unworried. He gradually increased his control, bringing blood from Ali's nose in the sixth and ending matters two rounds later with a couple of uppercuts, a body shot and a final left prompting referee Mark Lyson to step in. The new champion's target was now the Commonwealth belt won two weeks earlier by Ash Lane, the Bristol-based Midlander who had edged Paul by a single point earlier in the year.

In fact, his next outing was a short-notice area defence against a man who had been Commonwealth champion at the weights above and below, southpaw Jason Cunningham – and Economides had to travel to his rival's backyard to face him. Despite the sweltering heat inside the Doncaster Dome, both set off at a tremendous pace, the local generally successful at distance, but Paul relentless in his forward motion, scoring heavily at close quarters.

Economides was marking up around the right eye as Cunningham looked to be taking command – his manager-promoter, Stefy Bull, patrolled ringside exhorting more backing from the crowd – but Paul rocked his man with a right in the ninth and

Economides with the Central Area belt and cornermen Mike Jackson and Steve Goodwin

had the better of a torrid last only to fall one point short on the card of referee Phil Edwards.

After that crowd-pleasing display, the Welshman thought the phone would be ringing constantly with offers of fights, but the only calls came from people wanting him to box as a last-minute substitute. Those pleas were rejected and, in the absence of anything more substantial, 'The Spartan' has drifted into retirement – though a comeback is still not out of the question.

TIGER ELLIS
(1910-1981)

🥊 Welsh Welterweight Champion 1932

The fighting style of the miner from Ystradgynlais could be deduced from his nickname. They called him 'The Mad Mullah', after the Dervish leader, clearly regarded as an appropriate label for someone with such an all-action, somewhat uncontrolled attitude in the ring.

At the start Ellis Myrddin Davies, the son of mountain fighter Daniel, was something of a family project. Eldest brother Johnny looked after his training, while another sibling, Elvet, handled the management side. Although the family called him Myrddin, his other forename was preferred for his ring identity, presumably because it was easier for non-Welsh-speakers to cope with.

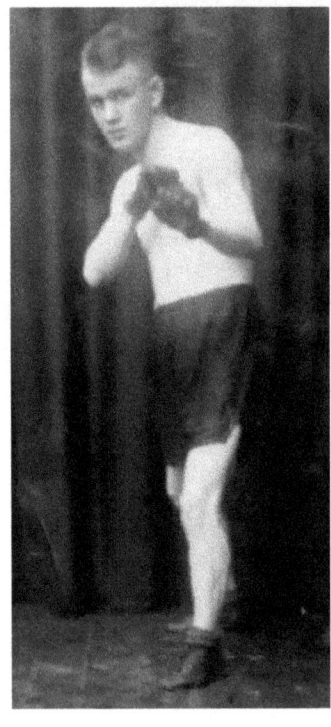

Tiger Ellis

Young Ellis, as he was originally known – the 'Tiger' tag came later, bestowed on him by English observers – threw his first punches at 15 at Ystalyfera Fair, earning a draw against Llanelli's Gwyn Thomas, a man good enough to go on and win the Welsh paperweight title.

There followed a series of victories, but then he ran into a roadblock. Young Dixie, a Rhondda boy based in Bournemouth, outpointed him at Swansea's Shaftesbury Hall; the pair met again twice over the next few weeks and on each occasion Ellis was disqualified. The referee who turfed him out the second time was former British bantam king Bill Beynon, from Taibach – and the following month Dixie showed scant gratitude, stopping the ex-champion in nine rounds!

Ellis made his first appearance across the border thanks to an old friend, Luther Thomas, a welter originally from Ystradgynlais, who settled in Kent and became a promoter. He hired his fellow-townsman to face Londoner Wally Gilbert at Margate Casino and after 15 rounds another Welsh exile, referee Percy Bevan, raised the teenager's arm in victory.

There was no shortage of excitement when the young miner was around, as the lucky fans at Llanelli Workingmen's

Club shortly before Christmas 1929 could testify. Ellis came up against Amman Valley lad Ike Lloyd, newly turned pro after four Welsh ABA titles, and found himself on the canvas four times. Lloyd was decked three times himself and eventually had to retire after seven rounds with a badly cut eyebrow.

A draw with South African middleweight Barney Kieswetter, in which Ellis might easily have become the first Welshman to defeat the Cardiff-based visitor, boosted the Swansea Valley man's confidence as he prepared to challenge Welsh welter king Danny Evans on March 19, 1932. Elvet, himself still only 27, had turned promoter to give his brother home advantage at Ystradgynlais Drill Hall, offering Evans 55 per cent of the gate. This, at least, worked out well for Danny, with the building packed to the rafters for the biggest sporting event the little village of Gurnos had ever seen.

The contrast between the two men was stark. The champion, making the first defence of the crown removed from the brow of the Rhondda's Billy Fry, was finely built and perfectly balanced, the epitome of elegant boxing; Ellis, broader of shoulder, relied more on workrate and non-stop effort, one pundit comparing him to Jack Dempsey as opposed to Evans's Gene Tunney.

The challenger should be given credit for not allowing Danny's dazzling skills to deflect him from his aggression, although Evans also retained his self-control, even when dragged over as Ellis stumbled in the second. And the Glanamman man looked on the way to a clear points verdict when, in the fifth, he threw a right to the body. Tiger stepped back a pace and the punch's downward trajectory meant it now landed below the belt, the recipient tottering for a moment before crashing to the boards. Evans was immediately disqualified by referee Will Bevan, just as the bell rang to end the round.

Still a cub, Tiger poses in his garden

The new ruler consolidated with a couple of knockout wins over Ferndale southpaw Ashton Jones, a former Welsh lightweight challenger, but could not long delay the inevitable rematch with Evans. They met for the second time at Llanelli Workingmen's Club on July 30, 1932. And, after barely four months in charge, the Tiger's reign came to an end.

Giving away weight, height and reach, Ellis maintained a fast pace, but had no answer to Evans's movement and ability to score on the retreat. His counters repeatedly rocked the Ystradgynlais man, a left hook in the fourth sending him to the boards, but, both then and in the eighth when Ellis was again groggy, Danny let

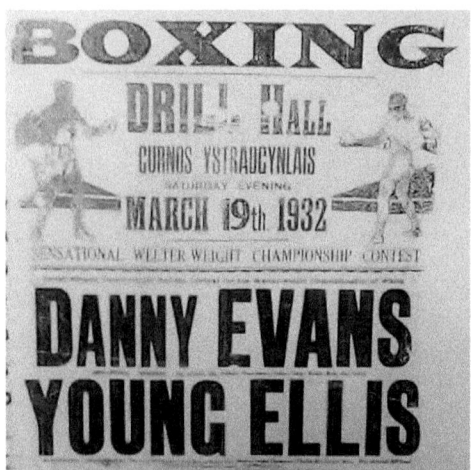

Bill for a big night in Ystradgynlais

him escape. After a flash knockdown in the ninth, the holder was flattened by a thumping right in the 11th, but once more Evans could not end matters; it almost cost him dear when he shipped a left to the body in the 13th, but he regained his composure to take a clear-cut decision.

Six weeks after he was dethroned, Ellis picked up a significant scalp when he halted future legend Tommy Farr in five rounds, but, in reality, it was not quite as impressive as it sounds. Four days previously, Farr had had to retire against Trebanos trier Hopkin Harry with a bad gash over his left eye; Ellis, naturally, made the injury his target and when it began to bleed again the referee called a halt.

In some contests Ellis seemed to go through the motions, lacking the ferocity that had seen him dubbed 'Tiger'. One scribe suggested he had "been fed on milk, rather than meat".

But he was still regarded as a top contender for domestic honours and was included in an eliminating tournament for a chance at his old crown. First up was Caerau's fast-rising Ivor Pickens, in front of a packed house at Swansea's Mannesmann Hall, but it was all over in 30 seconds.

Ellis forced Pickens to the ropes and went to throw a body punch, only for Ivor to move in to clinch; that meant the blow landed south of the border, leaving the Llynfi Valley man rolling over, clutching his groin. Referee C.B. Thomas was in no doubt, promptly disqualifying Tiger, who made his feelings known both vocally and by trying to punch Ivor, by now seated in his corner. Pickens's seconds pushed him away, while the irate loser's own acolytes ushered him from the scene.

There was further trouble when the pair met again in a 12-rounder at Ystradgynlais. When the referee gave the verdict to Pickens, some locals tried to drag the official from the ring, the police coming to his rescue and clearing the hall.

There was still to be another opportunity to reclaim his old throne, however. Having displayed an unusual fondness for the left jab in outpointing Jack Morgan, from the Tirphil fighting family, in a final eliminator, Tiger faced old foe Pickens – who, like Ellis, had upset Danny Evans on a disqualification – on January 30, 1935, at the Market Hall in Haverfordwest.

It was a hard-fought contest, with little between them throughout, although Pickens floored his rival for a brief count in the 14th round. In the end Ivor's tidier punching was enough to see him through – and provide a full stop to Tiger's career.

He had long been hampered by a bad knee, damaged in an accident with a coal dram at work, but he was also disillusioned with the way the sport was run. In later life he rarely even bothered to watch boxing on television, but he certainly never lost his fighting instincts.

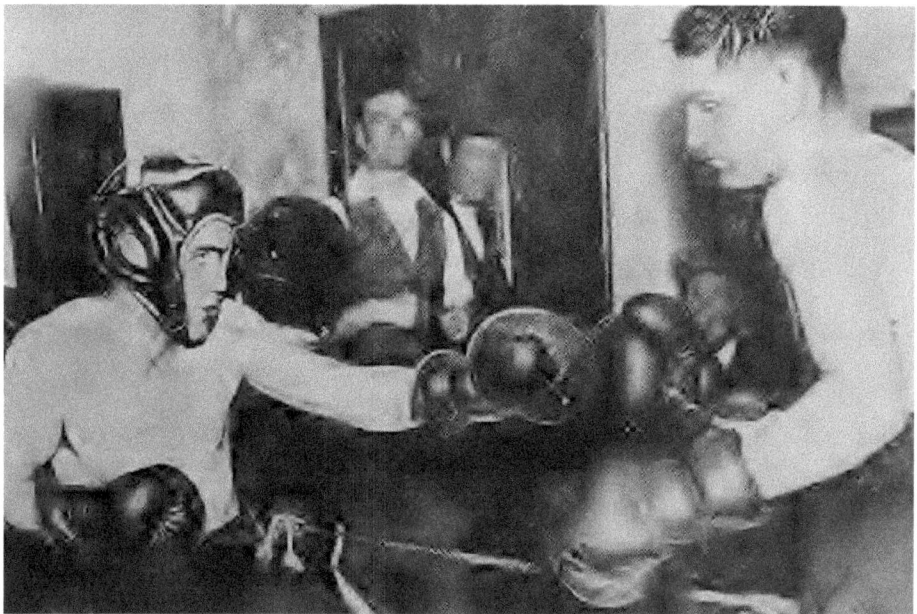
Tiger (left) spars with heavyweight champion Big Jim Wilde

In late middle age he was working as a school caretaker when he asked some electricians to use a side door to avoid tramping mud through the main entrance, but returned to find footprints all over the hall. He made his feelings known and the foreman, a strapping lad in his thirties, moved towards him with his fists clenched. One punch from the still ferocious Tiger and he was spark out!

DALE EVANS
(1991-)

- British Welterweight Challenger 2015, 2017
- Commonwealth Welterweight Challenger 2015

Sometimes it needs a special dedication to become a boxer. Everyone who makes it in the ring knows the blood, sweat and tears expended to get to the top. But for a few there are logistical obstacles to overcome as well.

An inner-city youngster with the urge to pull on the gloves may well have a choice of gyms within walking distance. When young Dale Evans was growing up in St Clears, it meant a 60-mile round trip to the Merlins Bridge club in Haverfordwest, four times a week. Even when he was given a motorbike for his 16th birthday, it could only reach 32 m.p.h., so it was still a long slog.

But it was worth it for the fistic education handed down by Graham Brockway, the doyen of Pembrokeshire trainers. A British junior title was followed by a couple of shots at the Welsh seniors, but after his second bid was ended by Fred Evans, an Olympic silver medallist the following year, Dale – billed as 'Big Boy', an ironic name given him by mother Joanne when he was a small toddler at nursery school – turned pro with Aberystwyth-based Nick Hodges.

There was to be plenty more travel involved, but Evans started strongly, only a draw with Amman Valley youngster Leon Findlay interrupting the 'W's on his early record. They included the first two rounds of a Prizefighter tournament in Wolverhampton, but unbeaten Wearsider Glenn Foot pipped him in the final.

By now Dale was guided by Gary Lockett, a former WBU champion making a name for himself as a coach. Three more victories followed, alongside a Technical Draw with

Dale Evans

Sam Eggington's height advantage is evident as he and Evans meet at the weigh-in

Mark Douglas in which the Berkshire boy floored him before a head clash left Evans too badly cut to continue. His successes had caught the eye of the powers-that-be and he was matched with Nigerian-born Larry Ekundayo in a British welterweight eliminator. 'The Natural', long based in London, had home advantage at the York Hall and overcame a second-round cut to deck Dale in the fifth, his follow-up barrage forcing referee Marcus McDonnell to jump to the Welshman's rescue.

Evans bounced back by going to Sheffield and hammering former British light-welter challenger Adil Anwar, clubbing the Leeds man to the canvas with big right hands in the sixth and twice in the last to take an eight-round decision and earn himself a Board nomination for another eliminator, this time against one-time Commonwealth ruler John O'Donnell. Young London promoter Olivia Goodwin won the purse bids and the bout was set for Bethnal Green, only for O'Donnell to cry off injured.

Dale, whose twice-weekly travels to Lockett's gym in Cardiff meant both expense and time off his day job at a cement works, was considering knocking the game on the head when Lady Luck's frown turned into a smile. As often in boxing, it needed someone else's misfortune: Evans was preparing for a routine four-rounder at the

Mike Towell, whose death destroyed Dale's love for the sport

Newport Centre when the phone rang. Frankie Gavin, the former world amateur champion, who was due to challenge British and Commonwealth welter king Sam Eggington in a much-hyped 'Battle of Brum' on October 17, 2015, had pulled out after a Tesco van reversed over his foot. Did the Welshman fancy taking his place? Having already beaten Sam in Prizefighter, you bet he did!

The money was good, but it was not the only incentive. With the cheque came the possibility of acquiring two significant titles and the certainty of topping a major bill live on Sky. And while the belts stayed in the Midlands, Evans's heroism in defeat at the Barclaycard Centre earned the respect of viewers who had never been aware of his existence.

With limited time to prepare, it was inevitable that Dale would have to go looking for an early finish, but when he was decked by a big right hand in the second it looked as if that plan had rebounded. The Welshman's vision was clear as he rose, however, and he battled back into contention.

"We're not here to win on points," said Lockett, all too aware of the likelihood that his charge would tire, and the situation became worse when a head clash in the ninth brought blood from Dale's left eyebrow. Eggington moved up a gear and battered the challenger as the round ended, a dominance he maintained through the next two sessions.

Lockett came within a whisker of pulling his man out before the last, but stayed his hand. And his decision was more than justified as Evans went after the champion, rocking him with a couple of head shots before Sam again took command. The indomitable West Walian grinned through the gore as the fight ended, with two judges giving Eggington a seven-point margin, while the third had it one point closer. No matter. It was the courageous Evans who emerged with his reputation hugely enhanced.

When Dale was matched with Scottish champion Mike Towell in a 12-round final eliminator, he faced it with confidence, despite having to travel to Glasgow and the historic St Andrew's Sporting Club, based at the Radisson Blu Hotel, where 'Iron Mike' had collected five of his 11 wins. That self-belief was enhanced when the Welshman dropped his rival with a sharp right counter in the opener.

The heavily tattooed and bushy bearded Dundee man rebounded to take the second and held his own in the next two sessions. But as he charged in midway through the fifth Mike ran on to a series of hooks which floored him once again. Pulling himself up by the ropes, he obeyed referee Victor Loughlin's request to walk towards him, but was quickly under fire again and the official stepped in.

The brave Towell insisted he could continue, but his legs suddenly gave way and Mr Loughlin gently lowered him to the canvas, where he was given oxygen. Tragically, he never regained consciousness and died in hospital 24 hours later.

The boxing world's sympathy, accompanied by a generosity which quickly raised funds for his partner and their two-year-old son, was extended to the others involved: Evans, the unwitting instrument of tragedy; his trainer, Lockett, who, just six

Evans – with a waistband tribute to Towell – never got to grips with the lanky Skeete

months earlier, had seen his British middleweight ruler, Englishman Nick Blackwell, hospitalised after losing the title to Chris Eubank, Jr; and referee Loughlin, who, by appalling coincidence, had also been in charge on that occasion.

For Dale, who had frequently come close to quitting the sport out of frustration following lengthy spells of inactivity, there was anguished reconsideration before he decided to continue boxing, encouraged by Towell's family, vowing to win the Lonsdale Belt in honour of his fallen foe.

After a rust-removing victory in Swansea, where he wore shorts with 'Iron Mike' across a saltire on his waistband, Evans was picked to tackle Eggington's conqueror, Bradley Skeete, at the Copper Box on London's Olympic Park on July 6, 2017. As well as the longer notice, there were other factors that had improved from Dale's previous challenge: then he had been travelling from Carmarthen to Cardiff after a full day's work "on the concrete", but a split with Lockett had seen him link up with Tony Borg in Newport, while new sponsorship had enabled him to focus full-time on boxing and move in with a sister-in-law at Magor, a 15-minute drive from the gym.

In the end, the changes made little difference; nor did studying tapes of Colin Jones's conquest of Kirkland Laing for the same title 37 years earlier. The 6ft 1in Skeete, aiming to win the Lonsdale Belt to keep, proved simply too tall, too mobile and too clever. Evans could never manage to get inside, his sporadic successes coming when he landed overarm rights, notably in the fourth.

Mike Towell's friends and family were represented in the crowd, but even their support could not stem the tide. Cornerman Borg repeatedly urged Dale to push the Londoner back and let his hands go, but execution was a lot harder than instruction, especially as Bradley, uninterested in seeking a stoppage, was content to keep matters at long range. His supremacy was underlined by the judges' scores, with the Welshman given just one round on two of the cards.

A fatal accident inquiry in 2019 revealed that the unfortunate Towell had been advised to quit boxing early in his career after several suspected seizures. He had also withheld from the pre-fight doctor the fact he had been suffering from headaches. The Sheriff Principal leading the inquiry emphasised that Evans was blameless, but added that he was sure he would always be haunted by the events of that night.

That was something Dale had long realised. In February 2018, he went on social media to say he was retiring. He had been offered a European title shot in Spain and began training in a gym in Oxford, where he was working on the railway. But there was something missing: instead of hunger and determination, there was just "worry and fear". For a man who admitted lying in bed, picturing Towell's fatherless son, and weeping uncontrollably, it was perhaps a decision that had been waiting to be made.

In his announcement, Evans admitted he had not achieved what he wanted from the game – a house, titles and fulfilment. He wondered if he had, perhaps, set the bar too high or that, simply, he was not as good as he had thought. But, as numerous replies insisted, he was a decent fighter operating at the highest level in Britain. Dale may not have won the belts he craved, but he did get to fight for them – and only the best do that.

DANNY EVANS
(1906-1993)

- Welsh Welterweight Champion 1931-32, 1932-34
- Welsh Middleweight Champion 1935

Danny Evans had a lot to live up to when he took up boxing. After all, big brother John had been the first Welshman to win the British ABA heavyweight title – and he captained the Neath rugby team as well. But the Glanamman youngster surpassed his sibling when it came to using his fists.

He first laced up the gloves at 14. Six years later he was the amateur welterweight champion of Wales, the boom in boxing locally demonstrated by the fact that the four men he beat to claim the prize included two of his Amman Valley clubmates.

In 1929 he joined many of his neighbours as a pro under the guidance of Johnny Vaughan. There was no gentle introduction – he went straight in with some of the best around. Only Rhondda veteran Gordon Cook, in his second spell as Welsh lightweight king, emerged victorious, while Evans saw off the likes of Trevor 'Tate' Evans, Billy Nicholas, Dai Beynon and Ashton Jones; there were also draws with Jones and the vastly experienced Billy Fry.

This form earned Danny a Welsh title eliminator against Nicholas and, despite his previous win, it was regarded as "a mild sensation" when he again outpointed the Blaengwynfi warrior. Billy had the longer reach, but could never contain Evans's speed and crisper punching, ending the contest with both eyes badly swollen.

The victory saw Evans matched with another old foe for the vacant Welsh welter throne. "Old" was the operative word: when Fry stepped between the ropes at Pontypridd's Palais de Danse on November 10, 1930, he was 35 and in the 17th year of a career which had brought him Welsh feather honours as far back as 1918. In contrast, Danny, just six when his opponent made his debut, had been a pro for only 17 months.

Experience was to overcome youth. It was fairly one-sided, too. Evans was badly cut over the left eye in the middle rounds, but was already behind, Fry

Danny Evans

controlling matters without ever producing anything spectacular. The old-stager from Blaenllechau did well to survive the second, which saw him fall through the ropes, but then took over, feinting with rights to the body and instead throwing lefts to the head. Referee Bob Hill had to halt proceedings in the fifth to calm opposing factions at ringside, but the Rhondda crew ended the happier as their favourite took a clear-cut decision.

It was really a last hurrah for Fry. Evans beat neighbourhood rival Arthur Rees, his victim in the 1927 Welsh ABA final, to guarantee another crack at the belt and faced Fry again on September 19, 1931, Danny this time having home advantage at the Pavilion in Ammanford. Despite the holder's clever defence, Evans was on top until a rusty Billy finally found his rhythm in the seventh. The revival did not last, however, Danny battering the champion for the next few sessions. Fry dug deep to stage a strong finish, but Evans was the fitter, stepping up the pace to walk through Billy's jab and hand out some solid punishment. He lacked the power to end it and had to settle for a wide verdict from referee Jack Leyshon.

The fight was watched by world bantam champ Panama Al Brown, who was introduced to the crowd along with Rhondda-born local hero Ginger Jones, prior to their meeting at Mountain Ash two days later.

If Fry's 10-month tenure had been brief, it was longer than Evans managed. His first defence, against Tiger Ellis, on March 19, 1933, saw the belt snatched away – not by the challenger as such, but by referee Will Bevan. Ellis, on home ground at Ystradgynlais Drill Hall – his brother was the promoter – hurled himself forward recklessly, but was regularly impaled on Danny's left. Tiger (though still billed as Young Ellis at that stage) relied heavily on a right hurled from around hip level, which was so erratic that he was given three warnings.

But late in the fifth another right, this time from the champion, strayed low as Ellis took a pace back. The recipient crashed to the boards and Mr Bevan immediately ordered Evans to his corner amid confusion as the bell sounded. Tiger did not seem greatly hurt and Danny had been in total command. But he still lost his title.

A rematch was inevitable and Evans took his revenge at Llanelli Workingmen's Club on July 30, 1932. As Tiger pressed steadily forward, Danny repeatedly countered effectively, decking his man with a left in the fourth, rocking him in round eight and putting him down again in the ninth and 11th. He could not finish the job, however, and was in trouble himself from a body shot before recovering to have his arm raised at the final bell.

Reinstated as national champion, Evans celebrated by becoming the first Welshman to beat his South African counterpart, Barney Kieswetter, who had been undefeated in 19 bouts with locals since his arrival. The success earned Danny a silver cup.

His reputation was spreading – helped by a draw with former two-weight British titleholder Harry Mason – and Evans was matched with Scottish No 1 Willie Hamilton in an official eliminator for a shot at the Lonsdale Belt, the Welsh authorities allowing him to put off a domestic defence against Ivor Pickens. The Glaswegian had given Danny what he confessed was "the lacing of my life" when they first met in Leeds a year earlier and travelled to Llanelli full of confidence. Yet, after a tame opener, the Glanamman fighter began to fire out his left in the second, disconcerting Hamilton sufficiently for him to leave a gap for the right hook, which sent him crashing. Up at nine, the Scot was promptly returned face-down to the canvas, this time by a left to the ribs, and was counted out, his head lolling on the bottom rope.

The veteran Mason was tempted to Swansea's Mannesmann Hall for the final eliminator, but even the backing of the crowd did not help Evans. Although Danny did well early on at distance, picking off the London-born Yorkshireman with one-twos, Harry countered effectively and his overall ring generalship proved decisive, even if many observers disagreed. In fact, some went so far as to storm the ring and police encircled the referee, Tom Murphy, from Newcastle, until they dispersed and he could be escorted to safety.

Evans (left) greets Barney Kieswetter after becoming the first Welshman to beat him. Manager Johnny Vaughan looks on with pride

While Mason went on to reclaim his British crown, his victim was soon to lose the Welsh equivalent. Finally facing the patient Pickens at the Vetch Field on July 7, 1934, he dictated the first few sessions, displaying his superiority in pretty much every department. But referees in those days showed little leniency if a fighter infringed the rules: when Danny sent a shot below the belt and the Caerau lad dropped to the deck, the third man instantly disqualified the holder. Ringsiders were disgusted, but Danny's second reign had ended in the same manner as his first.

Now relieved of obligations at home, Evans began to take advantages of the bigger purses on offer in London. A draw and a loss to welter contender Moe Moss were accompanied by two defeats to another East Ender, Archie Sexton, a former middleweight challenger whose career was ended when a fight injury left him blind in one eye – bizarrely, he then became a referee!

Now settled in the heavier division, Danny became a two-weight champion when he outpointed middle boss Billy Thomas at Newport's Pill Labour Club on April 29, 1935. Monmouthshire man Thomas, a noted ring general, possessed a greater variety of punch than the somewhat stolid challenger, but his timing was awry, while he slipped over on several occasions. Evans dropped him legally with a left to the body in the sixth on his way to the decision.

But he was losing interest in the sport. After a sixth-round stoppage by Cardiff-based South African 'Panther' Purchase, he gave up his newly acquired status before formally announcing his retirement the following year. There was a brief reappearance in Ammanford against Dai 'Farmer' Jones on a show to raise funds for the local hospital; any thoughts of a permanent comeback were dispelled when Jones halted him in nine.

Danny's voice was permanently impaired after a punch in the throat, but his sociable nature meant he was a popular companion around the pubs of the Amman Valley into his old age. A family man, he had three great-grandchildren by the time he died peacefully, aged 87, at his son's home in Loughor.

KEVIN EVANS
(1976-)

- World Amateur Bronze Medallist 1999
- Commonwealth Games Silver Medallist 2006
- Commonwealth Games Bronze Medallist 1998, 2002

Who was the first British boxer to win a medal at the world amateur championships? David Haye? Carl Froch? You will see both mentioned from time to time by the London-based media. But, while the two Englishmen reached the podium at the 2001 tournament in Belfast, a Welshman had beaten them to it.

Two years earlier in Houston, Kevin Evans made history. The solitary Welsh entrant – to get there at all, he had to overcome a certain reluctance on the part of the Welsh ABA – faced a fellow Celt in his first contest, Irishman Stephen Reynolds. The stocky Sligo man worked well inside to begin with, but Evans's height and reach advantage saw him take the verdict and move into the heavyweight quarter-final.

Kevin Evans with the first world championship medal ever won by a Brit

One more victory would guarantee a medal, but that victory was hardly a gimme. Kevin was drawn against the previous year's European gold medallist, a strong Milanese called Giacobbe Fragomeni. But the Carmarthen man kept his jab in the Italian's face for the first two rounds and even though he had to ship steady punishment in the closing sessions, the judges saw him through by a two-point margin.

It was a rather dubious privilege, landing Evans a semi-final against six-time world champion Félix Savón. In fact, boxing brilliantly, he led at the halfway stage before the Cuban landed a body punch which changed the course of the contest and his cornerman, Newtown trainer Keith Gallier, pulled Kevin out midway through the fourth and last round. Ironically, Savón and his light-middle team-mate were to be withdrawn from the finals in protest at a horrendous decision awarded against a Cuban in an earlier bout.

Houston nevertheless marked a turning point for a youngster who might well have made a name for himself on the rugby field. As a blind-side flanker, he had been part of a Grand Slam-winning Wales Youth side, but was also enjoying success in the ring.

"I wanted to go to the worlds to see what my level was," recalls Kevin. "If I wasn't good enough, I'd pack it in and concentrate on the rugby."

Returning home as a medallist settled that argument and he soon left the oval ball to his three brothers. Even while the two sports were competing for his attention, the strapping West Walian amassed

All dressed up – the Welsh Commonwealth Games team for 2006: Back, from left: Jamie Crees, Kevin Evans, Aaron Thomas – son of football legend Mickey – Darren Edwards and Robbie Turley. Front: Mo Nasir, Matthew Edmonds and a 17-year-old Chris Jenkins

a collection of Welsh junior honours and he continued his domestic domination at senior level, claiming no fewer than nine consecutive Welsh ABA titles, twice seeing off future British pro champion Scott Gammer in the final. Kevin also garnered four golds in Four Nations tournaments, defeating future pro stars David Price (twice) and Dereck Chisora en route.

Throughout his ring life he switched between heavy and super-heavy and that also applied to international competition. His success at Houston came in one of four visits to the world championships, while there were also two cracks at the Europeans and four at the Commonwealth Games, three of which saw him return home to Cwmffrwd with medals.

Perhaps there was a touch of fortune about the first bronze, at Kuala Lumpur in 1998, when a cuts stoppage of Northern Ireland's Ben McGarrigle was enough to see him to the semi-final, but that luck deserted him in Manchester four years later. After outpointing another Ulsterman and a Mauritian, Evans was 7-2 up in the first against England's David Dolan, when a fussy doctor decided to halt matters because the Welshman's nose was bleeding. Dolan, inevitably, went on to strike gold.

At least he was invited to a reception at 10, Downing Street, and, with it, a tale to dine out on. Kevin defied a ban on cameras to smuggle one in and then asked a passing waitress to take a picture of him with gold medallist Jamie Arthur, which she did. Only then did he discover that she wasn't a waitress, but the prime minister's wife, Cherie Blair!

Back in the ring, Evans kept trying and finally reached a final in Melbourne in 2006. Three victories – two of them via stoppage – saw him battling for gold against old

Coach Kevin with his Welsh ABA champion, Samson Leyson

rival Price, but the Liverpudlian giant avenged his earlier defeats and halted him in the third thanks to the 20-point difference rule that then applied.

Evans, with a family to look after, hung up his gloves and bought himself the gym which now hosts his Prizefighter ABC. But there was a last hurrah four years later, when he was offered one more shot at Commonwealth glory as a late substitute for Trostre heavy Owen Harries. Unfortunately, his left arm became entangled in a rope while sparring and the bicep muscle was torn from the bone. Using only his right hand, he managed to impress in a pre-event trial, but once in Delhi the handicap proved too much and he fell at the first hurdle.

Kevin then focussed on passing on his knowledge to others, including nephew Calum Evans, who won a Welsh elite title in 2013. But the raising of the upper age limit prompted dreams of a fifth Commonwealth Games and he came back to claim a record-equalling 10th Welsh title in 2014, nine years after his last. Unfortunately, the selectors did not share his dream and left him out of the squad for Glasgow.

These days his ambitions are channeled through his seven children. The four oldest (three of them girls) are already boxing, while the younger ones must wait until they are old enough. The name Evans is likely to feature on the local sports pages for a good while yet.

MARK EVANS
(1981-)

- Welsh Super-Featherweight Champion 2013-18

It is testament to the lack of promoters willing to stage shows in the north in recent times that the self-styled "slugger" from Holyhead boxed only once in Wales in six years as a pro – and even won his national honours in Blackpool!

Mark Evans began boxing as a 10-year-old at the local Red Dragon club, from where he soon won a Welsh schools title before taking a six-year break from the sport. He had a few unsuccessful attempts to repeat his national success at senior level, eventually deciding he might as well ditch the vest and look to add a few bob to his earnings on the building sites.

Nobody local was interested, so Evans signed up with Manchester-based Steve Wood and moved to that city, training at Irlam with Gary Booth, although former Holyhead puncher Tom Welsh looked after him when he was on home ground. His debut came in Wigan, just three months before his 30th birthday, bringing a points success over Rhondda southpaw Chuck Jones.

It began a seven-bout winning streak that only ended when Scott Moises, a six-footer from Norfolk who went by the name of 'The Iron Duck', held him to a draw at the atmospheric Liverpool Olympia, built a century earlier to host a circus. Legend has it an elephant which died after a performance was buried under the building to avoid the expense of moving it!

Mark was keen on claiming a Welsh championship and manager Wood agreed to promote his attempt, but there was a shortage of suitable super-featherweights available to oppose him. Eventually, the area council, keen to keep the titles busy, opted to allow former victim Jones, despite a spotty record, to fulfil the role. The pair faced each other in front of holidaymakers at Blackpool's famous Winter Gardens on June 7, 2013.

Ferndale boy Jones, brother of British title challenger Barrie, was better than his statistics suggested and fully justified the authority's decision in a thrilling encounter. The stocky underdog roared out, guns blazing, and a mid-ring collision in the opening session brought blood streaming from a gash on Evans's

Mark Evans

Mark shows off his Welsh belt with trainer Gary Booth

hairline. That prompted the slightly panicked Anglesey fighter to abandon caution and go toe-to-toe with his rival.

But by the third Mark, who realised he was unlikely to stop the durable Jones, began to outbox his man from distance, though when a left hand reopened the cut that tactic was abandoned and full-on war resumed. Chuck, 10 years the younger man, was on the receiving end in the next few rounds and began to mark up on the left cheek.

But he dug deep and found enough energy to keep his lead right hand in Evans's face until the closing stages, when Mark's determination and drive saw him move away on referee Wynford Jones's card, although the official's three-point margin did scant justice to the South Walian's efforts.

The islander's new status caught the eye of top promoter Frank Warren, who booked him as a test for unbeaten prospect Mitchell Smith at the York Hall in London's East End. Smith, from across the city in Harrow, had won seven in a row, his last action seeing him claim the Southern Area crown. The prospect floored Evans twice in a second-round demolition and went on to capture the English and WBO European titles in his next two outings before losing his way.

Mark was suddenly vulnerable. Worcester journeyman Michael Mooney dropped him on the way to a four-round verdict and Manchester-based Californian Adrian Gonzalez – though on the canvas himself in the first – decked the Welshman three times and ended matters in the third. Evans took five months out and lowered his sights: none of his six remaining foes could boast a winning record.

He was still Welsh champion, however, and when Wood decided to put on a show at Venue Cymru in Llandudno – the first pro bill in the resort since 1948 – the original plan was for 'Little Marky' to put his belt on the line. There were no takers, however, and Lithuanian trier Simas Volosinas was called up for an eight-rounder. The man from the Baltic dropped Evans with a counter in the opener, but the home fighter recovered to take a clear decision which brought him the decorative but meaningless International Classic Challenge belt.

Plans to drop in weight for a North Wales clash with Deesider Paul Economides in Liverpool never materialised and when Mark flattened Scouser Ricky Starkey in three at the Tranmere Rovers football ground it proved to be the final act of his career. He has not been lost to boxing, however, and now coaches youngsters at Holyhead and Anglesey ABC.

ROCKY FELICIELLO
(1963-)

- Welsh Light-Middleweight Champion 1984
- Welsh Welterweight Challenger 1986

South Wales has no shortage of boxers with Italian blood; Joe Calzaghe and Enzo Maccarinelli, both world champions, were preceded by a series of Rossis, Granellis, Colarussos and other sons and grandsons of migrants from the Mediterranean.

The North, not so much. But Rhyl – where Sidoli's, opened on Wellington Road in 1910, is believed to be oldest Italian café in Wales – is an exception. Heavyweight Carl Gizzi is the stand-out name, but the brothers Feliciello made their own contribution to the resort's pugilistic history.

The four sons of a couple from Naples all laced up the gloves, but Raffaele was the best. Known as 'Rocky', no doubt to the relief of MCs across the land, he wore the colours of Rhyl Star to a Welsh junior title and reached a senior ABA final in 1982, only to be disqualified against Pontypool's Gary Gething.

The teenage Feliciello opted to join the paid ranks and signed with Liverpool-based former pro Pat Dwyer. The decision was vindicated, with only one defeat – by just half a point – in a year in which his eight bouts included an appearance on the first show staged at the Deeside Leisure Centre in Queensferry.

Even a stoppage loss against Londoner John Andrews was the result of a cut eye and did not dissuade the Welsh Area Council from matching the youngster with Swansea's John McGlynn for the vacant Welsh light-middleweight throne, Rocky enjoying hometown advantage for his big opportunity.

He could also draw on the memory of an amateur victory over McGlynn. And when they met again at the Ffordd Las Social Club on February 17, 1984, a repeat success looked likely from the first bell, the local ripping through his rival's guard with an early flurry of left hooks.

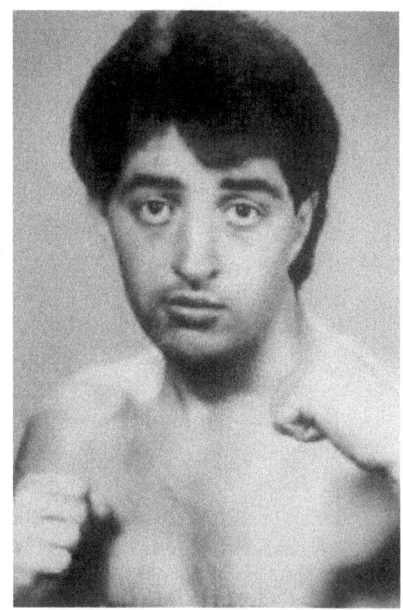

Rocky Feliciello

Feliciello, tackles Rocky Mensah in his first fight after moving to London

Further head shots in the second pierced McGlynn's rudimentary defence, though the visitor lacked nothing in courage and determination and hurled himself into the fray with an enthusiasm seemingly undimmed by the punches coming his way. But even when John looked for a moment to be getting on top in the fourth, Feliciello landed a sharp right which sent him lurching into the ropes.

The fifth saw Rocky target the body for a change and, despite isolated aggression from the South Walian, the contest was becoming distinctly one-sided. McGlynn somehow withstood constant attacks in the next two sessions, but a left hook at the start of the eighth drove him back into his own corner and his hands dropped, prompting referee Jim Brimmell to step in.

Rocky had become Rhyl's first Welsh champion for nearly two decades – and the last local hero, Gizzi, was at ringside to congratulate him.

The belt increased Feliciello's marketability and he began to venture further afield, winning in Yorkshire and the Midlands before a trip home to Prestatyn, where he took all eight rounds against previously unbeaten Dutchman Wim Thijssen. By this stage, Rocky had attracted the interest of the cartel who dominated British boxing at the time. He signed with manager Terry Lawless, moving to London, and duly outscored Ghanaian namesake Rocky Mensah on a Mickey Duff-Mike Barrett promotion at the Albert Hall, topped by Frank Bruno.

There was also a step down to welterweight, with Feliciello – still champion in the division above, though he relinquished the honour soon afterwards – actually scaling less than light-welter king Michael Harris when they met on a Solihull dinner show. In an eight-round thriller, Harris did just enough to earn the decision.

It marked the end of the relationship with Lawless, who had insisted on him dropping the 'Rocky' tag. The Rhyl man returned to Dwyer and promptly reclaimed the nickname. When he halted unbeaten local Peter Ashcroft on familiar ground in Liverpool he was even lighter than for Harris and there were suggestions that he might seek a rematch for his conqueror's 10st crown. (Ironically, the Swansea man was heading the other way and won the light-middle belt three years later). Points wins on Merseyside and in Colwyn Bay maintained his momentum.

But Solihull seemed to have it in for Feliciello, hosting defeats to Simon Eubank (brother of Chris) and, by stoppage, future British light-welter monarch Tony McKenzie. Despite those setbacks, Rocky's next outing was a bid to become a two-weight Welsh champion. It came at welter, where there had been a vacancy since Cardiffian Billy Waith retired two years earlier.

Once again Dwyer promoted it at the Ffordd Las; once again a Swansea man was in the opposite corner, this time former soldier Geoff Pegler. The outcome on March 24, 1986, however, was very different.

Having to shed a pound and a half at the weigh-in was not the best omen for Feliciello, but his speed of punch won him the opening session. Then things began to change: cut over the left eye in the second, he was dropped in the next by a body shot followed by a sharp right. With stamina a possible factor following the struggle with the scales, Rocky, cheered on by a packed house, tried to end matters in the fourth.

But Pegler kept him at bay with the jab and wobbled the Northerner in the fifth. With exchanges becoming increasingly one-sided, referee Adrian Morgan called a halt midway through the seventh.

Surprisingly, the new champion never boxed again, but Feliciello, still only 23, kept busy – after moving back up to light-middleweight – with two decision wins, although he had to climb off the canvas twice to hold off Geordie Graeme Ahmed in a battle which drew "nobbings" from the dinner-jacketed ringsiders at the National Sporting Club.

A trip to the land of his ancestors brought in some handy extra cash for Christmas at the expense of a points loss to Sicilian Giuseppe Cali. Defeats were becoming more frequent, most dramatically back at the NSC, when Brummie banger Martin Kielty demolished him in 83 seconds.

After a couple more bouts Rocky took a step back. There was just one bout in the next four years – he was outscored by future British title challenger Paul Wesley – before a last hurrah in 1991 under the guidance of former heavyweight Ron Gray. It began disastrously with a two-round thumping by Rhondda boy Kelvin Mortimer in Cardiff, watched from the balcony by singing star Tom Jones.

A month later Feliciello damaged a hand against Mike Reed, who also bit him on the shoulder! Referee John Coyle missed it, but at the end of the round was shown the evidence and crossed to warn the Midlander. "Somebody's been taking a bite out of the other bloke's shoulder," he told Reed, "and it isn't me!" Yet Coyle still gave the decision to the man with the wandering teeth...

It was enough for Rocky, but there was an unexpected last chapter. In Solihull to second kid brother Antonio, by now a pro himself, he answered the call of matchmaker Gray to step in as a late substitute and face Doncaster fight centurion Dean Bramhald – and he edged the verdict to finish his career on a positive note. (Toni also won, but joined his sibling in retirement despite only one loss in 13 outings.)

A qualified chef, Rocky was also a partner in a restaurant in his home town, called 'The Italian Touch'.

BOB FIELDING
(1911-1997)

Welsh Flyweight Champion 1932

The Fieldings were well known for their fistic prowess. Salford-born Billy boxed pro until his career was ended prematurely when he was gassed in World War I, while his brother Jack was also useful with his fists – family legend has it that he emigrated to the US and once faced three-weight world champion Bob Fitzsimmons in an exhibition.

Billy moved from the mills of Cottonopolis to the mines of the North Wales coalfield, setting up home at Caergwrle, a few miles from Wrexham. Robert William Fielding was the third boy in the family, arriving a couple of years before his father was sent to the Front.

Three more sons were to follow and all six threw punches for payment. All were useful, to a greater or lesser degree. George, in particular, did well enough to merit his own profile on the succeeding pages, while flyweight Jack, bantam Syd and feather Joe were popular figures on shows in the Wrexham area. Most of Syd's scraps were on the booths and therefore unrecorded, but did him no harm: he served in the Paras in World War II and lived until he was 95. Albert was much younger than his siblings and did not turn pro until the late 1940s.

But Bob was the undoubted star, becoming the first man from the north to claim a Welsh title.

The older boys trained in a stable, while fitting in boxing around their shifts below ground. With no other work available, taking a day off risked losing his job, so Bob frequently had to travel home from fights as far afield as Blackpool and Leeds in time for a 5.30 a.m. start down the pit. At first most of his contests took place locally at Wrexham Drill Hall, but the new prospect soon caught the attentions of the team at Liverpool Stadium and he became a regular at the Pudsey Street venue.

Some decent results against other Welshmen – he won and drew against Benny Howells, a Cwmavon collier who had moved north and settled at Llay, and drew with Rhondda boy Billy Howley before flooring and outpointing future Welsh fly king Charlie Hazel, from Pontypridd – brought Fielding to the notice of the powers-that-be, who duly nominated him for a series of eliminators.

Bob Fielding

Bob (left) greets Amman Valley boy Cliff Peregrine before their final eliminator

When he travelled to Llanelli to meet hometown hero Gwyn Thomas, it was his debut in South Wales. But there were no nerves – far from it! Bob took control from the first bell and the ringwise and gritty local was never able to work his way into the contest.

The northerner's two-handed assaults, with their speed and accuracy, reminded ringsiders of former British champion Johnny Basham, originally from Newport, but a man who made Wrexham home for much of his career. Thomas was usually at his best at close range, but even here Fielding was the master. At the end of 15 rounds and a display regarded as the best seen in the tinplate town for many years, Bob had won not merely a one-sided verdict, but the respect and admiration of the traditionally partisan 'Turks'.

Back in Wrexham they knew what to expect, so there was little surprise when their idol followed up with a dominant performance on home ground in the final eliminator, forcing the corner of Ammanford's Cliff Peregrine to throw in the towel during the eighth round. Peregrine, seemingly weight-drained, was never able to keep up with the home fighter's pace.

Fielding reached the summit by dethroning Freddie Morgan at Merthyr's Labour Stadium on February 6, 1932, ending the Gilfach Goch fighter's second reign as Welsh flyweight champion after 11 months. He proved completely superior to the fading Morgan, his height and reach advantage helping him keep his left in the holder's face, while nullifying the champion's own jab. But Bob lacked power in his right,

Bob (right) with brother Jack and their father, Billy

which frequently made solid contact with the Morgan chin without apparent effect.

Freddie scored with his own left in the sixth and had decent moments in the 11th and 13th sessions, but was otherwise a beaten man. Referee C.B. Thomas had an easy job in deciding that the belt was changing hands. Once again there were comparisons with Basham, based on similarities in the boxers' stances, both holding their hands away from the body, thus enabling them to be in punching range with minimal foot movement.

The best in Wales, then, but beyond? Next up was British and European fly ruler Jackie Brown before 8,000 Bank Holiday fans at Blackpool's Bloomfield Road football ground and it was soon clear there was a difference in class. Bob was decked in the first, saved by the bell in the second and down again in the third. He showed some resilience and landed well to the body in the fifth, but a thumb in his left eye in the sixth prompted him to retire.

It was more than a temporary inconvenience; it left him permanently blind in the left eye, though, with medical oversight rather haphazard in those days, he boxed on for a few more years. Merthyr's Jerry O'Neil had been nominated as his mandatory challenger, but the eye damage meant Fielding was unable to oblige him on the proposed date. At a time when even top boxers saw action at least once a month, the authorities were reluctant to allow a belt-holder too much grace and the concept of interim honours had, mercifully, not yet been conceived.

So, with no immediate idea when he might be fit to fight, Bob asked the Board for permission to resign, expressing the hope that he would be given another chance once he was over his trouble. It never happened. When Fielding announced that he was ready, he was told he would be considered as a leading contender; unfortunately, Bob suffered a relapse and wrote to the Welsh stewards to step down from his mandatory position.

Indeed, the Wrexham man had been out of the ring for 11 months by the time he returned with a points verdict over Stoke southpaw Tut Whalley at Hanley's Victoria Hall. A return visit a fortnight later saw Whalley stop him in 10 rounds.

Fielding kept going and was rewarded with a draw against future world flyweight king Benny Lynch after 10 toe-to-toe rounds at Liverpool Stadium; while the little Glaswegian had yet to reach his prime, he was on a 10-bout winning streak and the outcome demonstrated that Bob, despite his battering by Brown – another who went on to world honours, eventually being dethroned by Lynch – could in fact handle himself at top level, even with his handicap.

When the eyeball had to be removed, it meant an end to Bob's twin careers as boxer and miner, though he was still called up for World War II and served as a medic in the Far East. Back in civvy street he was a gardener for a while, but found his dream job working with dogs. He is said to have trained 50,000 over the years and is remembered by a generation of schoolchildren as the kindly old man who used his two Yorkshire terriers to teach them how to cross the road safely.

For a while he ran an amateur club in his own gym at Caergwrle and watched over his youngest brother, Albert. The family had decided that Abby, as he was known, should never have to work underground and encouraged him to use boxing as a way to escape that. With Bob in the corner, he had 11 pro bouts before he, too, had eye problems and was forced to hang up his gloves.

Albert, the youngest Fielding boy, was managed and trained by big brother Bob

GEORGE FIELDING
(1907-1992)

🥊 Welsh Featherweight Challenger 1932

The oldest of the fighting Fieldings did not actually bear that name. Born George Henry Barker in Manchester, he was still a toddler when his mother, Pembrokeshire-born domestic servant Emily, ran off to North Wales with mill worker Billy Fielding, living in lodgings in Wrexham's James Street before settling in the mining village of Caergwrle, a few miles out of town.

Unusually for the time – and given Billy's own boxing career – George was already in his twenties before his pro bow across the border at Crewe. There were a lot of draws in his first couple of years, but a fair few successes and no defeats – until a Scouser called Dave Craig dropped him twice to end matters in the first of a 10-rounder at New Brighton.

That setback was put firmly behind him as Fielding (the name he always used for boxing) set off on an unbeaten run which took in 19 contests – only two of them drawn – in a hectic nine-month period. The biggest scalp was Leicester veteran Len Wickwar, who already had well over 100 scraps on his record despite being four years younger than George! It must be admitted that this victory came when the Midlander retired after battling on for a round and a half with a dislocated finger.

When Blackpool's famous Tower Circus began a series of shows at the start of 1932, Fielding topped the bill against Sheffielder Tom Dexter. When it came to pure boxing, the Welshman had the edge, but Dexter had the power, flooring his man in the seventh before a big right lowered the curtain in the 13th. Nevertheless, hearing that the venue was to stage an open featherweight tournament over the next few Fridays, George was quick to put his name down.

In an eventful month he won the first three contests before hurting himself in a car crash the day after the semi-final – ruling him out of another bout scheduled for that evening – and

George Fielding

then he lost the final the following weekend when an ear was so badly damaged that the referee called a halt.

By now Fielding's exploits had caught the attention of the power-brokers down south and he was invited to challenge Welsh nine-stone ruler Ginger Jones on December 3, 1932, before an estimated 2,300 at the Workingmen's Club in Llanelli, almost home ground for the champion, who had left his native Rhondda to base himself in Ammanford. Ginger (his mother called him Bryn) had occupied the throne for more than three years, including a defence in Wrexham, where he had outclassed local Jim Crawford.

George, whose brother Bob was by now ruling Wales's flyweights, oozed confidence as he demonstrated an accurate straight left, jolting Jones's head back frequently in the first, but afterwards was rarely allowed to use it, the stocky southerner's defensive skills matched by his speed. The holder still walked on to a right uppercut in the fourth and shook his head violently while on the canvas in a bid to reclaim his senses before rising at seven.

It was an anomaly. From then on, Fielding was on the receiving end, slipping further behind on points. The climax was, however, unexpected. A left wobbled George and before he could recover his equilibrium, Ginger brought over a right to the point of the jaw. The Caergwrle boxer, who struck his head on the boards, lay on his back, immobile, for half a dozen seconds, before he attempted to rise only to crumple face-down as the count was completed.

George could at least console himself with his status as the main man in North Wales, an artificial honour said to be at stake when he faced the aforementioned Crawford at Wrexham Drill Hall on November 16, 1932, a few hours after Wales and England had drawn 0-0 at the Racecourse. Fielding despatched Jim in 12 rounds but fans caused so much trouble in and outside the building that the authorities banned boxing from the premises.

The loser announced his retirement following the bout and there was little left for the winner. He enjoyed a couple more wins and suffered a couple of losses, the last seeing him flattened in three rounds by a big right hand from Liverpool's Frankie Brown in what appears to have been his last action in the ring.

LEON FINDLAY
(1984-)

- Welsh Welterweight Challenger 2013

Leon Findlay

The youngster from Ammanford was a pretty useful amateur, but you will not find the name Findlay in the records. There he is listed as Leon Trott, using his mother's surname; when his Jamaican-born father died in 2010, he adopted his name in tribute and bore it with pride throughout his pro career.

It was his mother who introduced him to boxing, feeling that it would keep her 11-year-old son out of trouble. First gloving up at Hywel 'Cass' Davies's Towy ABC gym, Leon wore their vest to junior honours and a Welsh senior title in 2005, avenging the previous year's defeat by North Walian Aaron Thomas, son of football international Mickey.

In 2009 he switched to the Cwmgors club, where Ronnie Morris cracked the whip. Their partnership endured for the rest of his fighting life. The lad everyone called 'Lasha' – his dad's old nickname – crossed over to the paid side, with Briton Ferry-based promoter Paul Boyce taking the managerial role. A couple of wins and a draw (with future British title challenger Dale Evans) were followed by a shock reverse in his fourth contest.

Down in the bowels of Swansea's Oceana nightclub, Findlay was booked for a four-rounder against a teenage debutant called Sam Eggington, a Midlander with no great amateur pedigree who was expected to fulfil the role of "opponent", give the house fighter a decent workout and, of course, lose. Nobody had told Sam, who proceeded to earn a clear points decision and start a journey which has taken him to British and European titles.

At least Leon knew what he was up against when he travelled to Essex to face John Wayne Hibbert, a future Commonwealth ruler who had won eight of his nine bouts. The Welshman did well to last the 10 rounds – and to win two of them. Back on home ground, Findlay decked Swansea's unbeaten Darryn Bushbye twice in outpointing him and added a Technical Decision success over journeyman Jay Morris, from the Isle of Wight.

The Welsh Area Council were impressed enough to agree that he should face former national amateur captain Lewis Rees for the vacant Welsh welterweight crown. Rhondda southpaw Rees, who had won all six as a pro, had home advantage at Tylorstown on May 4, 2013. Few gave Leon much chance against the highly-touted youngster and the difference in class was immediately evident when the first punch thrown, a left down the pipe, sent the Amman Valley boy flying backwards on to the seat of his pants.

Findlay looks – rightly – apprehensive as Lewis Rees moves in

He touched down twice more in the opener, referee Wynford Jones ruling that neither occasion constituted a knockdown, and Findlay reached the bell, at which point Gary Lockett, Rees's second, protested volubly at the fact that his rival's manager was urging him on from the ring apron in a neutral corner.

Boyce's encouragement made little difference. The first exchanges of the second saw Leon's legs wobble and convinced the third man that it was pointless letting matters continue. The actual intervention came as Findlay was firing back, but it was still the correct decision.

Alas for Welsh boxing, Rees fell out of love with the sport and retired the following year. By then Findlay, too, had hung up his gloves. There was an impressive two-round dismissal of Swansea cage fighter James Lilley, but it was followed by a stoppage loss to future British title challenger Shayne Singleton and a points defeat by former English ABA champion Tamuka Mucha, both of whom had 100 per cent records at the time. Meanwhile a recurrent back problem – he had surgery back in his amateur days – was causing trouble again and he decided it was time to call a halt.

Armed with a sports science degree from Swansea University, he had a parallel life as a fitness instructor and these days looks after current students at the two gyms on campus. He has so far resisted the lure of a comeback, but hopes to help out amateurs locally once work commitments allow.

SCOTT GAMMER
(1976-)

- British Heavyweight Champion 2006-07
- EU Heavyweight Challenger 2008
- European Under-16 Silver Medallist 1992

Scott Gammer

A few years ago, at Cardiff's Holland House Hotel, a sad little scene was played out. A tactless MC, filling time between bouts, asked if anyone knew who the British heavyweight champion was. "No?" he went on. "Well, he's sitting over there."

An embarrassed Scott Gammer was then called into the ring to take a bow.

It was perhaps a reflection of a boxing landscape in which the country's best heavyweights often sidestep the once coveted Lonsdale Belt in search of international glory, but the Pembroke Dock man deserved better. As someone once said, you can only beat what's in front of you.

And he had certainly put in the work. From the age of eight, when he began training at the Pembroke club run by father Ralph, Gammer dominated the Welsh amateur scene. There were national honours in all age groups, while internationally he was named among a group of Welsh youngsters to travel to the first-ever European Under-16 tournament at Roseto, on the Adriatic coast of Italy.

There were only four entries at his weight and he reached the final with a points win over a Pole, despite an ingrowing toenail that had to be removed so that he could put his boot on to face England's Tony Dowling in the decider. Even without the offending nail, Scott found the Lincoln boy – later a pro who faced David Haye in an English title fight – clever enough to take the decision and leave the West Walian with silver.

As a senior, Scott won four Welsh ABA titles at three different weights, adding GB honours, but was unlucky on the wider scene. He went to South Africa for the Commonwealth Federation tournament and drew as his first rival a Kenyan called Omar Ahmed, a Commonwealth Games gold medallist who had also boxed at the Atlanta Olympics. Ahmed stopped Gammer in the third, which was a round further than his other two foes lasted as he stormed to the top of the podium. Then a hand injury ruled Scott out of the 2001 world championships.

He was gradually losing interest in the amateur game, admitting he cut a few corners in training, but decided he would give the paid circuit a crack and see where it took him. He linked up with Briton Ferry car dealer Paul Boyce as manager, with Dad continuing to oversee his preparation in the far west, a geographical isolation which meant a shortage of sparring and perhaps hampered his development at times.

Scott's determination to succeed was clear from the start. When he emerged for his debut on a Sunday show at Swansea Leisure Centre there was no sign of the flab that had disfigured his last years in a vest. The second shock came the way of Treharris's Leighton Morgan, a left counter and a right uppercut dropping him before he could settle. When Bristol-based Morgan turned his back as he rose, it was waved off after just 32 seconds.

Scott celebrates victory over Francis by proposing to girlfriend Jody

Three of his next four foes went similarly quickly. A draw handed to surprised Lithuanian Mendaugas Kulikauskas at Bridgend was the only stumble in a 13-fight gallop that soon brought him into title contention. The Board matched the Welshman with Chesterfield's Mark Krence in an official eliminator and, despite a hostile audience in Sheffield, Gammer upset the odds and forced the Midlander's corner to hold up the towel in the eighth.

Manager Boyce realised his charge needed more experience and persuaded former ruler Julius Francis to visit an agricultural showground outside Carmarthen, where 1,200 West Walians cheered their man to victory. Referee Mike Heatherwick gave Scott all eight rounds, which was harsh on the 40-year-old visitor, but the exercise had served its purpose. Scott completed a memorable evening by proposing to girlfriend Jody in a little ceremony at ringside.

Gammer had expected to face John McDermott in a final eliminator, but the Londoner was given a straight shot at Matt Skelton and beaten inside a round. Scott appeared on the undercard at the cavernous ExCel Arena and was floored for the first time in his life before scraping an unsatisfactory victory over Moscow-based Armenian Suren Kalachyan.

When Skelton relinquished the crown, Scott found himself paired with Krence to decide his successor – and this time Boyce made sure he had home advantage in the

Scott renews his contract with manager Paul Boyce

Gammer has Mark Krence on the back foot and becomes British heavyweight champion

big barn near Carmarthen on June 16, 2006. Butcher Krence had clearly cut back on the steaks, weighing in 12lb lighter than Gammer; a year earlier he had been 12lb heavier than the Pembrokeshire man.

The Midlander's greater mobility was evident in the early stages, but so was the fact that Scott, whose preparation had involved leaving the family home to live in a log cabin, carried the power, his successes prompting chants of "Gammer! Gammer!" which rattled around the corrugated iron walls. Krence tended to control the opening minute of each round, but when the home favourite stepped up the pace in the fifth Mark began to look flustered.

By the seventh Krence was slowing, while voluble trainer Richard Poxon fell silent. The ninth brought the climax: a left lead followed by a left hook dumped the Englishman beneath the bottom rope. He hauled his tanned body upright and was allowed to continue, but Gammer launched a barrage of blows which only ended when referee John Keane decided he had seen enough.

"He began to tire a bit around the sixth," said Scott. "I knew I'd catch up with him eventually, but it took a little longer than I thought."

Gammer was back in the ring four months later, when boxing returned to the Afan Lido for the first time in 15 years. Mandatory challenger Danny Williams was invited to the party, but declined as it coincided with Ramadan. His replacement was another rival Scott had already beaten. But that points decision 20 months previously was the only loss on the ledger of Micky Steeds, who had won all four fights since, picking up the Southern Area belt en route. It made little difference.

A surprisingly trim Danny Williams removes Gammer's crown

The bearded Thames waterman, his shorts reaching almost to his ankles, had brought plenty of vocal support from the Isle of Dogs, but was never in serious contention. Gammer's total domination was recognised on John Keane's card, while the other two judges gave Steeds two rounds, which at least saved him a total whitewash.

Scott was offered a fight with Olympic gold medallist Audley Harrison, but Boyce decided that he should first face Williams, at Neath Leisure Centre on March 2, 2007. Before fight week, there were many queries over the man who once halted Mike Tyson: having scaled 20st 8lb in losing to Skelton and split with long-time guide Jim McDonnell, Danny claimed he was being prepared for the Gammer showdown by a "mystery trainer". Old-timers shook their heads and feared the worst.

They – and Scott – were to be amazed. A flat-bellied Williams tipped the scales at just under 16st 5lb, lighter than for any bout since his debut; the Welshman, on the other hand, expecting the Danny of recent months, had bulked up to a career-high 17st-plus. Psychologically, it was a major blow.

A tentative Gammer gave away the opener, but discovered some rhythm in the second and kept on the move, firing in combinations to keep the full-house crowd on the edge of their seats. He stayed in command, with the 'Brixton Bomber' one-paced and predictable. Then everything changed. Williams came out for the fifth with a new determination, driving Scott into a neutral corner, and finished the session with lefts to body and head which brought a nod of acknowledgement from the champion. Danny kept his left in Gammer's face throughout the sixth and rocked his man with a right to close the seventh, only for the bell to intervene.

Suddenly, however, Scott reversed the trend, jolting Williams with a couple of uppercuts in the eighth, but when he began the ninth at speed he was abruptly slowed by a left to the side. The Londoner drove him to the ropes, ending a volley of hooks with a clubbing right above the ear which sent Gammer crashing. He dragged himself upright, but staggered backwards and referee Victor Loughlin completed the count. It was the end of Scott's reign – and his 18-bout unbeaten run.

The West Walian had been level on two of the cards at the previous interval and was still regarded as a viable contender, but the wide margin of an eliminator defeat to McDermott in Sheffield convinced him it was time to hang up his gloves.

His name still meant something, however, and lucrative purses were available on the Continent, tempting Gammer back to the ring. He travelled to Berlin to tackle German-based Italian southpaw Francesco Pianeta on August 30, 2008, for the vacant EU title. Scott damaged his right hand in the second and relied almost exclusively on the left, allowing the unbeaten Pianeta to move well clear on the cards. But Francesco was tiring and it was unexpected when the Welshman failed to emerge for the ninth.

A waving cheque-book tempted Gammer to Helsinki the following May to face another prospect with a 100 per cent record. Robert Helenius, later to become European champion, floored him with a right to the body in the first and repeated the trick in the sixth, with Scott narrowly failing to beat the count.

There was just one more attempt to hit the jackpot, Gammer entering a heavyweight Prizefighter tournament, only to be edged out in the quarter-final by Irish traveller Coleman Barrett. And that was that.

He and a friend set up a plastering business, but it was a struggle to turn a profit and when Scott heard of the money available to scaffolders at the local oil refineries it brought about a career change. The new job and its regular shiftwork meant an end to his sessions helping father Ralph at Pembroke ABC, but there are signs that a return to the fight game could be on the cards.

The two oldest of his four sons with Jody have already had the gloves on and although coronavirus led to closed gyms and the temporary end of amateur competition the name Gammer could yet feature in further chapters of Wales's boxing story.

CARL GIZZI
(1944-)

- Welsh Heavyweight Champion 1965-71
- British Heavyweight Challenger 1969

The idea that the nine-year-old Rhyl lad might become a heavyweight boxing champion would have been dismissed as ludicrous. Struck down by polio, he was paralysed from the waist down. As if that wasn't enough, he was suffering from a crippling bone disease in one hip. And his childhood also saw hospital stays for a ruptured hernia and double pneumonia. Yet Carl Gizzi's inner determination was undented.

When he watched on television with the rest of Wales as, on the final evening of the Empire Games in Cardiff, Howard Winstone saved the host nation's embarrassment by winning their only gold medal, the youngster realised what he wanted to do in life. And, as his health improved, he set about achieving it.

The Gizzis had arrived in North Wales in the 1880s, by a circuitous route. Michael Angelo left his home in the southern Italian town of Caserta with wife Nicolina and eldest son Giovanni, acquiring new children in Spain, Cheltenham and Swansea before landing in Rhyl, where Michael Angelo began to sell ice-cream to the holidaymakers. He also had a barrel organ, complete with monkey, while his wife told fortunes outside the town hall.

By the time Carl arrived on the scene, the family were well settled in the resort. Father Don set up the Rhyl Sportsmen's Club, with a gym at the Prince of Wales pub, and it was there that his son first laced up the gloves. The place was notable for a low beam above the ring that posed a threat to any boxer approaching six feet. In later years that was to cause problems:

Carl Gizzi

Gizzi was used to it, ducking each time he came near, but some sparring partners, such as future European title challenger Billy Aird, left with a collection of bumps and bruises that had nothing to do with Carl's fists!

Such problems were a long way off when the novice showed his innate talent by winning two Welsh schoolboy titles, followed by success at senior level, when he picked up some extra education from another North Walian, Barmouth-born former British heavyweight king Johnny Williams, while staying and working on his farm near Rugby. But Williams wanted to turn the boxer into a fighter and this rankled. After 18 months he headed for Merthyr and the more skills-based tuition of Eddie Thomas.

Like so many others before and since, Gizzi had his troubles with the Welsh amateur authorities, who dropped him from the national squad when his father insisted on travelling as his trainer to an event in Prague. It was time to go pro, Thomas the obvious choice as manager.

The newcomer had stuttered at the end of his amateur career – there was a shocking one-round stoppage loss against a Dutchman at Abercynon – but Eddie vowed he would make sure the underlying potential was fulfilled, promptly finding him a labouring job on the new Heads of the Valleys road. He also rejected the idea of putting the 20-year-old straight in with Bristol-based Len 'Rocky' James, a predecessor as Welsh amateur champion, until he had picked up some experience in the paid ranks.

Thomas certainly kept his protégé busy, his first nine wins coming in barely seven months, and the manager soon decided that his charge was now ready to face James, who, although 11 years older, had seen his tally of pro bouts overtaken by the workaholic North Walian.

'Rocky', originally from Pontypridd, gave things a good go at the Drill Hall in Cardiff's Dumfries Place, but Carl's improved skill-set earned him an eight-round decision. There was immediately talk of the pair meeting again for the Welsh heavyweight throne, unoccupied since Tommy Farr's second-time-around retirement in 1953. But Gizzi was still being shown off around the country and it was four months before the rematch.

On a Howard Winstone undercard at Carmarthen's Market Hall. Gizzi ended the career of Wolverhampton's portly Tony Smith after a single round, following up with outings at Liverpool Stadium and Wembley Pool before finally facing James for the belt at the National Sporting Club in London's ornate Café Royal on July 28, 1965.

The veteran, wild, but enthusiastic, swung for glory from the start, but Carl evaded the blows with ease, picking his man off with lefts to build an early lead. By the fourth, 'Rocky' was very much on the receiving end and a few punches into the fifth a solid right dropped him for nine. Gizzi piled on the pressure and eventually top referee Harry Gibbs jumped in to rescue James, who was struggling with a damaged rib, and crown the 21-year-old Rhyl man as the new king of Wales.

The handsome young heavyweight was getting seen in the right places. He outscored talented Londoner Dave Ould on the Earls Court undercard of stablemate Winstone's first collision with Vicente Saldívar, but had to prove his durability in climbing off the canvas to edge out Poplar southpaw Roy Enifer in Cardiff. Gizzi's winning streak had been extended to 21 when he hit a bump in the road.

Ray Patterson, the younger brother of former world heavyweight boss Floyd, had moved to Sweden to escape his sibling's shadow and campaigned regularly across

Gizzi takes revenge over Floyd Patterson's brother Ray

Europe. His first appearance in Britain saw him face Carl at the National Sporting Club in a short-notice replacement bill-topper after a Winstone bout fell through.

The New Yorker, once he became accustomed to the luxurious surroundings and silent, dinner-jacketed clientele, had that little extra class throughout and there were no complaints when referee Bill Williams raised the American's arm.

Gizzi responded with a points win over the much lighter West Ham southpaw, Ron Redrup, before taking on his conqueror again at the Afan Lido. This time it was a different story. With hundreds locked out of the seaside venue – a triumphant debut promotion for Cyril Thomas, Eddie's brother – the 3,000-plus crowd cheered to the echo as Gizzi kept his left in Patterson's face throughout. Despite a last-ditch recovery by Ray, the Welshman maintained his dominance for a clear decision and full revenge.

It was something of a false dawn, however. Twice in quick succession Carl faced foreign imports on London dinner shows; twice he lost on points. First Italian-based Brazilian Renato Moraes, despite conceding a stone and a half and several inches in height, proved awkward enough to outscore him on a charity card in Mayfair and then, two weeks later, Argentinian José Menno repeated the feat at the NSC, although the members disagreed (in genteel fashion, of course) with Pat Floyd's verdict.

It was clear that all was not well with the Rhyl fighter. A recurrent back problem had hampered him for some time, his hectic schedule not helping, and it was to be seven months before he reappeared in the ring. Despite the inevitable rust early on, Gizzi came through to edge a 10-round decision over roly-poly Italian Olympian Bepi Ros, only to take a step back at Liverpool Stadium next time out, boos from the Scouse

Gizzi and Bodell meet for the right to challenge ringside observer Henry Cooper

faithful drowning the cheers of his North Wales fans when referee Harry Warner ruled that Carl had sneaked home against Antiguan-born banger Rocky Campbell, who screamed for a return.

He never had his wish, but there was a second chance for Ros, when Gizzi travelled to the land of his fathers and repeated his points success with Italian officials in charge. With manager Thomas in Mexico – Winstone's third shot at Saldívar was the same night – Carl had agent Paddy Byrne in the corner and the Irishman was promptly swamped with offers for further dates on the Continent.

Victories over American Hubert Hilton and old foe Walford kept the pot boiling and the Welshman was being mentioned as a serious contender for a Lonsdale Belt. When Jack Solomons matched him with another prospect, Walsall's Billy Gray, at London's Grosvenor House, it came after the Board had introduced two new weight divisions – junior lightweight (now super-feather) and junior welter (later light-welter, now super-light). Taking advantage of the alternative meaning of "junior", the promoter announced that the two 23-year-olds – Gizzi was three days the older – would contest the "junior heavyweight" title, with a belt at stake. The authorities quickly vetoed that idea, but 'Jolly Jack' had achieved his publicity and a live TV audience watched the Welshman jab his way to a clear-cut 10-round decision.

The winner was rewarded with an official British final eliminator against another Midlander, Jack Bodell, with Solomons providing Carl with home advantage (even if Rhyl is actually further from Cardiff than Swadlincote, where Bodell lived) at Sophia Gardens Pavilion on November 27, 1968. Big Jack was massively more experienced and had already had one crack at the British and Commonwealth crowns, losing in two rounds to champion Henry Cooper. But the Derbyshire pig farmer had re-established himself with a stoppage of former holder Brian London and began a solid favourite.

Watched by champion Cooper, Bodell started strongly, but Gizzi made him miss so comprehensively that the Englishman flailed helplessly for a few seconds. Halfway through the opener, however, a head clash brought a large balloon beneath Carl's left eye, expert cutman Thomas banging the ring apron in frustration at what seemed a repeat of the injury that had cost Winstone his world title against José Legrá a few months earlier.

In the interval the maestro worked desperately to force the swelling away, with some success, only for another coming together to open a gash beneath the right eyebrow. Southpaw Bodell rapped home a concussive right-left combination which may have encouraged referee Gibbs to step in and call a halt as the blood flowed. Thomas promptly called for a rematch, but Jack, with a triple-belt opportunity awaiting – Cooper had added the European crown since their first meeting – was never likely to agree.

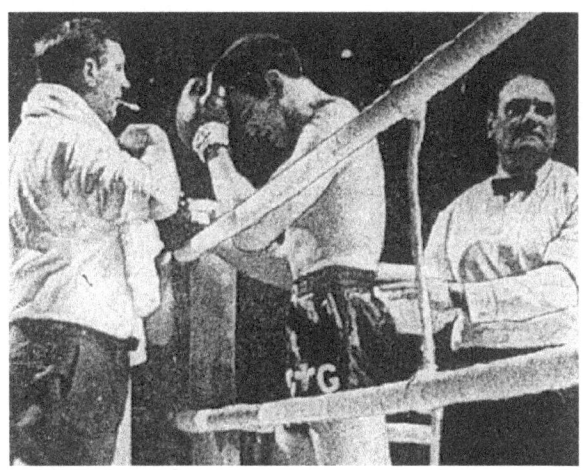

Referee Harry Gibbs escorts a beaten Gizzi back to cornerman Eddie Thomas

Springtime in Paris provided Gizzi with some consolation and a fourth-round stoppage of French Olympian Bernard Thébault, and when Cooper decided to relinquish his domestic crown Carl looked a shoo-in to face Bodell for the vacant position. First came the formality of dealing with giant American Jack O'Halloran over 10 rounds at the World Sporting Club. Most in attendance thought he had done so; referee Bill Williams disagreed. The patrons threw programmes and coins to supplement their catcalls and jeers.

The Board shared the general incredulity, ordering Williams to attend an inquiry; the Londoner opted to end a 16-year career rather than do so. And, happily for Gizzi, the authority duly went ahead and matched him with Bodell, as expected, to decide Cooper's successor. Solomons talked of staging the clash at Porthcawl, where fans had flocked to see Winstone-Legrá, but in the end he linked up with local Reg King to put it on at Nottingham Ice Rink on October 13, 1969.

It was by no means as one-sided as some had forecast – Bodell had won four since their first meeting, ending the career of the popular Billy Walker on the way – and became a gruelling battle in which Carl scored to the head while shipping punishment to the body. The pair had a welcome breather after the fifth when Gizzi's torn right glove was replaced, the MC taking the opportunity to ask the crowd not to make so much noise, as the fighters could barely hear the bell!

Each man paid brief visits to the canvas, as much through exhaustion as the power of the shots they had taken, while Scots referee George Smith had cause to warn the Midlander for low blows and careless headwork. When Jack's arm was raised at the end, the Welsh contingent were not best pleased, police having to restrain an attempt to get to the ring, but most neutrals seemed content with the verdict, if not the surprisingly wide margin.

From then on it was all about the money for Gizzi. He won only once in his seven remaining contests, but the losses came against some top operators. Unbeaten

Bodell drops Gizzi ien route to a points victory and the vacant title

South African Jimmy Richards won on points in Johannesburg, while Italian Mario Baruzzi, also undefeated and a former European amateur gold medallist, halted him in Rome before Carl, now managed by Byrne, wound down with a who's who of British heavyweights of the day.

Joe Bugner, two months before his controversial victory over Cooper, took a 10-round decision, as did Ulsterman Danny McAlinden, who went on to dethrone Bodell. Richard Dunn made it three future British champions in a row, before Gizzi bowed out with a defence of the Welsh title.

Cardiffian Dennis Avoth, big brother of light-heavy star Eddie, challenged him in the NSC ring where he had been crowned six years earlier, and did enough to take a close verdict from referee Joe Morgan. Some observers thought Carl unfortunate, though the man himself now admits he only went through the motions. It reflected a loss of love for the game and Gizzi duly announced his retirement.

After a spell living in the US, he returned to his home town to focus on his family and develop a window-cleaning business, still wielding his chamois leather into his seventies.

RAY HOOD
(1962-2004)

- Welsh Lightweight Champion 1983-85

Boxers have always fancied a tattoo. After all, when you have a toned body on display each time you go to work, why not illustrate it? But, while sleeves and other displays of unending ink are common these days, back in the 1980s most confined themselves to the odd football club badge and the wife's name. Not the lad from Deeside. For Ray Hood a jab was as likely to be received from an artist's needle as from a glove.

Ray Hood

Both passions began in his youth, the boxing side being nurtured at Buckley ABC, but there were no great expectations when he made his pro bow as an 18-year-old, drawing with fellow first-timer Alan Tombs on a dinner show at Southend. Future activity was closer to his adopted home in Liverpool, where former pro Pat Dwyer guided his development.

And it worked well. His next 15 fights included a dozen victories before the opening of the Deeside Leisure Centre in his native Queensferry brought the opportunity to fight on home ground. Propitiously, he had just outscored Swansea southpaw Andy Thomas at Liverpool's Rotters nightclub – manager Dwyer's first venture into promoting. He quickly matched the pair again at the new venue, with the vacant Welsh lightweight title on the line.

Thomas had been unhappy with the refereeing first time round and was well up for a rematch. From Dwyer's standpoint, he was ideal: someone who would put up a decent, competitive display, good enough to obtain Welsh Area Council sanction, yet someone Hood had shown he could beat. Confidence in the Hood camp was further boosted by the fact that Andy had been stopped in two of the three bouts he had fitted in since their first meeting.

The pair came together again on March 4, 1983, and two thousand flocked to watch the first pro event in North Wales for years. They were not disappointed. Thomas flicked out his right lead and kept on the move as Hood stormed in, roared on by his enthusiastic followers. Perhaps the excitement they transmitted to their hero had a negative effect when he trapped Andy on the ropes in the second, only to miss wildly as he tried to give the crowd the spectacular finish they wanted.

Thomas took advantage of an unusually large ring and his mobility saw Ray fly past him through the ropes in the fourth, the count reaching four before he clambered back to the business area. Later in the session, however, Hood landed a solid right and, as Andy's hands dropped, scored with three more.

On this occasion the South Walian withstood the volley, but in the seventh his legs sagged as another right thundered home. Understandably, Thomas began to focus on survival and referee Jim Brimmell had to call for more action in the eighth, an appeal which prompted some bonus exchanges after the bell.

Andy launched some desperate attacks in the ninth, but the aggressive local forced him back and continued to dominate until the final gong, when Mr Brimmell had him five rounds clear. The new champion, however, was never to defend his title – indeed, he never faced another Welshman and, after one more win in Queensferry, never again boxed in his homeland.

Any hopes he had of using his new status as a launchpad towards a shot at the Lonsdale Belt did not last long. A shock loss to Hartlepool counter-puncher Ken Foreman at Nantwich was followed by points defeats to Najib Daho and Kevin Pritchard, both future British champions at super-featherweight.

Worse followed when Ray travelled to Edinburgh to face local prospect Ian McLeod. A body shot dropped the Welshman in the opener, but the outcome was determined by a vicious right uppercut in the second which brought blood pouring from the recipient's mouth. Hood pulled out in the interval and headed for an X-ray which revealed a jaw broken in two places.

After eight months' recuperation, Ray reappeared in Stoke, but faded after a strong start to drop a six-round verdict to another Scot, Paisley southpaw Dave Haggerty. He did not box again for eight and a half years.

By now based in Crawley and looking after his own affairs, Hood began his comeback at Swindon, with Croydon-based Trinidadian Anthony Wanza in the opposite corner. Wanza had won only once in seven outings in the Caribbean, so hardly posed a great threat. Yet a sharp right put Ray on the canvas in the first before he regrouped to take the decision.

There was no such recovery when he took on unbeaten Jason Rowland at the York Hall. Dropped twice by head shots, Ray failed to beat the count on the second occasion and, while East Ender Rowland went on to glory as British and WBU light-welter king, referee Mark Green's waving arms had signalled the end of Hood's career.

He was not to enjoy his retirement. Despite a steady job as a baggage handler at nearby Gatwick Airport, he found life too much and committed suicide at the age of just 41.

CHRIS JENKINS
(1988-)

- British Welterweight Champion 2019-21
- WBC International Light-Welterweight Champion 2014
- British Super-Lightweight Challenger 2015

There is something to be said for toiling in obscurity when you are learning your craft. Nobody outside your immediate circle knows much about you. So, when the young man from Garnant was handed a last-minute invitation to take part in one of Matchroom's popular Prizefighter tournaments, few involved had heard of him.

When the revised betting list appeared, Jenkins was dismissed as an outsider. Welsh punters leapt at the opportunity, cashing in gleefully as the latecomer took every round on the way to a final which saw him stop Cassius Connor in the second.

The bookies' generosity was surprising, considering Chris had won all eight as a pro, albeit against men with losing records. But even following his impressive arrival in the public eye, the stylish Welshman continued to be overlooked and underrated. That does not unduly worry someone who has never courted the spotlight, but his semi-anonymity has been reflected in his financial return from the sport, with the result that he, his wife and three sons still live in rented accommodation near Ystalyfera.

Boxing can at least take credit for providing direction to a child in danger of going off the rails through the boredom of life in a mining village which had seen its last significant pit close in 1936. Once the 12-year-old Jenkins began attending Cwmgors ABC, run by his great-uncle, Ronnie

Chris Jenkins

Success in Prizefighter gets Jenkins noticed

Morris, his dedication and new-found discipline was rewarded with trophies.

Junior success led into a senior career which brought Welsh titles at flyweight, bantamweight and light-welterweight, along with trips to two Commonwealth Games – in 2006 he was, at 17, the youngest Welsh boxer ever to compete – two world championships and a European, plus a host of multi-nations tournaments.

Known in the amateur ranks as 'Six Jabs Jenko', he adopted the tag of 'Rok'n'Rolla' when he turned pro at 23 with manager Paul Boyce, Uncle Ronnie still looking after his preparation. After Prizefighter, staged at the famous old York Hall, brought him to the attention of Matchroom boss Eddie Hearn, other doors began to open.

When Hearn opted to showcase the fast-rising Lee Selby in a European title challenge at Cardiff's Motorpoint Arena on February 1, 2014, he decided to give Chris, too, the chance to win a belt. The WBC International light-welter throne was vacant and the Welshman was matched with France's Christopher Sebire to find a new occupant.

The man from Rouen, rocked in the fourth, dug in and finished the 10 rounds, but Jenkins's superiority was reflected in the scores, two judges seeing it as a whitewash, while their colleague gave the visitor a share of one session. Yet the acquisition of a supposedly significant honour was no launchpad to the big time.

Instead, there were a pair of first-round finishes in Merthyr, while when Matchroom returned to Wales he suffered the indignity of being a "floater" – one of those bouts without a specific slot in the programme – and therefore having repeatedly to warm up in case he was called. And, without enough early finishes in the TV-designated fights to create a suitable gap, he ended up being rushed into the hall as the main-event stars – and most of the crowd – were departing the scene. Chris took out his annoyance on Barcelona-based Nicaraguan Miguel Aguilar and halted him in seven rounds.

But behind the scenes his achievements had been noticed: Jenkins was matched with London Olympic captain Tom Stalker in a British light-welter eliminator. Frank Warren, the Liverpool man's promoter, won the purse offers and scheduled the bout for the city's Echo Arena. Then, with four weeks to go, Chris was told of a change of plan: Stalker was pulling out to go for bigger things. It turned out to be a shot at the spurious WBO European bauble, on the same Merseyside card, while Jenkins was left hanging.

The Board agreed he should have a direct shot at champion Willie Limond – but nothing in the Amman Valley fighter's ring life has ever been straightforward. The pair were booked for a Manchester bill to be topped by local favourite Anthony Crolla's bid for a world title, but Crolla was badly hurt trying to detain a couple of burglars and the whole show was scrapped.

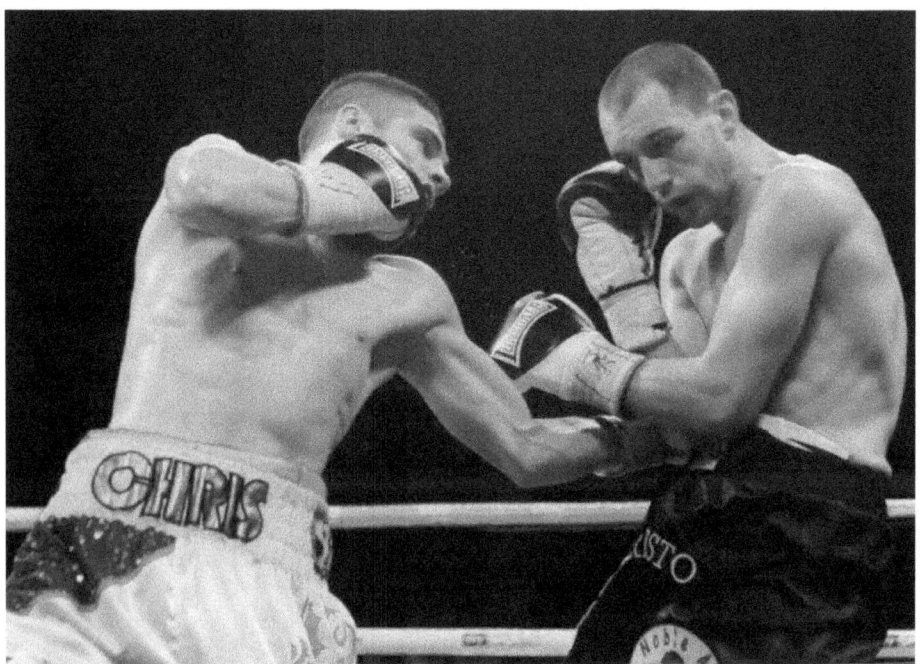
Jenkins outclasses Christopher Sebire in Cardiff

The Limond fight was rearranged for Leeds, but then the Scot hurt a shoulder and withdrew. He was persuaded to give up the throne and Yorkshireman Tyrone Nurse stepped in to contest the vacancy. But staying on weight through repeated postponements had left Chris dangerously dehydrated and three days before the showdown, he collapsed in the gym and was rushed to hospital, where he was kept on a drip for 24 hours before being allowed home.

Jenkins had been inactive for 10 months by the time he entered the Manchester Arena ring for the rescheduled bout on July 18, 2015. It showed. He was unable to find his range early on, the slippery Nurse evading his punches and keeping a long left lead in his rival's face. But as Chris settled, maintaining consistent pressure, Tyrone seemed to slow and stayed on the ropes for long periods, as if the body shots were taking their toll.

Inside the ring, however, the situation was not quite what it appeared to the crowd. Jenkins, nicked by an accidental head clash in the opener, was now finding it difficult to see out of his left eye; blood was streaming from a gash on the eyebrow, while damage in the inside corner of the optic was aggravated as the surrounding flesh began to swell.

Nurse found a second wind to take the closing sessions and immediately raised his arms at the final bell. Chris, by contrast, did not. The first score, that of judge Howard Foster, had a surprising five points between them, but the MC did not name the lucky boxer before revealing that the other two arbiters had the pair level. Foster's generous margin, it transpired, was for Nurse, but no matter; the draw meant the duo would have to do it all again.

Frustration for Jenkins and Nurse as their showdown is declared a draw

The rematch was at the same venue on November 21, 2015, by which time the Board had for some unfathomable reason rebranded the light-welter division as "super-lightweight". Once more the Welshman was bleeding early on, an errant elbow from a missed punch by Nurse opening a wound on his left temple that even ace cutman Mick Williamson was never able to seal. Despite the distraction, Jenkins unloaded a solid right in the fifth and floored Tyrone, who grabbed his rival around the legs as he fell. He negotiated his way to the bell only to be greeted in the corner by a furious harangue from his father, Chris Aston, urging him not to get involved.

Jenkins landed a straight left in the sixth which brought a nod of acknowledgement from its recipient, but Nurse was gradually growing in confidence and proving an elusive target. A coming together of heads in the tenth left Chris gashed near the right eye, which seemed to take him out of his stride, although he composed himself and finished much stronger than in their first meeting.

It was to no avail, however. Two judges had Nurse three points up, while Terry O'Connor scored it a bewildering 116-111. Even the new champion agreed that the margins were too wide, but that was little consolation.

Looking to regroup, Jenkins bade farewell to Uncle Ronnie and headed for the Gary Lockett gym in Cardiff. There was to be no easing back into things, the pair flying to Belfast for a 10-rounder against Philip Sutcliffe, Jr, son of a legendary amateur star and himself an Irish champion in the vest. Beaten just once, in Germany, as a pro, the Dubliner had the perfect start, dropping Chris with a left in the opening seconds.

Jenkins hurt Philip to the body in the second and enjoyed a good spell in the middle rounds, when his sharper work stood out. But the Irishman battled back in a torrid finale, both feeling they had done enough. Referee Hugh Russell, Jr, opted for Sutcliffe, but his 98-93 margin was way out of line.

A trio of tick-over victories was a pretty poor return for 2017, but the following year was worse.

At three weeks' notice, Jenkins was offered a date with unbeaten local Akeem Ennis Brown in Gloucester. It was a 10-rounder for the vacant WBC Youth strap, intended as a gift for the 22-year-old hometown hero; Chris, at 29 above even the somewhat flexible age limit, could (presumably) not have claimed the title himself. The matter became academic in the third when their skulls crashed together and left a red stream flowing freely from above Jenkins's right eye.

He threw himself desperately into toe-to-toe exchanges, which inevitably meant both that the cut became worse and that 'Riiddy Riiddy Rival' picked up enough points to be in front on all three cards when referee Victor Loughlin finally called a halt in the fifth and sent the verdict to the judges.

Then Chris was booked for a six-round warm-up leading into a Welsh title meeting with Kieran Gething, but plans changed abruptly when Scottish veteran Limond had to pull out of a show in Glasgow and the Welshman was invited to step in and face world-ranked Aussie southpaw Darragh Foley in a 10-rounder. Bizarrely, it was considered by the WBA – always a law unto themselves – as a defence of Foley's Oceania title, even though Jenkins was patently not eligible. As it turned out, both finished frustrated as another coming together of heads, in the second session, left Chris with a split right eyebrow and unable to continue beyond the third, leaving the result as a Technical Draw.

To add insult to the facial injury, the hospital doctor who treated him made such a shoddy job of it that the camp had to consult a specialist, who reopened the scar and put in 20 stitches, eight of them internal. The problem ended any lingering possibility of the Garnant man facing Pontypool youngster Gething or anyone else for the time being.

The situation had Jenkins pondering retirement, but wife Helen joined Lockett in persuading him to carry on. Their insistence soon proved justified.

He began 2019 with a six-round rust-remover and was presented with a crack at newly crowned British welter king Johnny Garton as boxing returned to the Albert Hall after a seven-year absence. Garton was highly thought-of, not least by promoter Warren, but the expected steamrolling of the Welsh challenger never happened. The Lonsdale Belt was carried into the ring by the champion's stablemate and predecessor, Bradley Skeete, who then watched from ringside as all their plans turned to dust.

Jenkins settled immediately, while Johnny looked tense, and the second saw the unexpected: the Londoner was being forced on to the back foot. Chris's major concern came from Garton's head and he broke off one sixth-round exchange to wipe his brow to check for blood. But this time there was no damage to distract the Amman Valley boy.

By the ninth, 'The Pexican' was looking dispirited, himself nicked below the left eye, while Jenkins, boxing brilliantly, landed repeated right hands to silence the once-

Jenkins overcomes hot favourite Garton to become British champion

raucous crowd. Despite a desperate late assault by the local, Chris maintained control down the finishing straight and his supremacy was recognised by margins of four, five and 10 points.

When imported American MC Thomas Treiber announced "the new…", Jenkins shed tears of joy, while new manager Mo Prior bounced across the ring in jubilation at his first British champion. Chris had become the fifth Welsh boxer to perform the feat in the imposing building, following Johnny Basham, Frank Moody, Robert Dickie and Joe Calzaghe.

His first defence – with the vacant Commonwealth title also at stake – came in very different surroundings, with 10,000 vociferous Ulstermen filling a specially built outdoor arena in Belfast's Falls Park, not far from the home of opponent Paddy Gallagher. Jenkins boxed brilliantly to control the early sessions, but was shocked when the local produced a left to the body which dropped him in his own corner at the end of the sixth.

The bell prevented any follow-up and the Welshman recovered his composure until a head clash in the eighth split his left eyelid – a similar incident had brought blood from his right eyebrow three rounds earlier – which referee Howard Foster and the ringside medic agreed was too bad for him to continue. It was with a degree of relief that the holder's camp heard that all three judges had their man ahead by a slender 86-85 margin.

The BT commentators had missed the second collision – as did others – prompting loud protest, not all of it with Irish accents, that Gallagher should have been given a stoppage victory. Trainer Lockett began a one-man mission to rebut the idea, waylaying

Coach Gary Lockett and manager Mo Prior celebrate Jenkins's title triumph

doubters with film on his phone proving that the second wound had indeed been caused by the head.

There was no need for him to repeat the exercise following the equally bloody end to Jenkins's November encounter in Birmingham with mandatory challenger Liam Taylor. After an even opener, Mancunian Taylor began to land right hooks early in the second and, as Chris tried to duck ever lower, a final blow behind the left ear tipped him over; up instantly and clearly unhurt, the champion nevertheless found himself losing the session 10-8. Jenkins looked to edge a competitive third and was doing well in the fourth when Liam charged in, head down, and caught his foe with some force. Chris turned away, a telltale red stream flowing from his right eyebrow; one look from the ringside doctor was enough and the bout was history.

The finish came just four seconds from the bell which would have meant the scoresheets being consulted, as with Gallagher. Instead a Technical Draw allowed the Garnant product to leave the ring with his reign intact.

With one more successful defence enough for Chris to keep the beautiful belt for twins Jaxson and Jacob and their baby brother, Jenson, he was keen to be back in business once the latest wound had healed. But it would be nearly 20 months before he boxed again. A rematch with predecessor Garton was set for mid-April; by then the world was in lockdown and the resultant postponement prompted the Londoner to hang up his gloves rather than wait for a resumption of the sport.

Jenkins and Essuman exchange leads

Next came Conor Benn, newly installed as mandatory challenger. His promoter, Eddie Hearn, came up with an offer acceptable to both Jenkins and Lockett, only for manager Warren – perhaps not wishing to see one of his champions appearing on a bill promoted by his biggest rival – to advise waiting for purse offers. Days before the envelopes were opened, Benn pulled out, incurring Welsh wrath on social media.

The Board replaced him with Ekow Essuman, but the Midlander, while holding the English title, lacked the public appeal of a legend's son and there was no rush to stage it. It was finally set for a Warren show in London, but a perforated eardrum sustained in sparring meant the Welshman had to cry off.

Essuman had managed one bout during the pandemic, a dominant points win over dangerous Frenchman Cedric Peynaud, and this contributed to his installation as a 3-1 on favourite with the bookies when the pair eventually faced each other at Wembley Arena on July 24, 2021, with recently relaxed restrictions in England meaning 2,000-odd fans were in attendance.

The fight was to turn on one right hand in the second session, not that this was immediately obvious to those watching. It was thrown by the challenger, landing with enough force to snap a couple of ribs and, although Jenkins showed no obvious distress at the time, it left him in constant discomfort.

The Welshman's ringcraft and movement, coupled with a pin-point left jab and an occasional right over the top, built an early lead, but as the rounds passed it was noticeable that the wounded warrior was keeping his left arm tight to his body as an extra barrier. The pain also hampered Chris's breathing and he was unable to respond when Ekow, though himself unaware of the injury, began to increase his workrate.

When it came, just 43 seconds into the eighth, the ending was still a shock. The Nottingham man threw a series of head shots, but few seemed to land clean and yet referee Ian John-Lewis jumped between them. Any question marks over the action were immediately dispelled, however, as Chris leaned to his left, grimacing in agony as he made his way back to his corner.

Essuman, born in Botswana to Ghanaian parents, was duly presented with the Lonsdale Belt his rival had hoped to claim outright. Once the truth emerged, Jenkins was deservedly showered with praise for his courage. He – and, importantly, promoter Warren – insist he will be back. The story is far from over.

KEVIN JENKINS
(1970-)

🥊 Welsh Flyweight Challenger 1991

Back in the early days of UK satellite television there was a channel called 'Screensport'. They broadcast regular shows under the label 'Pro-Box' and at the end of each season one scrap would be lauded as their fight of the year. In 1991 the prize was awarded to two Welshmen: one would go on to become a world champion, the other was an unsung journeyman from the Amman Valley.

Kevin Jenkins was always keen on the sport, but there were no active gyms within reach of his Garnant home, so he and his mates used to take their one pair of old gloves down the local park, wear one each and spar in the sandpit.

But when he was 16, Kevin was able to get a lift to the Towy ABC in Llandeilo, where he learned the basics from Wil Phillips. The new boy picked things up quickly enough to win the Welsh ABA flyweight title just a year later, outpointing Newport southpaw Alan Ley in the final before going down to the legendary John Lyon in the British semi-final.

The following year, while still a teenager, Kevin signed pro forms with Hywel Davies and soon learned that, as a member of that stable, there would be a lot of travelling involved. His first four bouts included two trips to Glasgow, where he handed a first loss to future European title challenger James Drummond, although the Kilmarnock man avenged it two months later when Jenkins, badly cut over the left eye, retired after five rounds.

He and trainer Ronnie Morris then found themselves in Helsinki, where Kevin rocked Finnish Olympian Antti Juntumaa a couple of times, but lost a four-round decision. Then, on successive weekends, he appeared on a world title undercard at the Albert Hall and – at the other end of London boxing's social scale – the York Hall, losing on points each time.

His ninth contest was his first before a Welsh audience, facing much tattooed Ceri Farrell at Penyrheol Leisure Centre on a show promoted by Llanelli farmer Les Cooper. Giving away nearly six pounds and five inches in height, the 5ft 2in Jenkins edged the verdict by half a point, confirming a date with the watching Robbie Regan for the vacant Welsh flyweight title.

Kevin Jenkins

THE BOXERS OF WALES

Kevin with long-time mentor Hywel 'Cass' Davies

The pair met on February 12, 1991, at Cardiff's National Sports Centre, where the fans were kept on the edge of their seats as the pair went at it from the start. It's not as though the result was in any serious doubt, with the supremely talented Bargoed boxer always that much better. But, as Tom Lyons wrote in *Boxing News*, "if bravery were rewarded, he (Jenkins) would have gained a bonus point at the end of every round".

The unbeaten Regan, in the early days of a career that took him to domestic and world honours, had speed and variety in his armoury, his accuracy winning him the rounds despite the workrate and aggression of his stocky rival. Kevin gritted his teeth and kept ploughing on, but in the seventh Robbie uncorked a vicious right to the jaw which dropped him. Up at nine, he somehow reached the bell, holding on and smothering Regan's efforts to end matters.

It was the only occasion on which Jenkins was in serious trouble, although referee Roddy Evans credited him with just two shared sessions on his scorecard. Despite the wide scoring, the fact that Screensport's end-of-year judging panel voted for it confirms that it was a special contest.

As Regan moved on to greatness, Kevin went back on the road. At one stage he was matched with old amateur foe Ley in a proposed Welsh title showdown, with the area council happy for it to be at either fly or bantam, given that both were vacant. A decision was never made; the fight never happened.

In fact, there were just nine bouts left for Jenkins, with only two draws to break the sequence of defeats, but he was taking on some top opponents.

Hitchin's Danny Porter had already challenged for British and Commonwealth belts and tried for the European in between two scraps with Kevin; both ended in stoppages, although the second came on a split lip when it seemed Porter was in worse trouble with a gashed eyebrow. The Welshman put reigning British bantam king Joe Kelly and Irish southpaw Noel Carroll on the deck before losing on points each time and then drew with future Commonwealth ruler Darren Fifield.

And he finished off with two world champions-in-waiting. Paul Weir outpointed him just two months before winning the WBO mini-fly belt – he was to add the light-fly version in due course – and Jenkins's last outing came in Mansfield against an unorthodox and controversial young man named Naseem Hamed. The 'Prince' won in three rounds and Kevin called it a day.

ALAN JONES
(1976-)

- IBC Middleweight Challenger 2005
- British Middleweight Challenger 2005

Growing up on the family farm at Llanon, an active outdoor life came with the territory. But it was to be an indoor sport that introduced Alan Jones to the world beyond rural Ceredigion, though it took some time for that to become apparent.

He represented Aberaeron Comprehensive School at rugby, while captaining the Welsh junior cross-country team. He did give boxing a try at 17, but before he could have a competitive bout he suffered a serious back injury on the rugby field, requiring surgery. Throw in a few years at Reading University, where he graduated with a degree in agriculture, and Jones was 23 before the put the gloves on again.

As a member of Aberystwyth ABC – run by Nick Hodges, born at Hemel Hempstead, but a local resident since he was 12 – Alan won 21 of his 26 contests and reached the national semi-finals before deciding to turn pro. Hywel 'Cass' Davies filled the managerial role, with Hodges continuing as trainer.

Jones's relative anonymity meant he was picked as an ideal opponent for Martyn Woodward, a beanpole Cardiffian with two British schools titles to his name, to make a splash on his first appearance on the pro scene. Any nerves would not have been eased when they both arrived in the same colour shorts and Alan had to rush back to the dressing-room to change. No problem: he dropped the prospect twice in the opener and finished matters in the third. Woodward never boxed again.

The West Walian, on the other hand, was soon back with another stoppage victory over another debutant in Kenny Griffith – and the man from Llanrug, too, promptly retired from the ring! And even though Jones continued to be employed as the out-of-town "opponent", he carried on upsetting his hosts.

He went to Wolverhampton and outscored Midlander Peter Jackson, at that point 5-0 as a pro, and drew in Northampton with locally-based Scot Allan Foster, who had won all eight and went on to box for the British super-middle

Alan Jones trains in the makeshift gym on the family farm

Jones (left) and British champion Scott Dann before things got real

crown. Alan finished 2002 in Birmingham, where he halted future English champion Donovan Smillie in the sixth.

On home ground at Theatr y Werin, on the campus of Aberystwyth University, Jones took all eight rounds against 37-year-old southpaw journeyman Leigh Wicks, and although things were closer when he faced another left-hander, Jason Collins, back in Birmingham, it was another win. There was a similar one-point margin in the Welshman's favour when he travelled to Belfast to face car dealer Jim Rock, a migrant from south of the border.

The 'Pink Panther' floored Jones in the opener and hotly disputed referee David Irving's decision, but the Irishman tired in the later sessions and most observers were content with the judgment. Alan took time out to have some gristle removed from his left elbow and it was eight months before he was back in action, claiming a repeat win over late replacement Collins on a Matchroom show in Hereford, the first pro event in the cathedral city for 55 years.

Jones was less than impressive against the awkward Midlander and looked fortunate to get the nod, but Scottish fight figure Tommy Gilmour – a promotional partner of Matchroom – still took over the managerial reins and the Cardi was soon back at the same venue, where he was much improved in outpointing previously unbeaten Hungarian Szabolcs Rimovszky.

He was rewarded with an invitation to tackle newly installed British middleweight king Scott Dann, though it meant travelling to the holder's Plymouth backyard on an off-TV card promoted by Jamie, 25-year-old son of Dann's manager, Chris Sanigar. The Pavilions, where Scott had won the vacant title five months earlier, was packed when the pair came together on February 4, 2005, with 150 Welsh fans adding their voices to a raucous atmosphere.

Jones prepared for southpaw Dann in Belfast, sharing a ring with WBU welter boss Eamonn Magee and staying with his sparmate's mother, a trip arranged by her eldest son, Terry. The former European title challenger, now living in Ammanford, had become involved in Alan's training, which did not sit well with long-time guide Hodges.

Nick feared that Jones, who had begun boxing too late to have the basics embedded in his muscle memory, would find himself in trouble if he tried new moves in the biggest fight of his career. Magee was insistent that Alan should take care to keep his left foot outside the lead leg of his southpaw rival, whereas Hodges, who had seen his charge deal comfortably with a wrong-way-rounder at Dai Gardiner's gym, thought it unnecessary. In the event, according to Hodges, Jones had been looking at Dann's feet when he was caught by the left hook which ended the contest.

In fairness, the Welshman never really looked at ease. While sensibly operating from range, he seemed wary of moving in – with cause, as when he tried he was greeted by left hands which had him clinging on. The second session brought more of the same, one clinch ending with a cut over the visitor's right eye. The third saw the curtain dropped when two lefts drove Jones into his own corner, where a right hook and a follow-up left dropped him against the post. Although he rose at eight, he stumbled to his right and referee Mark Green completed the count before grabbing the stricken fighter to prevent him falling again.

Alan's British title dream ends in disaster. He made it to his feet, but referee Mark Green completed the count

It is typical of modern-day boxing that someone comprehensively beaten in a British title clash should find himself contesting a world crown in his next outing, even if few would regard the International Boxing Council as worthy of much respect even among today's alphabet soup of sanctioning bodies. But the match-up itself had a lot going for it.

Jim Rock was still unhappy about the decision going against him two years earlier and was happy to be back in his native Dublin for a second encounter with Jones. Before a sell-out crowd at the National Stadium on October 14, 2005 – most, admittedly, there to see Bernard Dunne – the 'Pink Panther' gained his revenge with a unanimous decision.

Alan was always competitive, but found himself forced on to the back foot for most of the bout. He was able to put some pressure on Rock in the middle rounds, but the judges all favoured the local, two by four points and the other by five. There were no complaints from the loser, who promptly retired from the ring. He has since focussed on the farm.

DAI 'FARMER' JONES
(1914-1969)

🥊 Welsh Middleweight Champion 1936-43

Many of Wales's fighters in the last century hewed coal for a living, the arduous work below ground packing muscle on frames small enough to manoeuvre in the confined spaces in which they laboured. But, alongside the pit, there was another wellspring of fighting talent: the farm.

Dai 'Farmer' Jones

Above the mining valleys, there has always been agriculture. And it, too, produced strong and athletic men, often physically bigger than their collier friends. The first boxer to win a Lonsdale Belt at middleweight, Tom Thomas – who was actually born near Llandysul – lived such a life on a mountain overlooking the Rhondda, and the same division saw success for David Samuel Jones, whose background was acknowledged by his nickname, 'Farmer'.

Born and raised at Llwynyronen Farm, above Betws, Dai grew up at a time when the Amman Valley was a hotbed of boxing. The Jones boy had just one contest as an amateur, losing a Welsh ABA prelim to Alf Ford, a Monmouthshire man on his way to the first of five consecutive titles. His victim promptly joined the successful stable of former pro Johnny Vaughan.

Effectively learning on the job, Jones suffered a few early setbacks, including two defeats by Bert Bevan, a Swansea scrapper who became something of a benchmark of the newcomer's progress. Bevan won their first encounter inside five rounds, but had to settle for points when they met again. Even when Jones embarked on an unbeaten streak which included triumphs over the likes of Ocky Davies, Trevor 'Tate' Evans and Cyril 'Bunny' Eddington – all Welsh title challengers – he could only draw in two further clashes with Bert.

But he came good when it mattered. In an official middleweight eliminator at the Mannesmann Hall in Bevan's home town, Dai showed how much he had improved, his solid leads keeping Bert at bay until he took complete control from the fourth onwards. After the local was floored by a right to the body in the sixth, it became a matter of time. He finally subsided under a constant barrage in the ninth; in total Bevan beat six counts before the seventh reached its inevitable conclusion.

Back at the same ramshackle building on the banks of the River Tawe on February 24, 1936, Jones took on titleholder Billy Thomas. Any confidence the Deri man brought to the ring vanished on receipt of a right to the midriff early in the opener. From then on, he adopted a totally negative role and suffered the predictable consequence of allowing a big puncher to have free rein. After a one-sided second, Dai found a right hook halfway through the third which penetrated Billy's guard, landed plumb on the chin and deposited the champion on the deck for the full 10 seconds.

The Amman Valley fighter was now being seriously considered as a threat to the British throne and faced top Scot Jackie McLeod in an official eliminator at the Mannesmann. Dai took a blow to the left eye, which began to swell, and clearly did not want to risk it getting worse; he went after the Leith man in the second and flattened him with a right hook. McLeod rose, but a thunderous left dropped him again and this time it was all over.

The final hurdle before a shot at the Lonsdale Belt was the hard-hitting Jack Hyams, three months later at Earls Court. It proved too big an ask, with the East Ender in charge throughout the 15 rounds. Jones relied on swings from distance, which allowed Hyams to score regularly with left counters as the Welshman moved in. Some Londoners were unhappy with their man's no-risk strategy, but they could hardly blame him for a tactic that earned him a shot at British ruler Jock McAvoy.

Before he met Hyams, however, McAvoy stepped up to light-heavy, overcoming an early knockdown to flatten Eddie Phillips and claim a second belt. His first opponent afterwards, before the mandatory middle defence against Hyams – he stopped the Stepney man on cuts – was in fact the man who lost the eliminator. The 'Rochdale Thunderbolt' met Dai over 10 rounds at Bristol's Colston Hall and turned on a masterful performance, with only the Welshman's courage enabling him to see matters through.

Jones was still top dog at home, however, and defended his belt against Merthyr prospect Tim Sheehan, a previous victim, at Carmarthen's Market Hall on August 2, 1937. The challenger looked nervous as he flicked out a few early leads while keeping an eye open for Dai's feared right. The threat came from the other side, however, with a thunderous left felling Tim for eight midway through the second. He survived the round, but the next session saw him visit the canvas four times, the last prompting the referee to call a halt.

Five months later Tim was dead, having suffered a heart attack following a sparring session. He was only 21.

Jones did not defend his crown again for another year, not that he was idle. He beat Cuban Cheo Morejón – a former conqueror – but was twice outpointed by Fijian Ben Valentine, while also coming second on a visit to Hamburg to face German middle king Jupp Besselmann. Former British welter monarch Dave McCleave twice outscored Dai, but the Welshman put up a sterling show in dropping a decision to the outstanding Scouser Ernie Roderick, who went on to win British honours and last the distance in a world title challenge to the legendary Henry Armstrong.

When the time eventually came to risk his domestic laurels, back in Carmarthen, the opposite stool was occupied by Elfryn Morris, originally from Tiryberth, but based in the Midlands for several years. A packed Bank Holiday house saw the taller holder stake an early claim to the centre of the ring, following his left lead with powerful rights.

The second saw Dai draw Morris on to another solid right, which dumped the Rhymney Valley product for a count of three, but he was fighting back by the bell. Elfryn seized the initiative in the third, working the body, but 'Farmer' responded with a right hook before a left downstairs put Morris back on the seat of his pants for six seconds.

The challenger returned to the attack early in the fourth, but was quickly repelled and Dai took advantage of momentary confusion to launch his pet right to the stomach. Morris dropped instantly, rolling over in agony. Somehow he scrambled to his feet at nine, but referee C.B. Thomas ruled that he was in no state to box on.

Jones's roster of exotic foes was extended when he beat Egyptian Mohamed Fahmy, who stunned the Earls Court crowd by standing in his corner throughout the intervals (unheard of) and wearing white shorts (unacceptable; Board officials made him don coloured ones after two rounds).

Dai headed west on March 27, 1939, to bid for a second national crown. Former middleweight boss Glen Moody had followed the example of big brother (and two-weight British champion) Frank and left his native Pontypridd to run a pub in Pembrokeshire. Frank was mine host at the Royal Hotel, Milford Haven, while Glen pulled pints at the Globe in Fishguard. Midway between the two is Haverfordwest, where Jones faced the younger Moody with the vacant Welsh light-heavy belt at stake.

Turning 25 just five days earlier, Jones had comparative youth on his side; Moody had reached 30 and, in fact, had announced his retirement three years before, only to be seduced back into the ring. And now he was to enjoy an Indian summer.

Dai had outscored Moody at middleweight in 1936, but this time he was drawn into a gruelling encounter, in which the veteran's experience and ringcraft proved decisive. Glen was totally in command at close quarters, while he did well enough at range to win by a narrow margin.

Four months later came the career change that effectively ended Jones's exploits as a boxer. 'Farmer' became 'Copper', joining Carmarthenshire Police as a War Reservist. There were a couple more fights, but when police duties meant he had to withdraw from a planned date with future British champion Dick Turpin it became increasingly obvious that the two jobs could not be combined.

Over three decades Dai served the communities of Llanelli, Laugharne and Pontyberem, retiring as a sergeant in 1969. Less than nine months later he died of cancer at his home in Myddynfych Drive, Ammanford. He was 55.

EMRYS JONES
(1931-2011)

- Welsh Lightweight Champion 1955-56

Farm boy Emrys Jones was born a few miles from the Montgomeryshire village of Four Crosses, where boxing would not normally be considered a likely leisure activity. Indeed, his father and uncles favoured music, the youngster later adding his tenor voice to the songs of Parti Wern Ddu as they entertained the community.

Yet an interest in the sport was there from the start, with Dad waking his five-year-old son to listen to radio commentary on Tommy Farr's brave challenge to world heavyweight king Joe Louis. But it took the success of local man Dennis Powell a decade later to show what was possible, even in the most rural of areas.

With little amateur activity around, the 17-year-old Jones had just one bout – against a mate, after their opponents never turned up – before joining the paid ranks with Powell's manager, Bernard Thomas.

There were only two losses in his first 21 contests, both of which he reversed, while 11 of his wins had come inside two rounds. But manager Thomas, conscious of Emrys's comparative inexperience, was not disposed to rush him, while trainer Billy Roberts worked to add technique to the obvious power.

Regular action provided ample opportunity for him to hone his skills, but also saw defeats increase in regularity, including a one-round dismissal by Derby veteran Sam 'Darkie' Sullivan. If it was becoming clear that a Lonsdale Belt would remain beyond his reach, championship dreams within Wales were a different matter.

Even if four victories over someone called Peter Cardiff were of little significance in this regard – the guy was a Lancastrian – Jones had seen off Neath's useful Mel Wathan and although newcomer Darkie Hughes outscored him over six rounds the

Emrys Jones

THE BOXERS OF WALES

Emrys on his first love, a scrambling bike

Cardiffian was a bit special, a former British ABA champion who went on to fight for the same honour as a pro.

A draw against another fighter from the capital, Teddy Best, caught the attention of the Welsh Area Council and the pair were asked to face each other again in a lightweight final eliminator at Newtown Drill Hall on May 1, 1954. It had a fairly unsatisfactory outcome, with Best thrown out in the eighth for persistent holding, but that crime is usually a pretty good indication that the other feller is getting the better of things.

Three weeks later, coincidentally, it was another disqualification that installed Crickhowell's Willie Lloyd on the national throne, with redheaded former Olympic reserve Parry Dando, from the Gwent valleys, red-carded for a low blow. It took a year before Emrys, by now living across the border at Trefonen, was finally given his date with Lloyd on a bill at Carmarthen Drill Hall in May 1955, but the champion was halted in four rounds by Geordie Johnny Miller in Liverpool and an accompanying broken nose meant he had to withdraw. The would-be challenger had to settle for a 10-rounder against German-born Devonian Kurt Ernest; a demotivated Jones struggled to a draw.

West Wales promoter Ben Davies rearranged the title showdown for the same venue on September 26, 1955, and it proved worth the wait, particularly for Emrys. His constant forward motion nullified Lloyd's greater skill, even if the Montgomeryshire fighter wasted his height and reach advantage by relying on round-house punches.

Willie was keen to work inside wherever possible, but found no respite there, with Jones matching him at close quarters. Lloyd took a tumble in the fifth, but it was ruled a slip, and neither seemed to have the power to repeat it so that it counted.

But there were no complaints from an enthralled audience as the pair maintained a tremendous pace throughout the 12 rounds and ended with a torrid session which had the fans on the edge of their seats. Come the final bell and the referee decided Emrys had done enough to become the second man from his village to call himself champion of Wales.

The Jones boy celebrated his new-found status by demolishing Bobby Gill inside a round at Blackpool – though only after hitting the deck himself – but that was to be the last time his arm was raised in triumph. Over a five-week spell, he was outpointed by Irish duo Pat McCoy and Leo Molloy, sandwiching a loss to Brummie Johnny Mann. A few months later he confirmed that his career was done, blaming a recurrent problem with his back, the result of a couple of spills from his scrambling bike.

Emrys returned to life as a farm labourer, but that was badly hit by the foot-and-mouth outbreak of 1967 and he took a job at Whittington Dairy; it later became the Cheese Company in Oswestry, where he remained until retirement. He and wife Ivy had four children: although neither of his sons followed him into the ring, the older, Graham, inherited his love for motorcycles, becoming a professional speedway rider.

Dad was always the main man, though. When the Oswestry Sports Hall of Fame was set up in 2019, eight years after his death, Emrys Jones was one of the first honoured, alongside golfing superstar Ian Woosnam and World Cup winner Alan Ball.

Emrys in later years

HENRY JONES
(1975-)

- Welsh Bantamweight Challenger 1997
- Welsh Super-Featherweight Challenger 2006

The amiable Pembroke southpaw was a journeyman. But, like many of the breed, when given decent notice and a belt on the line he proved he could box a bit. Not well enough to win a title, perhaps, but certainly well enough to let his supposed betters know they had been in a scrap.

Henry Jones

Henry Jones's talent was soon obvious as a schoolboy with the local club. Guided by his father, Tommy, and Ralph Gammer, the youngster picked up a selection of national age-group championships and a gold medal at the Gaelic Games, adding a senior Welsh ABA triumph before turning pro as part of the Glynne Davies stable.

There were wins and losses – notably one 80-second blast-out of Plymouth trier Danny Lawson before diners at Cardiff's City Hall and a similarly early defeat by unbeaten prospect Francky Leroy on the French coast – before Henry was matched with an old rival for the vacant Welsh bantam crown at the Brangwyn Hall on December 2, 1997.

The Jones boy had beaten Tredegar's lanky Ian Turner when both were juniors, but the Monmouthshire man had his revenge when they came together again in a six-rounder at Ebbw Vale. The rubber match would have a belt as added incentive. Prior knowledge perhaps encouraged the early caution on both sides, although energy-saving might also have influenced two boxers who had never been beyond six rounds. Turner, with three wins and a draw to his name since leaving the amateur ranks, gradually began to bring his jab into play, his height and reach advantages almost guaranteeing its success.

But the stocky West Walian's workrate kept him in contention into the middle rounds and he was given a boost in the sixth when Turner was gashed on the left eyelid. Cornerman Dai Gardiner did a good job with the swabstick, however, allowing Ian to focus on the task at hand and slowly take command.

Halfway through the eighth, Turner uncorked a left uppercut which wobbled Henry and two supplementary rights helped his victim on his way to the canvas.

Jones looks relaxed backstage at the Brangwyn Hall before facing Dai Davies

Jones was up at six, his eyes clear, and began to fight back, but another sharp right to the jaw brought the intervention of Maesteg referee Mike Heatherwick. Manager Davies, himself involved in the last title fight at this weight 17 years previously, objected vigorously, but to no avail.

Henry, beset by injuries and also busy with work as a mechanical fitter in the oil industry, fought only twice in the next five years, eventually coming back with Aberystwyth-based Nick Hodges, while Graham Brockway handled the training side. Jones was on the welter limit when he returned – far too heavy for someone barely five feet tall – but slimmed back to super-feather over the next three years. His success on the scales was not matched in the ring, his only two victories in that time coming over Brummie Jason Nesbitt.

But regular defeats were apparently no bar to contesting British Masters belts and Henry was employed as the fall guy for unbeaten Darren Johnstone in Glasgow. The Welshman deviated from the script and decked the Scot in the opener. Johnstone was given a suspiciously long count, allowing him to recover, and then landed low blows in the third and fourth, each of which prompted referee Victor Loughlin to give Henry time out to get his breath back. Immediately after the second pause, however, Darren hurled a left cross which felled the visitor for the full count.

There was some revenge over Scotland when Henry outscored Furhan Rafiq at the Carmarthen Showground before he was handed a second Welsh title chance in his new 9st 4lb division. It was again at the Brangwyn Hall on October 8, 2006, with manager Hodges dipping his toes into promoting with a Sunday afternoon affair and being rewarded with a decent turnout. Unfortunately, while his fighter played his part in a cracking contest, he was never able to contain Merthyr's talented Dai Davies.

Henry's task was made harder when a right in the opener drew blood from his left eye and a short left in the fourth added a matching wound above the right. Jones had some joy when he worked his way inside, but a jolting two-punch combination in the eighth discouraged him from such ventures and Davies controlled the later stages to take a four-point victory from referee Wynford Jones.

There was little left for Henry. A stoppage loss (somewhat premature, it must be said) at Neath to Ingle fighter John Baguley was followed by another in Scotland to unbeaten Gary McArthur, this time with the British Masters lightweight strap up for grabs. Enough was enough.

With his work taking him all over the place, there has been little opportunity for the fight game, but when he gets a break at home Henry usually finds time to call in at Brockway's Merlins Bridge gym and pass on a few tips to the kids.

IVOR JONES
(1954-)

🥊 Southern Area Bantamweight Challenger 1983

They called him 'Ivor the Engine', but the boy from Anglesey was more into horses than motors. In fact, he was more into horses than boxing, even though his Uncle Llew had a brief pro career.

The family were well known in the area: his father, Will, was a ship's pilot and coxswain of the Holyhead lifeboat for 30 years, honoured three times for bravery. But that love for our four-legged friends saw young Ivor leave the ferry port at the age of 15 and head for Newmarket to become an apprentice jockey.

Ironically, that meant exposure to the fight game too. Back in the day stable lads learned the noble art as well as how to handle racehorses and the Welsh-speaking youngster won their national competition three times, while adding a Home Counties title and two in the Eastern Counties. He also met the man whose story would be intertwined with his from then on.

Londoner Colin Lake was a useful performer whose career included a brave challenge to British junior lightweight champion Jimmy Anderson. Himself a former apprentice jockey, he first saw the Jones boy at informal sparring sessions in a stable loft and realised he had a talent worth nurturing. After taking his pupils to various local gyms, Lake set up Cheveley ABC, a few miles outside town, and it was their vest that Jones wore to his amateur successes.

By now boxing had supplanted racing as Ivor's passion and it was time to get paid for it. The pair left East Anglia to head for London, Lake finding him digs in Holloway, and he signed up with Danny Vary while his trainer qualified for a manager's licence.

A third-round stoppage of lanky Carl Gaynor was a promising start and was followed by five more victories before the run came to an end in what, amazingly, turned out to be his only contest outside the metropolis. Central Area bantam champion Steve Enwright faced him on neutral ground in

Ivor Jones with his father, lifeboat hero Will

Jones on the attack against fellow-Welshman Kelvin Smart

Birmingham and took a wide points decision, but Jones had been well below par. He was later – after retiring from the ring – found to have a thyroid problem, easily sorted by a daily tablet. At the time the medics were baffled and he was inactive for nearly a year.

He made up for lost time, picking up five wins in as many months, thrilling the fans with his all-action style. Then things began to go awry, just as he was given a slot on two major events. At the Albert Hall Ulsterman Davy Larmour took an eight-round verdict, while a couple of weeks later at Wembley Arena Ivor was outclassing Merseyside journeyman Jimmy Bott when he was shaken by a right counter in the sixth. Three trips to the canvas followed before referee Brian Anders waved it off.

Once his mandatory suspension was over, Jones returned to the Albert Hall – promoter Mike Barrett loved the number of tickets he could shift, with the racing fraternity travelling en masse from Newmarket to cheer him on – and this time flattened Irish veteran Neil McLaughlin in four and then, in the more homely surroundings of York Hall, edged out Eltham's Johnny Dorey by half a point in a fight-of-the-year candidate.

Six months later, on March 22, 1983, despite a hotly disputed points loss to that man Bott, he and Dorey – friends who had frequently trained together at the famous Thomas à Becket gym – were back in Bethnal Green to dispute the vacant Southern Area bantam throne. Ivor had been chief sparmate for Charlie Magri as the flyweight prepared for his world title triumph the week before and the new champion was present for his big night.

In a thriller to match their first meeting, Jones's aggression was met by sharp, accurate counter-punches and the Holloway-based warrior was soon bleeding from the nose and left eye. His constant pressure forced Dorey back, however, and the Londoner also suffered a nick on his right cheek. After a toe-to-toe final session, Roland Dakin gave his vote to Johnny by one point.

Unfortunately, some of Ivor's backers were unable to accept it. One drunken follower punched Dakin in the face, causing a gash across his nose which required hospital treatment. Another threw the contents of a cornerman's bucket over MC Billy Jones as he made the official announcement. Other, calmer ringsiders threw money into the ring in recognition of a cracking scrap that could have gone either way.

Ivor shrugged off his disappointment with a fourth-round win over Midlander Gary Roberts before facing two fellow-countrymen. Swansea's future British feather king Peter Harris was held to a draw, while a former Lonsdale Belt holder, Llanbradach flyweight Kelvin Smart, was blown away inside two rounds.

Next up was another man on his way to the top. Billy Hardy was coming off a shock stoppage loss when he took on Jones at the Albert Hall. It was, inevitably with Ivor involved, an enthralling battle and, while

Ivor celebrates with trainer and best mate Colin Lake

referee Nick White favoured the Sunderland man's skill, it was controversial enough for them to go at it again two months later at York Hall. But the Welshman, disillusioned by the outcome of the first encounter, was losing enthusiasm for the game and had no complaints when third man Roy Francis had Hardy clearly ahead at the bell.

Jug-eared Billy went on to be British champion at two weights, adding Commonwealth and Europe honours and challenging three times for world titles. For Jones, there was one bout left. It was, of course, exciting fare for the dinner-jacketed patrons of the National Sporting Club, but Shane Sylvester, from West Bromwich, finished in front after eight rounds which convinced both Ivor and mentor Lake that the journey was over. 'The Engine' had hit the buffers.

Not that his love affair with boxing has faded. He and his pal Colin are still passing on their accumulated wisdom to the amateurs of the Angel club in Islington.

MIKE JONES
(1984-)

🥊 Welsh Super-Welterweight Challenger 2017

The Wrexham man should, by rights, not appear in this book. There are many boxers across the years who have achieved more, but have missed out on inclusion. But Mike Jones's five-fight professional career included a bout sanctioned as for the championship of Wales, so here he is.

This is not to say that Jones was not a perfectly reasonable operator at his level. But the fact that the Welsh Area Council recognised someone with just four contests, two of which he had lost, as worthy of a shot at national supremacy seems as strange now as when the match was made.

In addition, all Mike's appearances had been over four rounds; normally, the authority insists on a prospective contender having experience over six at least before being allowed to step up to the 10-round title distance. And it's not as though he had a lengthy amateur career behind him.

Mike Jones

Michael Andrew Jones spent his youth in the south, studying at Newport's Hartridge High School, before moving to the Wrexham area at 20 and settling at Brymbo. It was another two years before he first climbed into a ring in the colours of Llay ABC, winning nine of 14 competitive outings before switching to the paid ranks.

Stoke-based Scott Lawton, a former English lightweight ruler who challenged for British, Commonwealth and European honours, held the managerial reins, while ringwise journeyman Peter Buckley took over the training side. Mike's first two engagements took him to Lincolnshire and Scotland; he failed to win a single round in points losses to a fellow-debutant and, more understandably, a former amateur international who had won all four previous fights. Strangely, neither man has boxed since.

Their victim, however, showed that he was learning, claiming the decision in his next two contests. It no doubt helped that each time he was in the home corner at Stoke's King's Hall, while his hand-picked rivals were not overly threatening. Jones won every session in handing Torquay trier Ali Wyatt his 30th defeat in 36 bouts, bur only scraped a one-point margin over Paul O'Brien, a Yorkshireman who had lost all 16 encounters.

Mike, a qualified plumber by now working as a galvaniser in a steel firm, was then inactive for 11 months before his eyebrow-raising chance to bid for the vacant super-welter throne. The show, at Merthyr Leisure Centre on March 25, 2017, was due to be televised by S4C, who wanted title action to launch their new venture. Crowd favourite Tony Dixon was to occupy one stool; eager to encourage the Welsh-language channel, the powers-that-be sanctioned Jones to take the other.

Jones (right) on his way to victory over Paul O'Brien

The outcome surprised nobody. A Dixon right dropped the Northerner in a neutral corner and another two knockdowns prompted referee Martin Williams to halt matters after just 109 seconds. Jones promptly announced his retirement. But he can always say that he fought for a belt.

STANLEY JONES
(1964-)

🥊 Welsh Lightweight Challenger 1985

The Yanks call boxing "the red light district of sports". It suggests that the normal rules do not apply. And the southpaw from Llandeilo has particular reason to lament the lack of logic – and, indeed, fair play – in the way the fight game is run.

Stanley Jones's unbeaten entry to the paid ranks earned him a crack at the Welsh lightweight championship in just his seventh contest. Holder Ray Hood had relinquished the crown and Rhyl donkey man Eddie Lloyd was expected to keep the honour in the north. Eddie's manager, Pat Dwyer, provided home advantage (near enough) by staging the bout at the Cee-J Club in Colwyn Bay on July 19, 1985.

A packed house saw Lloyd hustle the taller Jones out of his stride early on, but the West Walian soon settled and his greater skill began to cause Eddie problems. The middle rounds saw Lloyd regroup, one solid right in the sixth giving his rival pause for thought. Stanley came back to regain control, but an all-out assault in the last was enough to earn the crowd favourite a draw on the card of Rhondda referee Ivor Bassett. Jones felt hard done by, claiming that even Eddie's father thought he had won. Worse was to follow.

The *Boxing News* report left no room for doubt, insisting the verdict "means they must meet again". Lloyd, it appears, was not enthusiastic, but Stanley might have expected to face someone else. Instead he had to stand by while two other men met to decide Hood's successor, Gwent's Andy Williams outpointing Cardiffian Mark Pearce. Indeed, Jones was never given another chance at glory; Llandeilo still waits for its first ring champion.

Stanley's introduction to the sport came as a belligerent eight-year-old. After assorted street scraps, including one where he saw off six bigger boys in quick succession, his mother, whose father had boxed, decided he needed an outlet for his aggression and directed him to the nearby Towy ABC.

A string of Welsh schoolboy titles climaxed in triumph at the British finals in 1980, when he stopped Enfield's Dean Barclay to celebrate along with Welsh winners who included future pro stars such as Floyd Havard, the aforementioned Andy Williams, John Davies and Tony Borg.

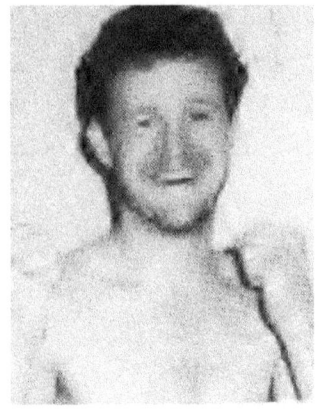

Stanley Jones

Stanley the trainer, in the corner of Robert Peel

As a senior, Jones reached the 1982 Welsh final, only to be disqualified for repeatedly holding David Griffiths as he tried to avoid a series of kidney punches which left him needing hospital treatment afterwards. Cardiffian Griffiths went on to represent GB at the Seoul Olympics; by then Stanley had already dipped his toe into the professional pool.

Joining the camp of amateur mentor Hywel Davies, better known as 'Cass', he found himself in the same predicament as his journeymen stablemates, having to travel for work. Usually, that means facing popular attractions in their own back yards, but the dinner-boxing circuit thriving at the time had no need to rely on local ticket-sellers: for their audiences, mainly businessmen and their clients, the bouts were just part of a night out and the identity of the participants was irrelevant.

So when Jones opened his account with a knockout victory in Southend, his victim, Frankie Lake, came from Devon. The neutral onlookers had value for money, with Lake putting Stanley on the canvas in the opener before a right to the jaw ended the argument in the fifth. Three points wins and two draws saw Stanley rewarded with the Welsh title shot against Lloyd and a third successive sharing of the spoils.

With no sign of a second chance at the belt, Jones grabbed a late opportunity to replace another Rhyl fighter, Rocky Feliciello, against Scottish champion Steve Boyle at Glasgow's St Andrew's Sporting Club. It proved a disastrous decision. The highly-touted Boyle, also a southpaw, dropped the substitute in the first before storming in to end matters; a barrage of body shots sent Stanley through the ropes. He crashed to the floor, landing on his head, and was counted out, a doctor preventing any attempt to rise.

Boyle went on to an unsuccessful tilt at Tony Willis's British throne – the Scot did win a Lonsdale Belt in due course – while Jones took 11 months out to ponder on life's lottery. A draw with Scot Steve Kiernan back in Glasgow, followed by a points success against Irish ruler Gary Muir in Gloucester, boosted Stanley's self-belief. But his place in the pecking order was underlined back in Scotland, where he was clearly outscored by unbeaten fellow-southpaw Alex Dickson, another who went on to British honours.

Promoter John Davies, wanting to showcase his son of the same name, brought boxing back to Carmarthen after a 20-year absence, and Jones was handed a spot on the Leisure Centre undercard. He duly outclassed Liverpool-based Ghanaian Junaido Musah before heading back on the road.

The first port of call was a familiar one, Glasgow, but so was the outcome, Stanley being floored and outpointed by Brighton veteran Peter Eubank. Yet when the Welshman agreed to face Chris's big brother again on his own patch in Hove, it was the visitor who came out on top – though it should be said that the loser was less than impressed with the verdict after a bout in which both made brief trips to the deck.

It was the last time the Jones arm was to be raised. In fact, his career had only three months to run. First he responded to a late call back to Hove Town Hall after the Mexican opponent of Commonwealth light-welter king Tony Laing dropped out. The non-title clash was scheduled for 10 rounds: it was over after 20 seconds, when a thunderous right sent Stanley crashing, his skull thudding into the canvas.

He had one more try when Frank Warren's *Seconds Out!* TV series visited Cardiff, but future European 10st boss Pat Barrett was far too good. He almost ended things even sooner than Laing, a right uppercut felling Stanley in the opening seconds. Somehow its recipient reached the bell, but two more knockdowns in round two brought referee Wynford Jones's intervention and the Llandeilo man's retirement from the ring.

He lost interest and stepped away from boxing, focussing on his trade as a laminator. But a decade later he took out a trainer's licence to guide former sparmate Robert Peel. After a further break, Stanley returned to the Towy gym, now in Ammanford, to teach amateurs including future pro Jake Anthony.

There was a change in the day job, too: he is now employed by a charity as a support worker helping look after people with learning difficulties.

CHRIS LAWSON
(1957-)

- Welsh Light-Heavyweight Champion 1978-80

Boxers tend to take things easy as a big fight approaches. At the top level, there may be a few media duties to fulfil – a light public workout, a press conference – but nothing too demanding on either mind or body. As a rule, they don't get married two days before defending a title. Chris Lawson did.

It was never intended that way. The fight had been booked for the previous weekend, with Chris then free to celebrate his 21st birthday on the Wednesday and enjoy his stag night on the Friday before getting hitched on the Saturday. But challenger Ken Jones was sick and the show had to be put back a week.

The social gatherings went ahead without him, but the wedding took place on schedule. And Jones was beaten on the Monday, so Lawson was able to fly off with Mags for their delayed honeymoon, sporting a black eye, but still champion of Wales.

Chris was actually born in Leeds, but the family moved to Tredegar when he was four and it was at the Deri Bargoed club that he first clambered into a ring. Migration further west, to Cardigan, followed and the youngster joined Narberth ABC before – once he had started work as a greenkeeper at a local golf course and could afford a car – switching to Pembroke Dock and coach Roy Witts, who was in his corner for the rest of his fighting life.

Already a junior champion, Lawson made an immediate impact on the senior amateur scene, claiming two consecutive Welsh middleweight titles only to fall foul of Londoner Dave Odwell in the British each year and miss out on an Olympic spot. In 1977, stepping up to light-heavy, he went all the way, demolishing the improbably named Placid Gonzalez – the glazier from Stevenage

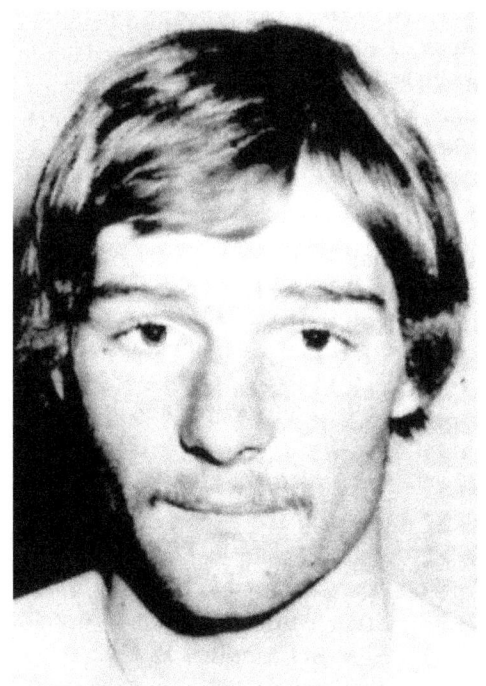

Chris Lawson

Chris and a battered Ken Jones following their first meeting

had Argentinian forebears – with a left uppercut inside two minutes of the British final. Although a crack at the Europeans ended with his first bout, against an East German who went on to the silver medal, professional eyes were watching.

Eddie Thomas, the maestro from Merthyr, was the obvious choice for a Welsh hopeful, but it was a long journey to the old Penydarren gym and most of the basic work was done locally with Witts. Even that short trip became tedious and Chris left the golf course to live in Pembroke Dock and work as a scaffolder.

A successful debut at a storm-lashed Afan Lido was followed by two more triumphs before the wheels came off at London's posh Grosvenor House hotel – ironically, against a fellow-Welshman!

Former pro Brian Anders was absurdly generous to Cardiffian Bonny McKenzie in giving him seven of the eight rounds (and a share of the other), but there was little suggestion that he had the wrong victor. And a return to the same Mayfair venue proved disastrous when Londoner Karl Canwell, half a stone heavier, stopped Lawson at the end of the fifth. There were a couple of wins, too, but one of them saw Chris pay two brief visits to the canvas before a knockdown of his own left unbeaten Blackpool boy Steve Hill with what turned out to be a broken ankle.

Yet less than a month after that eventful evening, the Cardigan man was Welsh champion. New promoter Pat Mathias invited him and old rival McKenzie to dispute the vacant throne at Swansea's Top Rank Suite on November 29, 1978. While Bonny started strongly, his former victim – despite two cuts dealt with expertly by manager Thomas – worked his way into the fight and began to hurt his Jamaican-born foe with body shots. McKenzie was rocked in the ninth and dropped in the last to clinch Lawson's victory by half a point for world-class referee Jim Brimmell.

Another stoppage loss, to Manchester-West Indian Eddie Smith, reminded the new monarch of his position in the wider pecking order, but there were no such problems when the new bridegroom defended against Gorseinon's Ken Jones, big brother of fast-rising Colin. In front of a 600-strong crowd at Haverfordwest's Market Hall, the West Walian controlled matters from the start; by the seventh Jones was bleeding from nose and eyebrow and although referee Brimmell cleared him to continue there was little doubt about Chris deserving his decision.

Reality struck across the border when Londoner Carlton Benoit beat him in two and after two wins and a draw improved the look of his record, future British and European ruler Tom Collins prevailed in four, while Dennis Andries, a world champion-in-waiting, did so in eight. It was on the back of these defeats that Lawson found himself defending his national supremacy again.

Ken Jones was back in the other corner at Gowerton, where the National Eisteddfod had just ended and Thomas hired the Pavilion for the night of August 12, 1980. With

Colin retaining his recently acquired Lonsdale Belt against Swindon's Peter Neal, Ken completed the family double.

Chris displayed his customary neat skills, but Jones maintained a hot pace and generally forced matters in a battle that climaxed in a toe-to-toe last round. This time referee Brimmell had the local man two rounds in front.

The deposed champion chased the cheques across the border for much of the remaining four years of his career, which meant losses to some useful men: future British title challengers Roy Skeldon, Trevor Cattouse and Keith Bristol all beat the Welshman, while former conquerors Canwell and Andries repeated their previous triumphs.

The Lawson passport saw some use as well, with trips to Germany, Denmark, Italy and as far as British Columbia. All ended with another 'L' on the record, but alongside a few top names, including future IBF king Slobodan Ka ar and four-time European challenger Manfred Jassman. But the Cardigan fighter also had two more shots at his old belt, each time vacant.

Chris Lawson immortalised in oils

The first came in London, beneath the chandeliers of the Café Royal, where the dinner-jacketed members of the National Sporting Club saw old foe McKenzie win their rubber match, according to the ubiquitous Jim Brimmell. The decision displeased many of the normally sedate ringsiders, while Witts – by now holding the managerial reins – insisted his charge would never again fight for the Welsh title.

He did, of course, although Mr Brimmell was not in charge when Chris took on Gilwern's Aneurin Williams at Ebbw Vale two years later. Caerleon schoolteacher Adrian Morgan, however, returned the same scoreline, in favour of the man from a few miles along the Heads of the Valleys road. In a thriller played out to constant chanting from both bands of supporters, the younger Williams's enthusiasm and energy gave him an early lead, which proved sufficient to withstand Lawson's late surge.

The last hurrah came with a points defeat by unbeaten Battersea southpaw Sam Reeson, on his way to British and European cruiser crowns and a tilt at world honours. Just 27, Chris had had enough.

Not that he was lost to boxing. He became a trainer at the recently formed Cardigan ABC, but eventually the demands of running his own scaffolding business forced him to take a back seat. These days he is the club's honorary president.

DUDLEY LEWIS
(1917-1993)

- Welsh Flyweight Champion 1938
- Welsh Bantamweight Challenger 1938

Breconshire was something of a barren area when it came to the fight game, but it was a popular staging post for the travelling fairs – and, with them, the boxing booths. And this was where Raymond Dudley Lewis first laced up the gloves.

He may not have acquired too many of the game's technical skills – he was always described as a "perpetual motion" character in the ring – but he discovered he could bang with both hands and that was enough to convince him that a career in the sport would be worthwhile.

To find a manager and trainer young Dudley had to head for Swansea and Dai James, who kept him busy, enabling him to learn his trade while building a reputation against domestic rivals. Even in defeat against Al 'Kid' McCoy the teenager looked good enough for promoter and booth owner Joe Gess to want to take him under his wing for a year.

With or without Gess's input, Dudley impressed the authorities enough to be nominated to face Rhondda namesake Dickie Lewis for the vacant Welsh flyweight title. More than 6,000 packed the Mountain Ash Pavilion on April 4, 1938, to see Dickie turn on a masterly display for the first four rounds. He looked set for victory, with Dudley relying on wild rights that rarely found their target.

But a toe-to-toe exchange in the sixth saw Dudley land a right to the chin and the Stanleytown stylist went down for five. He had hardly regained his feet when he was floored again, just beating the count. In the seventh Dickie hit the canvas once more, but the bell came to his rescue. There was another lengthy count in the eighth and after three more knockdowns in the ninth referee Bob Hill stopped the carnage. The triumph caused something of a stir in Brecon, a

Dudley Lewis

Dudley Lewis (left) poses with namesake Dickie before their Welsh title bout

normally placid market town, and he was presented with a wristwatch to mark his achievement.

Lewis's preparation for fights was not always as rigorous as it might have been. It is said that on one occasion he and a few friends stopped off at a pub on the way to a bout in Monmouthshire. After a few pints had been despatched, Lewis urged the others to put a few quid on him winning in the seventh round. He took some punishment early on, but duly stopped his man in the allotted session, only to find his mates had not placed the bet, believing he had drunk too much to deliver on his promise.

Dudley was furious. "I could have taken him out in the first," he said, "but I took a battering for six rounds just to make you some money!"

His elevated status meant the new champion was in demand beyond Wales and he travelled to Belfast to face Jimmy Warnock, a vastly experienced operator who could boast a non-title points win over reigning world champion Benny Lynch in his native Glasgow. Outdoors at the Glentoran football ground, Warnock gradually took control until a knockdown in the ninth and two more in the next brought the towel sailing in from the Lewis corner.

Dudley's reign was to be short-lived, although that was his own decision. Struggling to make the 8st limit, he relinquished the belt and was promptly matched in a bantam eliminator against Eddie Davies, of Cwmparc, who had outpointed him a few months earlier. When holder Mog Mason stepped down after sustaining an eye injury while boxing in Canada, the bout at Hereford Drill Hall on December 6, 1938, was upgraded to be for the vacant throne.

Different eyes saw different things: the *Boxing* reporter (possibly a Mid-Wales man) said it lacked colour and was somewhat monotonous, as Eddie concentrated on making Lewis miss, while doing little positive of his own until the later rounds, and claimed that the verdict had a mixed reception. The *Echo* writer, on the other hand, saw Davies winning convincingly, the complete boxer dominating the slugger. "He knew every move in the game and showed a versatility few present-day boxers possess," he insisted.

Only once was Eddie in trouble, when Dudley knocked him through the ropes in the ninth (an event *Boxing*'s bored scribe did not bother to mention) and although the Rhondda boy made it back in seconds, he was clearly shaken and struggled to reach the bell. Lewis also scored often enough to bring blood from Davies's nose, but a last do-or-die effort by the Brecon battler proved to no avail.

Further defeats followed, including a 10-round decision to Swansea's Len Davies, who went on to challenge three times, all unsuccessfully, for Welsh honours, before ill-health left Dudley on the sidelines for a spell. He reappeared with a seventh-round knockout of Jimmy Wilde – not the legend, of course, but a fairly ordinary operator from Oxford. A week later Lewis halted Eddie Davies, but this was not his title conqueror, but a lad from Cwm with the same handle.

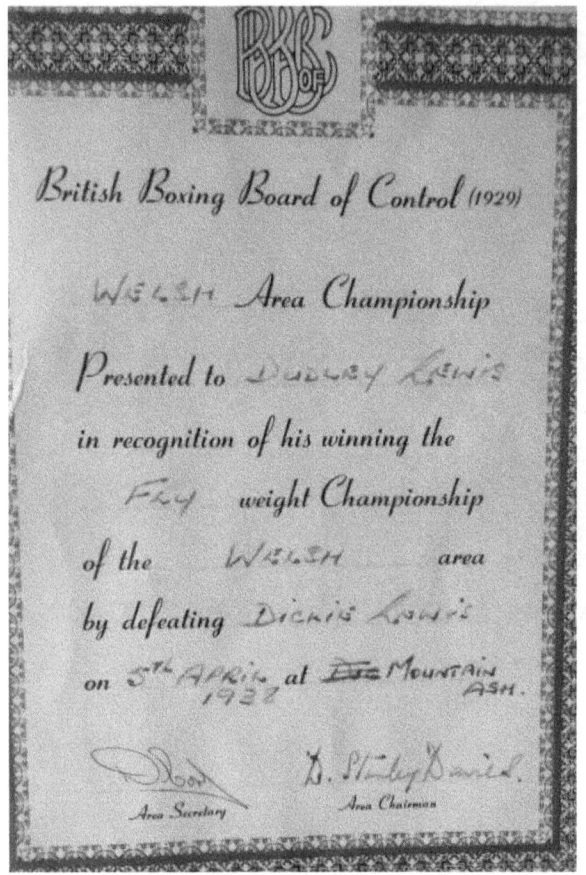

The certificate presented to Dudley as a token of his triumph

With World War II underway, Dudley left his job as a lorry driver to join the Army, but boxing still played an important and morale-boosting part in British life. Not that Lewis's personal morale would have had much of a lift when he was stopped by West Indian Ritchie 'Kid' Tanner, at the Racecourse in Wrexham, and knocked out by Scouser Gus Foran at Liverpool Stadium. Foran, who stepped up to replace the injured Peter Kane despite spending the previous night on guard duty, was decked in the fourth, but dropped Dudley five times in all, the last occasion seeing top referee Eugene Henderson count him out.

Facing future world flyweight champion Jackie Paterson on a big show at the Albert Hall was a similarly chastening experience. First the Welshman was fined for coming in over the agreed weight; then the talented Scot poleaxed him with a left hook and it was all over inside a minute.

There was little left when Lewis, now back in civvy street and living at Talybont-on-Usk while working at a sawmill in Crickhowell, tried again four years later. Lancastrian Bert Jackson and future Welsh title challenger Vernon Ball each knocked him out, as did Londoner Jackie Grimes. And even though Dudley halted debutant Gareth Bevan at Ammanford in 1948 – a result which convinced Bevan he had a brighter future as a trainer – it was a farewell gesture from the 31-year-old former champion.

That was it as far as boxing was concerned, although he still enjoyed a good scrap on the radio or television. After leaving the sawmill – where he had a thumb severed in an accident and reattached in hospital – he worked as a railway porter, an odd-job man at a British Legion home and finally in security at the Sennybridge army camp. Dudley Lewis, as quiet out of the ring and he was boisterous in it, died in Nevill Hall Hospital, Abergavenny, at the age of 75.

An artist's impression of Brecon's finest boxer

EDDIE LLOYD
(1963-)

- Welsh Lightweight Challenger 1985

- Welsh Super-Featherweight Challenger 1993, 1995

Nobody can have come closer to a Welsh crown without actually wearing one than the donkey man from Rhyl. After all, twice his arm was raised at the end of a contest for the belt. The only problem: so was that of his opponent. Each time the bout ended in a draw.

When you realise that only seven Welsh championship clashes since the establishment of the Board of Control in 1929 have finished level, Eddie Lloyd can have even more reason to curse his luck.

He had started early in the fight game, first heading to the Rhyl Youth gym when he was six before joining brother Robert, three years older, at the Rhyl Star club run by their uncle, Benny Lloyd, a former pro flyweight. The youngster proved a good pupil, with five Welsh schoolboy titles among his triumphs before he turned pro shortly before his 20th birthday.

His first three fights came in just 15 days: Eddie won two, but disaster struck when he was halted in 69 seconds by Londoner Paul Cook, who floored him with his first punch. Manager Benny, in his promotional role, brought him back with a win at his home town's Dixieland, but it was followed by another first-round loss, though this time, against Sheffield southpaw Jimmy Thornton, it resulted from eye damage caused by a clash of heads.

Even home advantage didn't help as Lloyd dropped two points decisions at Dixieland and the next 18 months brought more defeats than successes. But a draw with Monmouthshire boxer Andy Williams convinced the Welsh authorities that Eddie was an acceptable challenger for their vacant lightweight throne, with West Walian Stanley Jones in the other corner. The Rhyl man was now handled by

Eddie Lloyd

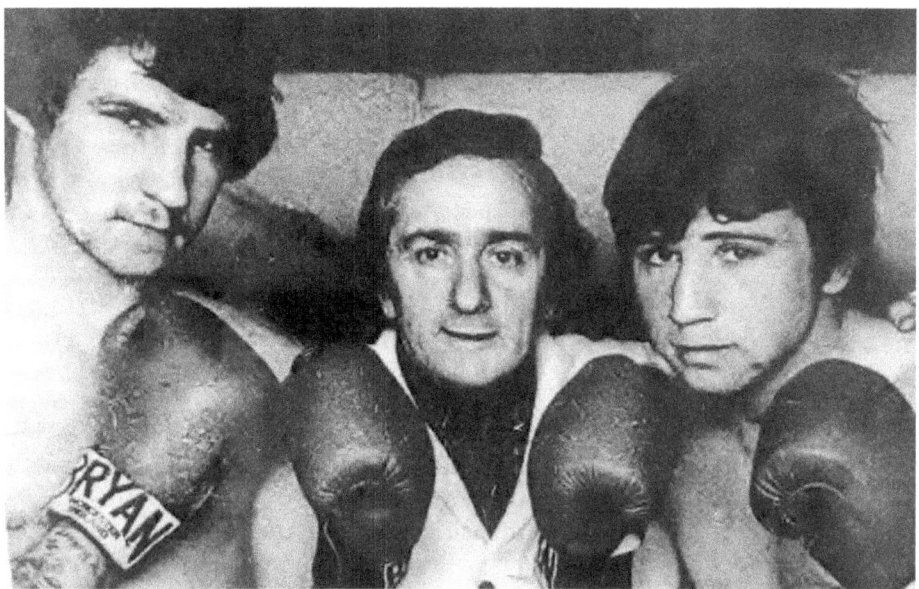
Eddie (right) with brother Robert and manager-uncle Benny

Merseysider Pat Dwyer, who secured the showdown for the Cee-J Club, on the pier at Colwyn Bay, on July 19, 1985.

In the height of summer, much of Lloyd's training involved running alongside the family's donkeys as they gave children rides along Rhyl beach, while his contemporaries elsewhere opted for a bike. Fitness was never going to be a problem.

Unbeaten southpaw Stanley, from Llandeilo, who had beaten Eddie as an amateur, had height and reach on his side, but he was shaken by his rival's early aggression, roared on by a full house. The away fighter began to find his range, but it was mostly toe-to-toe action and Lloyd went up a gear in the fifth. But Jones rocked his man in the next session and boxed beautifully in the seventh; he looked to be heading for victory, but a final-round fightback by the fans' favourite was enough to convince referee Ivor Bassett that he deserved a share of the spoils.

That performance boosted Eddie's reputation as a value-for-money attraction and he caught the eye once more when he decked Najib Daho, although the Moroccan-born Mancunian took the verdict. Two months later Daho knocked out two-weight British and European champion Pat Cowdell in a round to claim the super-feather Lonsdale Belt.

Lloyd's first outing in South Wales saw him outscored by Swansea's Keith Parry, a future Welsh lightweight boss. A decision over Scouser Sugar Gibiliru – later to dethrone British 9st 4lb king Robert Dickie – began a run of four wins, including two in Spain. But a shoulder injury forced his retirement against Midlander Colin Lynch after the pair had each visited the canvas twice.

His father's death led to four years on the sidelines – though he spent much of the time coaching kids at Rhyl Star – before a sparring session with Robbie Regan

In retirement Lloyd became a trainer

convinced Eddie to come back, with the flyweight's manager, Dai Gardiner, holding the reins. He returned in Cardiff against Dewi Roberts, a quarryman from Blaenau Ffestiniog, shrugging off any suggestion of ringrust as he felled the heavier Gwynedd man twice and stopped him in just 75 seconds.

Future lightweight ruler Mervyn Bennett was beaten on a cut and Lloyd was matched with new stablemate Steve Robinson to decide the new Welsh super-feather champion. But hours before their meeting at Barry, the title tag was removed because Robinson's brain scan certificate was out of date. Illogically – the Board changed their rules as a result – the bout still went ahead over 10 rounds, though Eddie was pulled out after eight.

Another chance at the 9st 4lb crown was on the horizon, however, against Llanelli's Barrie Kelley in the capital on January 19, 1993. But if the 20-year-old Kelley was on the face of it an easier proposition than Robinson, who captured the WBO feather title three months later, he still proved too much for Lloyd. Despite an early hand injury and facial damage, the youngster held off a late surge by the North Walian to be clearly in front at the bell.

With only one success – on cuts – in his next six outings, which included an inside-the-distance defeat in a London non-title clash with reigning British monarch and fellow-Welshman Floyd Havard, Eddie might have been forgiven for thinking his own dreams of national supremacy were long gone. But there was to be one more opportunity, against Kelley's conqueror, Pontypool puncher J.T. Williams, on a dinner show at Cardiff's City Hall on March 8, 1995.

Yet, almost a decade on from his first championship contest, history repeated itself: the same official, Ivor Bassett, returned the same scoreline, 98-98. In truth, it was difficult to pick a winner after 10 nip-and-tuck rounds and the reaction of the dinner-jacketed onlookers was more a reflection of their sympathy for the popular Lloyd than any serious disagreement with the referee. But it was a long trip back north afterwards.

A year after the Williams disappointment Eddie turned up at Dunstable to tackle world-class Billy Schwer, from nearby Luton. Predictably, Lloyd was well beaten, suffering a split lower lip, before manager Gardiner retired him at the end of the fifth. There was a date to face three-weight Australian champion Tony 'Mad Dog' Miller in Melbourne, but that fell through and the Rhyl man, now 33, decided to call it a day.

The donkey rides were among the traditional beach entertainments killed off when the local council increased their fees, but Eddie still has his day job as a gas mains engineer. He also trained youngsters at Clwyd ABC for several years.

WILLIE LLOYD
(1933-2019)

- Welsh Lightweight Champion 1954-55, 1956-57

National Service could help or hinder a boxer's progress. Which way it went often depended on where the two-year conscript found himself based. For the lad from Crickhowell the fates were kind: posted as a PTI to an RAF depot at West Kirby on the Wirral, he was within easy reach of Liverpool Stadium, one of the busiest venues in Britain. What better time to turn pro!

Although he made his winning debut in nearby Warrington, Lloyd, managed by local fight figure Tony Vairo, became a familiar name on the Stadium cards, building a reputation that saw him continue to appear there long after demob day.

Willie – the family actually called him by his second name, Malcolm – came from a more comfortable background than most fighters: his father was a bank manager, while Mum ran the town's Dragon Hotel. But he lacked nothing in his determination to succeed. Packing 16 contests into his first six months as a pro, he had boxed on home soil just the once. But a points verdict over former amateur star Parry Dando at Sophia Gardens Pavilion clearly caught the eye of the movers and shakers because they promptly paired them again to decide the successor to long-serving Welsh lightweight champion Dai Davies, who had retired.

The duo met back at the Cardiff venue on May 24, 1954. And neither wasted much time on the sport's niceties, going hell for leather from the off. Dando brought the greater accuracy, but the muscular Lloyd possessed the harder punches, particularly at close range.

Willie looked to have a slight lead when they reached the eighth, but it became academic when he dropped to the canvas in apparent agony. Referee Ike Powell clearly had no doubts about the illegality of the blow and promptly disqualified the Newbridge fighter. Lloyd was the new boss of the 9st 9lb division in Wales.

Back in Crickhowell, his first act was to go to the local bakers' shop and buy two cream cakes as a treat

Willie Lloyd

Willie went on to become a newsagent in London ...

after going without as he made weight. And the rest of his purse, as ever, was put towards his lifetime ambition to own a farm.

Back on Merseyside, Willie hammered Rhuddlan's Johnny Ritchie – whose son and grandson would both fight professionally – inside two rounds, but he lost three on the trot before two successful appearances in Blackpool inside a week restored any shaky self-belief.

But it was at Liverpool Stadium that Lloyd produced arguably his best performance to date. Former amateur champion Dave Charnley had won all seven as a pro, but Willie climbed off the canvas to drop the Dartford man twice and earn a draw. Next up was another highly touted prospect, Dagenham's Ron Hinton, faced at West Ham Baths. On the receiving end for the first three rounds, Lloyd nevertheless stuck at it and was so clearly in control at the end of the eight-rounder that when he was given the verdict it provoked not a murmur of dissent from the East End fans.

But a two-round battering by Geordie Johnny Miller left him with bruised pride and a broken nose, the latter forcing the postponement of a Welsh title defence against fellow Mid-Wales man Emrys Jones until September 26, 1955, at Carmarthen Market Hall. The fans had plenty of entertainment as the pair swapped punches for the full 12 rounds.

Lloyd showed the greater skill, but the lad from Four Crosses never stopped moving forward. Willie, the shorter man, tried to keep the action at close quarters, but found

Jones could at least match him in that aspect of the game. There were no knockdowns – Emrys slipped over in the fifth – but that did not detract from the combative nature of the bout, capped by a toe-to-toe last round, at the end of which the challenger was deemed to have done enough.

It sparked an unsuccessful period for Lloyd, prompting the decision to give up his day job as a lumberjack and move to London in a bid to revive his career. Coincidentally, conqueror Jones retired with a persistent back problem and Willie was matched with Cardiffian ex-amateur Darkie Hughes to fill the vacancy.

... and a publican in Ireland

They met at Maindy Stadium on July 16, 1956, in the outstanding contest on an excellent, if poorly supported bill. Hughes was the better boxer by far and in the early rounds consistently lured Lloyd in and countered him, building a decent lead by halfway. But he became rattled when referee Joe Morgan ticked him off for holding – it seemed Willie was equally guilty – and was further disconcerted when he injured his left hand in the ninth.

Lloyd's body assaults began to have an effect and he piled on the pressure in a grandstand finish. It was enough to earn him a close verdict, which brought catcalls from Mr Morgan's fellow citizens.

Willie was back at the open-air venue six weeks later to face old rival Charnley, who had lost only once in 21 fights. The 'Dartford Destroyer' was pencilled in to challenge British champion Joe Lucy once he passed his 21st birthday in October. Willie, himself only 23 despite his balding pate, put the mockers on that.

The ring was slippery from rain, which hindered both and contributed to Dave's brief knockdown in the third, although the sight of the Englishman on the deck brought a roar from the crowd. Lloyd's right hand was regularly in Charnley's blood-spattered face and, although he had to take a few himself from the seventh onwards, a storming finish convinced referee Ike Powell that he deserved the nod.

When he lost on points to a late substitute from Belgium, Louis van Hoeck, it led to a split with manager Vairo, Willie placing an advert in *Boxing News* to announce he was conducting his own affairs.

The Board handed him an eliminator rematch with Charnley at the Albert Hall on January 22, 1957. Since their last meeting the Kent man had overcome pneumonia, got married and outscored dangerous South African Alby Tissong. Whichever of those provided the most inspiration, Dave marched on towards a Lonsdale Belt and a world title shot. He dominated from the start and, despite a cut from a sixth-round head clash, the outcome was never in doubt. The brave Welshman may have edged a couple of the middle rounds when Charnley took his foot off the pedal, but was never going to withstand the onslaught he faced in the final session.

A hail of punches saw Willie fall to his knees for eight seconds. He gamely rose to face his fate and was taking two-fisted punishment on the ropes when referee Bill Williams stepped between them just 45 seconds before the scheduled final bell.

Things got no easier for Lloyd. Promoter Harry Levene put him in the Albert Hall ring with Guy Gracia, a Frenchman who had beaten three British champions, including Charnley, in three visits to London. Willie never looked likely to buck the trend. Sure, he broke the Parisian's nose early on, but Gracia decked him five times before referee Jack Hart ended the slaughter in the ninth.

When another Frenchman, Martinique-born Fernand Nollet, made his first visit to Britain two months later and halted him in eight, it was all over for Lloyd. He cancelled a Welsh title defence against Cardiffian Teddy Best and called it a career.

Staying in London, he briefly turned his hand to management, with Empire heavyweight king Joe Bygraves among his charges. He also ran a newsagents' near Victoria Station, where he met and married a neighbour, Maura Tallon, eventually fulfilling his early dream and buying a farm in her native Ireland.

Alas, it brought more pain than pleasure until the Lloyds changed tack, taking over a pub in the Wicklow mountains, which proved much more successful. In later years, they moved to the outskirts of Dublin to be nearer their daughter and her family and it was in the Irish capital that Willie Lloyd heard the final bell.

TERRY MAGEE
(1964-)

- European Light-Middleweight Challenger 1990
- All-Ireland Light-Middleweight Champion 1987-91

Terry Magee with the Irish belt

The four Magee boys were well known on Belfast's Ardoyne estate. Their mother was firmly of the belief that "boxing was as important as school" and her sons showed talent from an early age. Two went on to become Commonwealth champions: Eamonn ruled the welterweights for three years and went on to add the WBU title, while Noel, six years older, was briefly in charge at light-heavy, losing the crown to Cardiffian Nicky Piper. But the oldest lad found his success in Wales.

The seeds were sown when nine-year-old Terry, growing up in the middle of the Troubles and having seen innocent people on both sides suffer, promised his grandfather, Robert Magee, that he would never use a gun in the name of Ireland. And the way to avoid getting caught up in the conflict was to leave.

His destination was decided when he visited the Amman Valley as part of an Irish schoolboy team, to be greeted in Betws by a couple of youngsters who addressed him in Welsh; the presence of bilingual street signs added to the attraction. The boys were invited back the following year – and Magee stayed on for good.

With more than 100 wins as a lad with the Sacred Heart club in his native city, Magee had a handful of bouts with Llandeilo-based Towy ABC, even appearing for a Welsh Select line-

Magee in the corner with Leon Findlay

up in Germany. In 1982 he turned pro with Llanelli-based Glynne Davies, but after four bouts across the border joined North Walian Benny Lloyd. As a result, his first two paid outings in Wales came at Rhyl's Dixieland. A switch of manager to Stoke-based Pat Brogan then had him earning a regular crust in the West Midlands.

He had won 13 of his first 16 contests when an abrupt jump in the standard of his opposition saw him make his big-time debut at the Albert Hall, against St Helen's southpaw Gary Stretch, a former amateur star whose only loss in 10 fights had come on a cut eye.

The Merseysider's unusually long reach enabled him to land almost at will, while keeping him away from Magee's attempts at retaliation. Terry kept punching back and, indeed, enjoyed a little success in the sixth, but that simply prompted Stretch to a renewed onslaught which brought referee Reg Snipe's intervention as the bell rang to end the seventh. *Boxing News* editor Harry Mullan suggested the loser's corner might have spared him the last few sessions, although the boxer himself insisted he could have continued.

A falling-out with Brogan – unconnected with the Stretch defeat – meant 13 months on the sidelines as Magee waited for his contract to expire. His return saw him finally make his bow in West Wales, but with a nod to his background. Before a decent crowd at Swansea's Mayfair Suite (the renamed Top Rank) on June 23, 1987, he took on Derbyshire's bottle blond Seamus Casey for the vacant All-Ireland light-middle title, Casey qualifying through his Derry-born mother.

Seamus, with his distinctive lean-forward style, kept his left arm, bearing multiple Manchester United tattoos, in Magee's face in the early stages, but midway through the fourth Terry discovered the answer: he began to fire in uppercuts and Casey was soon looking flustered.

Solid rights – thrown despite a torn ligament – buckled Seamus's knees in the fifth and with a minute remaining in the sixth another right sent the Midlander sprawling. He sat there with a resigned expression as referee Ivor Bassett completed the count and Magee leapt high in delight.

The belt presentation was equally memorable: surely, in the long and varied history of boxing, never before has a promoter climbed through the ropes dressed as a leprechaun! It has to be said that the garb suited Teresa Breen, petite wife of manager Colin, rather better than it would most of the game's movers and shakers.

Magee was invited to South Africa to face national champion Charles Oosthuizen. The money was good, but so was Oosthuizen and Terry was stopped, still on his feet, in the eighth, having damaged a hand two rounds before.

When a planned contest between Magee and Cardiffian Kevin Hayde had to be bumped up to the main event on an Afan Lido show, promoter John Davies tried to have it sanctioned as for the vacant Welsh light-middle crown. The Welsh Area Council rejected the plea, ruling that Hayde was not good enough, something that almost came back to bite them as Kevin gave Terry fits before losing a close eight-round decision.

It was one of six straight wins for Magee, with future British light-middle king Wally Swift, Jr, also among his victims, and the Betws man was rewarded with a crack at European ruler Gilbert Délé in Paris on March 26, 1990. The West Indian-born southpaw was making the first defence of the title he had won four months earlier and proved clearly superior, the referee giving Terry two standing counts before cornerman Breen tossed in the towel in the third. Délé went on to win the WBA belt; Magee headed back to Ireland.

He took on Ray Close in Dublin for the All-Ireland strap up at super-middle, but the man who would hold WBO champion Chris Eubank to a draw stopped him in seven. There was another quick defeat against former European titleholder James Cook – though Magee floored him – but the transplanted Ulsterman was still nominated to challenge Cardiff's Wayne Ellis for the Welsh middleweight title.

Terry wanted to win it for Tommy Davies, who had worn the crown for nine years and lived just up the valley from his home. But Ellis opted to go down a different path and was eventually stripped, the Welsh Area Council matching Magee with Llandovery's Robert Peel. Before it could take place, Terry was forced to retire after failing a brain scan.

Strangely, he was still to acquire another title. More than two decades after the bout, Magee discovered that the vacant Northern Ireland area title had also been at stake when he beat Casey – and he now has a certificate to prove it!

Seeking to fill the void left by boxing, he took up marathon running and clocked up 31 in total, including three in a week, culminating in the New York event, to raise money for the city's firefighters following the horrors of 9/11.

A fireman himself for 14 years, Terry also helped coach a new generation at Towy ABC, in addition training young athletes as part of the 'Get Kids Going' charity. He was honoured by Carmarthenshire County Council in 2001 as their Volunteer of the Year.

MICKEY McDONAGH
(1998-)

- Commonwealth Games Bronze Medallist 2018
- European Under-22 Bronze Medalliat 2019

Boxing has traditionally played a significant role in the lives of boys born into the travelling community. Mickey McDonagh was never likely to prove an exception to that rule.

He first entered a gym as an eight-year-old, a few years after his family headed west from his Swansea birthplace and settled in Pembroke. His talent was clear from the start. Fast forward a couple of years and he won the first of three Welsh schoolboy titles in the colours of his local club. After moving up to junior level – where a couple more national championships came his way – he moved to Merlins Bridge ABC, where Graham Brockway imparts his wisdom.

Mickey McDonagh

At first the GB championships proved something of a barrier, with English lads Francie Doherty and Jimmy McDonagh halting Mickey's progress. There was still a trip to the European Juniors, where he reached the quarter-finals, but it was as a youth that the West Walian really broke through. This time two Welsh victories were followed each time by gold medals at British level, the second success also earning an invitation to join the GB squad in Sheffield, the only junior to have that privilege.

It brought regular experience in foreign rings, with trips to European and world age-group championships and although he was unable to reach the medal stages, it still, along with multiple appearances at multi-nations events, built a bank of experience to draw on as a senior. That was obvious when McDonagh strode to the Welsh ABA lightweight title in his first year as an adult, comprehensively outpointing the previous season's runner-up, Cardiffian Kane Shepherd, in the final.

The triumph virtually guaranteed a place in the Wales party for the Commonwealth Games on the Australian Gold Coast in April 2018. But Mickey underlined his quality by taking GB honours with two whitewash victories and adding golds at tournaments in Bosnia and Finland before heading Down Under.

One of the sound stages at the sprawling Oxenford Studios, where films in the *Thor* and *Pirates of the Caribbean* series had been made, was the Games boxing venue – and the Welshman's first call to action saw him up against a lad from Lesotho. McDonagh would have had more trouble trying to pronounce Quobosheane Molerepe's name than he did in the bout, emerging with a unanimous decision.

Next up was Papuan puncher Thadius Katua, a Commonwealth Youth gold medallist

Mickey has his arm raised after beating Irishman Pierce O'Leary in Chechnya

who began boxing at 12, using gloves that were older than he was. A confident start led to a superb display of movement and accuracy, rarely allowing Katua – on his 21st birthday – into the fight. The third round saw a clash of heads which left both men cut; the islander had to survive a doctor's check, but was allowed to reach the final bell.

Blood was dripping from the side of McDonagh's left eye as the one-sided scores were announced, but a medal was guaranteed – and, on the other side of the draw, England's highly-rated Calum French was eliminated by Indian Manish Kaushik.

But in the semi-final Mickey had to face the host country's Harry Garside, a southpaw who had reached the last four with victory over the superbly named Namibian, Tryagain Ndevelo. While the African left town – presumably to follow the advice his parents gave him – Garside had the support of the home crowd.

With both natural counter-punchers, most of the opening action, such as it was, came at range, the Aussie perhaps landing more as McDonagh's blows kept falling short. The second saw the Welshman enjoying some success, before they emerged for what looked to be a decisive final session.

Urged by cornerman Colin Jones to "let your hands go", Mickey increased his workrate, but found his rival hard to pin down. Despite throwing both arms in the air at the bell, he must have known it was a close-run thing – and the verdict went on a 3-2 split to Garside.

Analysis of the respective scores underlined how difficult it was to separate the pair. Apart from a Canadian who gave the winner all three rounds, the judges were all over the place. Although Harry had seemed to edge the first, three actually went for McDonagh. Mickey upped the pace in the second, yet all five favoured the Aussie. Three preferred the Welshman in the last – so he had, in fact, won two of the three rounds – but it still left him the loser overall.

Nevertheless, McDonagh had a bronze medal to bring home, plus the dubious consolation of losing to the champion, as Garside sneaked another 3-2 vote in the final

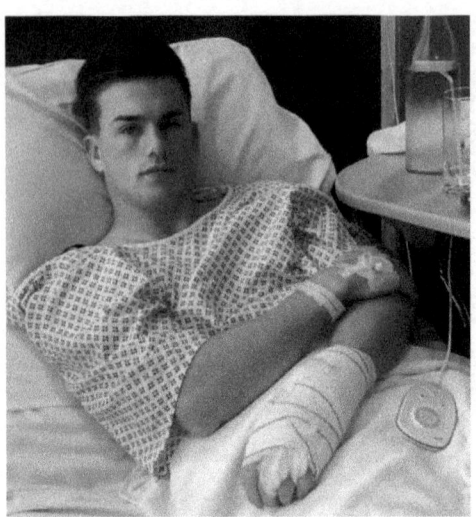
McDonagh rests after surgery on his troublesome hand

against Kaushik. Since then Harry has picked up a silver at the delayed Tokyo Olympics, so the defeat looks better in retrospect.

The following year saw Mickey step up to light-welterweight and – despite entering the competition with a torn ligament in his left fist – return from the Chechen city of Vladikavkaz with another bronze medal from the European Under-22 championships. Ireland's Pierce O'Leary – now an unbeaten pro – and Pole Damian Durkacz were dealt with pretty much one-handed, but Turk Tugrul Han Erdemir took a 4-1 decision in the semi-final.

Soon after arriving home Mickey went into hospital for surgery to repair the damage and was sidelined for several months before receiving the call to go back to Russia and compete in the worlds in Ekaterinberg. Going out with just three weeks' training was probably unwise and he fell at the first hurdle, losing on points to Thomas Blumenfeld – though he did enough damage to force the Canadian to withdraw from the next stage.

Then Covid arrived. The Olympic qualifier saw Geordie Luke McCormack confirm his place on the plane to Tokyo and McDonagh quit the GB squad. His mind was no longer on the sport anyway. A family tragedy hit him hard and he stepped away from the ring. It is hoped that one of the most talented youngsters of his generation will be back before too long.

IORRIE MORRIS
(1915-1944)

- Welsh Bantamweight Challenger 1937

The English never quite understood that someone could be called Iorrie. Frequently reporters – or their sub-editors – altered it to Lorrie, or even Laurie. Which is a pity, as Iorwerth Milton Morris was a good enough boxer to deserve the dignity of having his deeds attributed correctly.

The thirties were a boom time for the fight game in the Amman Valley, with the local amateur club providing a regular conveyor belt of talent. Not that success was automatic in an era when the threat of unemployment meant many top men with steady jobs were wary of risking that financial security by turning pro. One such was Cardiff gas worker Jackie Pottinger, who outpointed Morris in the 1934 Welsh ABAs; he went on to win five national titles and an Empire Games bronze, while selected ae a reserve for the Berlin Olympics.

Miners, however, seemed far keener to add a few bob to the family income; perhaps the combination of life below ground and a ring career was so ingrained in tradition that mine-owners had become more tolerant than other employers. So coal hewer Iorrie, with Pottinger standing in the way of his amateur ambitions, handed in his vest to join the expanding stable of former featherweight Johnny Vaughan. It took a few months for him to settle, but in due course the Ammanford teenager – the youngest of 14 children, whose father died when Iorrie was a baby – began to string together some decent results, beating the rival Lewises, Dudley and Dickie, Llanelli's tiny terror Gwyn Thomas and Rhondda boy Eddie Davies.

Any suggestions that the successes were undeserved were put to bed when he repeated his triumphs over Dudley Lewis and Thomas, although Davies did earn a draw in their rematch. By the end of 1936, it was clear that the lad from New Road was among the best bantamweights in Wales.

Iorrie Morris

Yet it was only when he had started losing that he was offered a chance to claim the national crown. The year had begun well, with Iorrie outpointing Neath's useful Dai Davies and Llanharan prospect Syd Worgan; within weeks both had avenged those reverses. Dudley Lewis, beaten three times by Morris, underlined the Ammanford man's slipping status as he handed him a third consecutive defeat. And it was now, bizarrely, that he was matched for the belt relinquished by Swansea ace Len Beynon.

In the other corner at Cardiff's Greyfriars Hall on October 20, 1937, was a former holder of the title, Mog Mason. The Gilfach Goch warrior – real name Tom Slater, he had adopted the nom de guerre of an old mountain fighter – had beaten Beynon on a disqualification only for Len to regain the throne 15 months later. With Beynon leaving the division to campaign as a featherweight, Mason was clearly lined up to be his successor.

And so it proved. More than four thousand packed the building to welcome home Tommy Farr, newly returned from his gallant challenge to world heavyweight champion Joe Louis. The contests themselves were something of an afterthought.

Not for Farr, though. He was cheering on Mason, a friend and protégé who was already booked to tour North America with Tommy the following month. And from the first bell there was little doubt that Mog would be making the trip with the added cachet of being the top 8st 6lb man in his native land.

It was a one-horse race from the off. Morris was outboxed and outfought: he was in distress several times before the punch to the jaw which ended matters in the third round. Iorrie was well gone, needing attention in his corner for a good 10 minutes before he was able to return to his dressing-room.

There was precious little left for the Ammanford fighter in or out of the ring. A handful of bouts brought mixed results before he hung up the gloves. And then, barely two years after marrying Nancy, Iorrie was dead from peritonitis. He was just 28 years old.

ROBERT PEEL
(1969-)

- Welsh Middleweight Challenger 1994, 1995

Ask a boxer how he took up the sport and the answers tend to follow similar themes. Copying Dad or a big brother, maybe. Learning to fight to deal with schoolyard bullies, perhaps. Or going to a gym to lose weight and discovering an unsuspected skill. For some, watching Muhammad Ali or the *Rocky* films proved the spur. Not Robert Peel.

"I was nine and living with my mother in Bournemouth," he recalls, "and Henry Cooper was in town to open a supermarket. I'd never heard of him – I thought Mum was talking about Tommy Cooper!"

But, instead of the Caerphilly-born comedian, Robert found himself meeting a former heavyweight champion.

"I got to shake his hand – and it was huge! He made a big impression on me. I wanted to know all about him. And I decided I wanted to box."

It was to be another decade before that dream came true – and in a different country. Birmingham-born Peel's family moved to Tenby when he was three, but a parental split saw him live on the Dorset coast for a few years before joining his father in Llandovery and becoming a boarder at the town's famous college.

At an establishment which has produced more than 50 international rugby players, he developed into a first-team flanker; it was only when he left school and started work as a welder in his Dad's business that he first laced up the gloves at the Llandeilo premises of Hywel 'Cass' Davies. He won around half his 20-odd contests, but his one attempt at the Welsh ABAs saw him outpointed by Simon Walters – despite flooring the Swansea boy three times!

Robert Peel

Peel drives Barry Thorogood across the ring

Unsurprisingly, Robert opted to turn pro, facing another Swansea fighter, John Kaighin, in his debut at nearby Gorseinon. This time he was given the decision, but Kaighin gained revenge three weeks later in Cardiff. There were a couple more points losses over the border – one (which Peel still insists he won) against future British title challenger Andy Flute – before he was stopped in four by Wolverhampton's Adrian Wright, who, like Flute, had a substantial weight advantage.

Next up was a rubber match against Kaighin at Ritzy's nightclub in Swansea. This time Robert earned the nod, despite a broken bone in his right hand which kept him idle for five months.

He returned against Jason Mathews – cousin of future world champion Robbie Regan – who stepped up as a late substitute despite conceding almost a stone. A toe-to-toe thriller had the crowd at Cardiff's STAR Centre on their feet before an unfortunate ending: referee Roddy Evans called a halt just 37 seconds before the final bell after Peel has sustained a gash over his left eye. It required 16 stitches; ironically, Mathews needed 13 to repair damage of his own. In addition, Robert suffered a perforated eardrum which meant another lengthy spell on the sidelines.

Once he returned to action, 1992 proved as busy as the previous year, but brought a series of defeats broken only by a draw with Merthyr's former amateur champion, Steve Thomas – and Thomas beat him in a rematch. A points success over Llanelli's portly Russell Washer broke the run, but it was a brief respite. In a 12-month period, as well as dropped decisions, Peel was halted within three rounds by future world title challengers Ensley Bingham and Adrian Dodson – the Bingham setback, in fairness, came on cuts – and Geoff McCreesh, who went on to wear the Lonsdale Belt.

The Welsh Area Council duly summoned him to Cardiff, his career in the balance, but he showed the meeting a tape of his most recent contest, against Dale Nixon, along with a *Boxing News* report suggesting he had been robbed; the council didn't just allow him to box on, they accepted him as a suitable opponent for Terry Magee to contest the vacant Welsh middleweight title.

It never happened, though, and Peel had a rematch with Taunton boy Nixon instead – which he lost in seven rounds. The Board's men stuck to their guns, however, and Peel faced Cardiffian Barry Thorogood for the still unoccupied throne in Cardiff on November 29, 1994. (Given Thorogood had been stopped in his last two bouts, denying Robert would have been a bit harsh.)

Thorogood already boasted two six-round verdicts over the West Walian and a dinner-show crowd at the Welsh Institute of Sport watched him repeat the feat over 10. He had to work for it: when Peel battled back to take the eighth and ninth from the tiring local, he looked favourite – Barry admitted afterwards that he was worried – but the capital city man dug deep to take the last and claim the belt.

It was close enough to merit a return, at Llanelli Leisure Centre on April 12, 1995, but this time Thorogood's superiority was beyond doubt. Robert caught the eye with a pair of knee-length shorts in a shade officially described as "grape", but the improving champion dominated the actual fighting. His left hooks soon had Peel marking up around both eyes before another raised a swelling on the temple. Another punch on the same spot at the start of the eighth sent Robert to one knee and when a follow-up assault put him down again referee Wynford Jones and manager Davies agreed they had seen enough.

Between the Thorogood contests, Peel had travelled to London's East End to outpoint unbeaten Yorkshireman David Larkin, but it proved his last victory. After a two-year break he tried again at super-middle and light-heavy, but 10 straight defeats, culminating in a neck injury retirement against rising Londoner Michael Bowen, convinced him to leave the ring for good.

These days he travels the world as a welding inspector, but home is very definitely West Wales. Actress daughter Ella is a familiar face on Welsh-language television. And her father boasts a tattoo proclaiming: "English-born, Welsh-bred – that's perfection!"

BRYN PHILLIPS
(1931-2017)

🥊 Welsh Lightweight Challenger 1957

The travelling fairs that visited Pembrokeshire each summer always drew in the local youths. And the boxing booths that invariably formed part of the entertainment were a particular attraction for Bryn Phillips and his mates from Goodwick.

Bryn's father, David, had warned him against getting involved, advice his son, who worked on his Dad's market garden, took seriously. But when his pals, who knew he could handle himself in a scrap, urged him to accept the barker's offer of a few quid to anyone who could last three rounds with his best man, he yielded to the temptation – and proceeded to knock the guy out!

The teenager had already shown his physical prowess as a gymnast, trapeze artist and weightlifter, travelling around West Wales with a troupe run by former strong man Tommy George, from Letterston. But all that was left behind as he continued to despatch hard nuts on the booths and even his father was onside when he decided to display his skills in a more formal setting.

The 20-year-old made his bow at Carmarthen's Market Hall and was shocked to find himself on the deck in the first round of his pro career. Phillips showed spirit to battle back and outpoint former British youth champion Harold Urch, from Cross Keys. But he lacked the contacts to keep him busy and did not box again for eight months – and then he had to travel to Walsall and was flattened in four by Brummie first-timer Norman Wormall.

The pattern was repeated with a victory on home ground at Haverfordwest followed by a knockout loss in the Midlands, but Phillips proved he could win over the border when he went to Liverpool and floored Bolton's Wally Barkess six times before stopping him in two. There was another quick defeat in Derby before recently acquired manager Bill Dixie despatched him to London to take part in a tournament backed by *Boxing News* to discover the best lightweight talent coming through.

And members at the National Sporting Club saw the young West Walian left-hook his way to the final with a second-round knockout of Doncaster's Colin Stables and a three-round decision over Portsmouth prospect Bob Murray.

Bryn Phillips

Two weeks later he was back in the West End for the decider, recovering from a slow start to drop Dagenham office worker Len Wilson three times for a stoppage that earned him a gold watch, handed over by former British heavyweight king Len Harvey.

The NSC invited him back to face vastly experienced Irishman Pat McCoy and, despite injuring his left hand, he drew with a foe he would meet again, before adding another victory on Merseyside, albeit when Bolton's Des Willis was thrown out for careless headwork after felling Bryn with a body shot in the opener.

His eyes set on the Welsh lightweight throne, Phillips spent several weeks with his increasingly troublesome left mitt in plaster. And, when he recovered, a points loss to Cardiffian Teddy Best at Carmarthen did nothing to speed his progress up the domestic ladder, although he did come on strong in the later rounds. Bryn would get the chance to put things right.

Bryn Phillips goes after Teddy Best

Not for a while, though. When he broke his lead hand again in sparring – the fourth time in all – it meant a spell in hospital to have a piece of his hip grafted on to the fragile area in a bid to solve the problem. He was out of the ring for seven months, returning with a decision over Birmingham's Johnny King at Malvern (at last a success in the Midlands) in which both men visited the canvas.

Old rival McCoy was tempted to Wales, where the pair drew again at Carmarthen before Bryn finally took the honours in a third set-to in front of 6,000 fans attracted to Aberystwyth's Park Avenue football ground by the presence of Newport heavyweight Dick Richardson in the main event.

Phillips reminded the Welsh authorities of his title aspirations when he wrecked the unbeaten record of Trinidadian Ronnie Rush inside a round in his adopted Cardiff, though this was admittedly only because Rush, later to train Steve Robinson and Robbie Regan to world crowns, was disqualified for a low blow!

Two months later Bryn was back at Sophia Gardens Pavilion to face former conqueror Best, then considered the leading challenger for Welsh honours at both lightweight and welterweight. But Bryn gave him all the problems he could handle before losing a close eight-round verdict. The winner scaled more than four pounds over the 9st 9lb limit and the Pembrokeshire man reckoned that if Best could not make lightweight, he should be the man to challenge Welsh champion Willie Lloyd.

In the event, Lloyd announced his retirement and Teddy, who had insisted he could shed the surplus if necessary, was matched with Phillips to decide his successor. He proved his point by scaling a quarter of a pound inside the limit when they met at Pandy Park, the Cross Keys rugby ground, on August 21, 1957. Best, whose Milford Haven-born cousin Tommy once led Cardiff City's attack, was a strong favourite; not

Phillips and Best are reunited more than 50 years later

only could he point to the two victories over Phillips, but since their previous clash Bryn had lost four in a row, twice being stopped by Londoner Arthur Murphy, whom Teddy then halted in six.

The pundits were justified, but the crowd enjoyed an all-out slugfest for the nine rounds it lasted. At first it seemed unlikely to go so long, with Phillips down twice in the second and once in the third, but he recovered to take the battle to Best. Matters were nip-and-tuck for several sessions, but the Cardiffian was beginning to take control when Phillips had to pull out at the end of the ninth, indicating a sprained thumb. Before leaving the ring, Bryn told those present that he would not box again.

Like so many others, he was to change his mind, but only to say farewell to his loyal Pembrokeshire supporters. After a six-round decision over West African Danny Lartey at Haverfordwest he hung up the gloves for good.

The following year he joined Pembrokeshire Police and when it was decided to bring in a dog section PC Phillips was given the task of looking after the first canine recruit. It was to open a whole new career path, which saw service in Bristol, Sheffield – where horses were added to his responsibilities – and finally Staffordshire Police, where he retired as a Chief Inspector in 1987. By this stage Bryn was the go-to man for dog training, writing a book on the subject and travelling as far as Pakistan to pass on his wisdom.

He and wife Sybil returned to live in Bristol and it was there that Bryn died in 2017, at the age of 86.

DENNIS POWELL
(1924-1993)

- British Light-Heavyweight Champion 1953
- Welsh Heavyweight Champion 1949-51
- Welsh Light-Heavyweight Champion 1949-53

It is unusual for a small rural village to produce a champion boxer. But there are two who can claim credit for a man who, though his time at the top was limited, won a Lonsdale Belt in a battle remembered as one of the most blood-spattered in the sport's history.

Llanddewi Skirrid, near the Gwent market town of Abergavenny, is where Dennis Powell was born. But father Harry worked the farms and the family were constantly on the move before settling, when Dennis was nine, in an equally insignificant speck on the map, Four Crosses, in Montgomeryshire.

The exploits of Tommy Farr first attracted Dennis to the fight game. He was 12, and stuck in a hospital bed when his hero tackled Joe Louis, but was allowed, as a special treat, to stay up and hear the radio commentary. Fourteen years later, he was to cross gloves with Farr himself. It seemed improbable at the time: the young Powell, with four sisters and no brothers, was restricted to pummelling an old onion sack filled with rubbish. Only when he joined the Royal Navy during World War II did he get the chance to try the game for real.

Back in civvy street, somebody entered Dennis for one of Jack Solomons's regular novices' competitions. A trial bout in the Solomons gym saw Irish Guardsman Jack Cooper flattened, but at the expense of an injured left thumb, which hampered the Welshman throughout his career. The damaged hand sidelined Dennis for nine months, but gave him time to think about the future. He

Dennis Powell

Dennis Powell (right) faces his idol, Tommy Farr

and a friend, Bernard Thomas, eventually to become his manager, spent hours thumbing through phone books for promoters' numbers. The first to respond positively was Johnny Best, and the Powell career was relaunched at Liverpool with a first-round victory over Blackpool's Dick Freeman.

Powell's unsophisticated attacking style brought him plenty of bookings. It also meant a fair sprinkling of defeats, some spectacularly brief. And there were problems outside the ring. Dennis, who was working in a timber yard at Four Crosses, found his employers increasingly unhappy about the time he took off for boxing – after all, he had 23 bouts in 1948 alone – so he switched to the maintenance staff of the GPO radio station at nearby Criggion. With the new job came increased success in the ring, bringing two Welsh titles in under a month.

Abertillery's Jack Farr had occupied the light-heavy throne for 14 months, but was basically a middleweight: he conceded almost a stone to the Montgomeryshire man on July 9, 1949, at the Newtown Pavilion. It took just 69 seconds before Championship No 1 was in the bag. Exactly four weeks later, Dennis faced heavyweight king George James at the Oswestry football ground, just across the border in Shropshire. The champion, from Ebbw Vale, a miner since the age of 13, was making the first defence of a crown won in 1939. A massive weight advantage was no substitute for youth and Powell despatched him in the second round.

British honours (at least in the lighter division) were now a possibility, and he took another step on the ladder by beating Londoner Mark Hart. The loser, later to be a top-class referee himself, questioned the verdict and immediately challenged Powell to a return. Dennis agreed, as long as it was recognised as a British title eliminator. Alas, it was Hart who came out on top in an Oswestry ring made slippery by pre-fight rain, although this time it was the Welshman's turn to query the decision.

Vulnerable eyebrows had already caused a few losses on Dennis's record and a five-month break failed to solve the problem. "It got so as I never went into a fight wondering if I'd win or lose," he recalled, "just when I'd get cut. As a left-hander relying on the left hook, I used to carry that hand low, leaving the left side of my face wide open. Really, I suppose I should have been a southpaw."

Powell entered 1951 with renewed enthusiasm, picking up three wins before climbing between the ropes at the West Midlands Showground in Shrewsbury to face a new candidate for the Welsh heavyweight title – none other than Tommy Farr. The 'Tonypandy Terror', making a financially driven comeback after 10 years out, weighed 20lb more than the man who had once idolised him. But he was also 12 years older than the 26-year-old champion and needed all his famed defensive skills to evade Dennis's confident assault. Then, in the fifth, a clash of heads split Powell's left eyebrow yet again; Farr, too streetwise to be sentimental, concentrated on the wound, and referee Ike Powell called a halt after the sixth. The dejected loser lamented, "My training programme was much harder than the actual fight."

Dennis underwent surgery to remove old scar tissue before sailing through the next year with only one defeat. One of his victims was a former British ABA champion from Stepney, George Walker, disqualified after a series of warnings from referee Frank Wilson covering almost every misdemeanour in – or rather outside – the book. They would meet again.

British light-heavy champion Randolph Turpin relinquished the crown to concentrate on his world title ambitions at middleweight, and Powell and Walker were controversially matched for the vacant throne. Johnny Best, the man who gave Dennis his professional start, won the purse offers and staged the bout at Liverpool Stadium on March 26, 1953, two days before the Grand National. Early Mist was to romp home at Aintree at 20-1; the odds on the fight itself were to fluctuate dramatically before the time came to pay out.

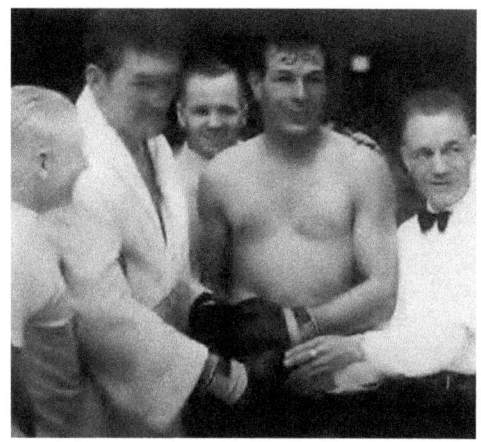

Farr (in white gown) and Powell pose with ref Ike Powell after the fight

The Welshman, ridiculed at the outset of his career for his lack of finesse, had developed as a boxer and neat footwork made the 23-year-old Londoner miss repeatedly. Dennis, by contrast, found his man easily and dropped him for eight in the second with a solid right. George was swollen beneath the left eye by the fourth, but suddenly found a right which drove Powell into the ropes; a second right split his eyebrow, a third had him sagging at the knees and a fourth sent him to the canvas for a count of nine. He hung on, literally, until the closing seconds, when another series of blows had him down again, Walker tripping and momentarily joining him on the deck. The bell was a welcome sound.

Dennis kept on the move, picking up the points, but the seventh almost brought an end to Welsh hopes. For all the surgeon's handiwork, that left eye had been seeping blood again, and now deteriorated rapidly: one of Dennis's seconds glanced across at referee Vic Green, but the official was too busy filling in his scorecard to notice. Reprieved, Powell leapt back into the fray for the eighth, and suddenly Walker was the man in difficulty.

A fairly subdued programme for one of the most blood-spattered British title fights ever seen

Powell (right) watches for Walker to make his move

His own left eye was tightly closed, and he did well to survive. Only courage kept the Stepney man coming forward, but Powell too was exhausted, and a right to Dennis's chin at the bell spurred Walker to a last-ditch effort. However, his injuries – his right eye, too, was no more than a slit – meant he never saw the left hook with which the Welshman sent him reeling in the closing seconds of the 11th. George slumped on his stool and offered no protest when his chief second, Dave Edgar, signalled his retirement.

The Lonsdale Belt – a new one, its predecessor having been stolen – was fastened around Dennis's waist, and 3,000 Welsh voices soared in celebration. The singers were unaware of the panic in the Powell camp on the eve of the bout. Faulty scales had convinced Dennis he was over the 12st 7lb limit – "I went across to the gym and cooked myself," he said. "I didn't have a drink or anything. Then at the official weigh-in I found I was only 12st 3 1/2lb." It could so easily have proved decisive in a battle as brutal as any in the barefist era.

It was nearly six months before the new champion returned, beating former middleweight king Albert Finch in a 10-round non-title affair at Oswestry. Then it was back to official business against Alex Buxton, the third of four boxing brothers born to a war hero father from Antigua and a mother from Watford. Eighteen months younger than Dennis, he was vastly more experienced, his 87 bouts including clashes with the likes of Randolph Turpin and Dave Sands. Reg King clinched the fight for October 26, 1953, at the Nottingham Ice Rink, a venue favoured by the Buxton camp – although when Alex and manager Jim Wicks arrived at their hotel the night before all they could find to eat were ginger biscuits.

The restricted diet clearly did the challenger no harm (the portly Wicks may have been less happy) and he proceeded to expose Dennis's limitations. His left lead was rarely out of the Welshman's face, and when Powell was able to work his way inside, Buxton scored well with the uppercut. The inevitable cut eyes soon marred the Welshman's film-star looks: referee Tommy Little visited Powell's corner at the end of the ninth, but allowed Dennis a last attempt to save his title. When a clubbing Buxton right brought the blood gushing forth again, 44 seconds into the 10th, the official had seen enough.

Dennis, suffering from a heavy cold, had been outboxed and outfought, his longer reach and 10lb weight advantage irrelevant, his defence in tatters. Alex's mother, crippled and partially blind, had been ferried to Nottingham in the back of a furniture van to be present at her son's coronation. While the Buxton family rejoiced, the Welshman drove disconsolately home.

He had a brief flirtation with management, Dennis's camp including Paul Brown, remembered by quiz compilers as the heavyweight who knocked out Joe Bugner in the St Ives man's pro debut. Then the gentler pursuits of ballroom dancing and a spot of golf took over as his main outside interests.

He looked back with fondness on his career. "My record's nothing special – I won some, lost some, drew some. I was only a Sunday afternoon fighter, travelling around with my punchbag in the car, a pair of gloves and a skipping rope, doing a bit of training when I could. But I enjoyed it."

Dennis Powell may not go down in history as a great champion, but no-one who was there will forget the titanic struggle in which he won the title. George Walker, son of a brewery drayman and himself a former Billingsgate fish porter, became one of Britain's wealthiest businessmen, as well as guiding the crowd-pleasing career of heavyweight brother Billy. His conqueror lived out his years more quietly, still weighing 12st 9lb despite more than 20 years running the pub at Willenhall in which wife Olive was brought up. Its name seems appropriate for an ex-fighter: The Bell.

Powell (left) showing signs of wear as he heads for defeat against Alex Buxton

JAMES PROBERT
(2000-)

- Commonwealth Youth Silver Medallist 2017
- European Junior Bronze Medallist 2015
- European Schools Bronze Medallist 2014

Boxing is a testing vocation within and beyond the ropes. As well as the regular challenge of stepping into the ring to face an equally driven opponent, risking damage – occasionally to health, always to reputation and self-esteem – there is the day-to-day routine of exercise and sacrifice in order to be ready for combat.

For youngsters who first lace up the gloves when their age is still in single figures and find that success brings with it not merely a chance of glory, but the pressure of expectation, there often comes an urge to reclaim their everyday lives.

Some turn their backs on the game despite making substantial strides in the professional ranks – Gilfach Goch duo Gareth Lawrence and Russell Rees were both unbeaten and approaching championship contention when they opted out of what had become a grind. Fellow Rhondda prospect Lewis Rees lost his love for boxing, but tried to ignore it until defeat by a journeyman convinced him that this was not an enterprise to undertake half-heartedly.

Even more who have excelled as juniors reconsider once teenage temptations come calling. When your friends' weekends are dominated by parties, it is difficult to focus on the distant prize of sporting fame and fortune.

For Pembroke youngster James Probert the moment of truth came when four judges at the Commonwealth Youth championships decided

James Probert with his Commonwealth Youth silver

he had lost his final against the world No 1, an Indian who goes by the single name of Sachin. One judge – and the majority of the others in attendance – favoured Probert.

"I lost heart after that," admits James. "I'd been at the Welsh camp in Cardiff four days a week, training several times a day, and it no longer seemed worth it."

When he lost another split decision in Ireland it was the last straw. Still only 17, he packed it in.

That young Probert would take up boxing was almost inevitable. His father, Nathan, who had won a couple of Welsh ABA titles himself, ran the local amateur club and James was a regular there from the age of seven.

His first attempt at a national tournament saw him beaten in the schools final, but – unlike his dad, who was also a runner-up at that level – James bounced back to top the pile in the next two seasons. The second triumph earned selection for the European championships in Hungary. It was the first time Wales had sent a team and the venture was justified when they won two bronze medals – one for the Pembroke lad.

Just a few days after his 14th birthday, Probert saw off foes from Turkey and Romania before losing in the semi-final to the eventual winner, a Russian with a famous fight name, Nikita Golovkin.

It was not the only event of 2014 that marked him out as one to watch. When Wales were hammered 10-1 in a mixed-age match against Scotland in Merthyr, James, the first to box, won his bout and then watched as every one of his older team-mates crashed to defeat.

The following year brought a step up to the junior class and James took both Welsh and British titles before heading to the Ukraine, where he eliminated Italian and Armenian rivals, only to lose a split decision to Romanian Cosmin Girleanu and have to settle for another European bronze.

The West Walian retained his Welsh crown in 2016, but, despite home advantage, he struggled through his GB semi and was still below par when outpointed by England's useful Eithan James in the final.

Moving on to the youth section, James added another two Welsh vests via walkovers, with nobody wanting to face him, but Englishman Ibrahim Nadim came out on top in the GB tournament. There was still to be a trip to the sun, with those Commonwealth Youth championships being held in the Bahamas. Probert became one of four Welsh medallists, defeating a Sri Lankan and Ulsterman John Moran to reach the final, where that highly contentious defeat to Sachin left him with the silver – and the disillusionment that prompted his early retirement.

These days he has other things on his mind. Now married and father to recent arrival Lavinia, James lives with his wife's people at Evesham, though returning home regularly to work as a roofer. But once things have settled down on the family front, there are plans to return to the gym. Nathan took a few years out at 19 before returning with new enthusiasm; it seems likely that his son, too, will be back to see where his talent can take him.

BILLY QUINLAN
(1911-1982)

- British Lightweight Challenger 1934
- Welsh Lightweight Champion 1932-34

A big punch is a valuable tool for any boxer, particularly if they aspire to great things. But there are many who became champions without one. Welsh stars Howard Winstone and Joe Erskine reached the top through superb technical skills, while Johnny Owen made it thanks to the non-stop energy which earned him the tag of 'Bionic Bantam'.

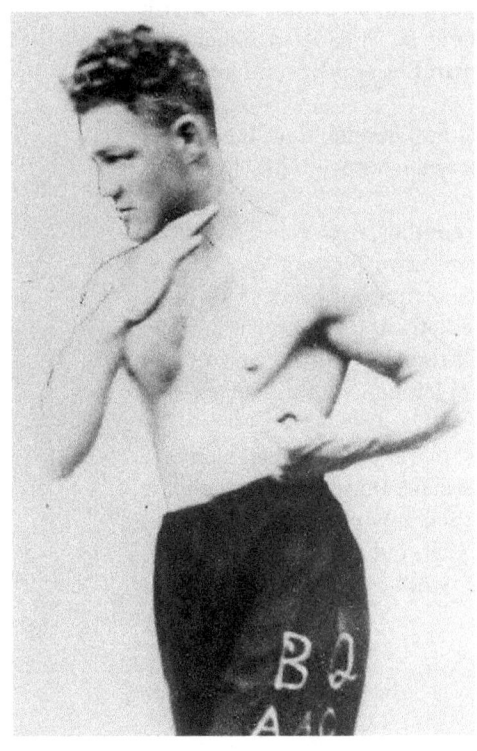

Billy Quinlan

Billy Quinlan falls into the second category. His hands and feet were never still, his perpetual motion more than compensating for a lack of destructive power.

The oldest of the eight Quinlen children – that's the correct surname, although the fight world invariably spelled it with an 'a' – entered this world in the Cwmbwrla area of Swansea, where his father, also William, lived with the family of his recently acquired bride, tailor's daughter Mary Elizabeth Morley. The young couple soon took their first-born to Garnswllt and it was in the Amman Valley that Billy learned to box, like so many, on the fairground booths.

He was 17 and already working alongside his father at Wernos Colliery when he made his bow, appropriately on Boxing Day, with a victory over the experienced Tich May impressive enough to see him taken on by top manager Johnny Vaughan. It started an unbeaten run which lasted almost until the following Christmas, finally being interrupted by a cut eye which forced him to quit against Treorchy product Oliver Cullen. Once the injury was healed, Cullen was tempted back to Ammanford and soundly outpointed.

Manager Vaughan was sure enough of his charge's ability to enter him in an open featherweight competition at Holborn Stadium. Billy repaid that faith by reaching the semi-final before losing to the tournament's eventual winner, Tommy Lye. He was to avenge that loss, twice beating the taller Londoner, and be also reversed the only other setback he suffered in 1930, against Merthyr's useful Billy Evans.

"Putting the record straight" was something of a habit for Quinlan. Once again a pre-Christmas defeat, this time by Rhondda boy Nobby Baker, was followed by a New Year victory over the two-time Welsh title challenger. Such form had put the Amman Valley prospect, now a lightweight, in contention for his own shot at national supremacy; a confident Vaughan dipped into his wallet and came up with the cash to persuade holder Alby Kestrell to leave his native Cardiff and give Billy the advantage of contesting the belt on home turf.

Billy (left) spars with Ginger Jones., who left the Rhondda to join the Amman Valley camp

There was a packed house in the Ammanford Arena on May 7, 1932, to watch Kestrell, his height advantage exaggerated by his upright stance, tackle the stocky local, who boxed with a slight crouch. Perhaps the occasion affected the home fighter, who seemed tentative in the early rounds, Alby's left constantly in his face. But he gradually settled to the task at hand and the more he scored, the more the visitor covered up, ceding the initiative.

As they went past halfway, the city slicker – he had needed a Turkish bath to make the weight – was tiring, while Quinlan was now dominant. But the ending was still a surprise: late in the eighth, as he was driven back to the ropes, Kestrell shipped a vicious body shot which saw him pitch forward, writhing in agony. He was still on the floor when the count was completed.

Alby insisted that the vital blow had landed south of the border and was granted his desired return at Judge's Hall, Trealaw, seven months later. This time there was no such controversy, Quinlan overcoming a slow start to take control and the former holder did well to hear the final bell.

Between the two Kestrell bouts, Billy was keeping busy in and out of the ring. The day after outpointing Billy Burnham in Swansea, he married Elizabeth Walters; the following weekend he was in Glasgow, being sparked by Scottish feather boss Johnny McMillan. The same month he lost a decision to teenage sensation Ernie Roderick, a future two-weight Lonsdale Belt holder, on the first bill at the replacement Liverpool Stadium, built on the site of the demolished St Paul's church, and replacing the iconic old hall on Pudsey Street, itself knocked down to make way for a cinema.

An attack of jaundice delayed Billy's mandatory defence against Evan Lane, but the pair finally clashed at Llanelli Workingmen's Club on June 6, 1933. The Dagenham-based Rhondda man boxed well at long range and seemed to have built a decent lead, but Quinlan proved stronger down the straight and was handing out some severe punishment in the closing stages. It proved enough for him to take the verdict and retain his laurels.

Billy was back at the same hall three months later for a British title eliminator against Scottish champion Tommy Spiers. Most of the 4,000-odd in attendance considered the Ammanford fighter, clearly faster than his rival, had done enough to merit the verdict after 15 rounds, so the draw handed down by London referee Jim Kenrick was not well received.

A rematch was required, but a broken jaw Quinlan suffered midway through the first meeting meant it did not happen until the following year. Even then, the Swansea crowd did not get a definitive answer regarding supremacy. Not that they cared too much: after seven evenly contested rounds, Spiers emerged for the eighth to target the body, one punch strayed low and the Glaswegian was promptly disqualified by the referee, a neutral from Watford.

The victor had to travel for the final stage in his bid to challenge Harry Mizler, but the outcome was the same. Sunderland's Douglas Parker, who ruled the Northern Area, was in the other corner at St James's Hall, Newcastle, but a thrilling encounter ended abruptly in the sixth when a left from Parker landed below the belt, Billy fell to the deck, clutching his groin, and Glaswegian referee Bill Strelly handed out the ultimate sanction to the unfortunate Wearsider.

Normally, in that era, the title bout would have followed fairly swiftly. But there were tales that Quinlan was asking too much money, though three successive defeats as he awaited the outcome of negotiations did little to improve his bargaining position, amid talk of a rift with mentor Vaughan.

A month later than the original Board deadline, on August 4, 1934, Mizler and Quinlan finally found themselves in the Vetch Field ring to contest the Lonsdale Belt, with the touring Australian cricketers among a disappointing crowd. Billy, with Swansea trainer Dai Curvis in the corner, showed little to counter those who by now were loudly questioning his right to be in there.

In fact, Mizler was far below his best. He was apparently unwilling to risk attacking the body in case he, too, became a disqualification victim, although English journalists present made a point of stressing that in no way did Quinlan try to "engineer" a low blow by jumping into it. In fact, it was Billy who suffered repeated lectures from the referee for hitting with an open glove.

The Welshman landed some sharp and legal blows when he moved in close, but his wilder – and wider – swings were often slaps. Mizler, by contrast, kept his left lead in Quinlan's face, with the challenger seemingly overawed by the occasion. In the sixth Billy finally seemed to relax and began to gamble more, but the champion, even though he rarely used his right, did enough to gain the verdict. It was not one with which the majority in attendance agreed – and they made their feelings known.

Billy's decline was by now irreversible. Scouser Jimmy Stewart halted him in eight, while Londoner George Daly took a points decision that meant the Welsh champion went into the next defence of his crown having lost seven in a row. Boyo Rees had been beaten when they first met two years earlier, but things were different on October 29,

1934, at the Mountain Ash Pavilion, just up the Cynon Valley from Rees's Abercwmboi home.

The oldest of four boxing brothers, Rees was soon in command, rocking his foe in the eighth and ending matters in the following session with a body shot that sent Quinlan rolling in agony until he fell from the ring and was counted out at the feet of the timekeeper. A fifth of the show's takings were given to a fund set up after the previous month's disaster at Gresford Colliery, which killed 266 men.

Billy was to win only once more – a commendable repeat success over former victim Parker in Newcastle – but further defeats followed before he signed off with a draw in his home town against Rhondda journeyman Billy Pritchard. With baby Yvonne adding to his responsibilities, Quinlan decided to focus on work down the pit, although a rock fall which broke both legs was to see him restricted to lower-paying tasks on the surface.

There was a brief spell managing kid brother Reg, but by the time Billy died at the age of 71 he had lost interest in the sport that had made him famous.

REG QUINLAN
(1924-1976)

Welsh Lightweight Champion 1949-51

When the best Welsh boxer of his generation tells you to do something, you do it. And following the instructions of world lightweight challenger Ronnie James made Reginald Phillip Quinlen a Welsh champion in just 75 seconds.

The colliery blacksmith's striker from Ammanford caught James's eye when the newly retired Swansea man opened a gym at Pontardawe and began to venture into management. He soon noticed that Reg seemed reluctant to use his right hand, which had been hurt in one of his early bouts. The former British champion convinced the youngster that he would need both fists if he wanted to emulate big brother Billy and soon had him spending hours learning to hook with his neglected weapon.

When Quinlan (his name, like his brother's, was invariably mis-spelled with an 'a') finally found himself in the ring with long-serving Welsh lightweight boss Warren Kendall over the border at Hereford Drill Hall on November 16, 1949, James told him not to nurse the right, but to throw it from the first bell. Reg obeyed, using the mitt to floor the Rhondda man inside a minute; he then kept hammering away until Kendall hit the canvas again. This time referee Jerry Walsh stepped in and halted the slaughter. The satisfied smile on Ronnie's face was as broad as that of the new monarch.

Reg was born at Garnswllt in 1924, although he always claimed it was the following year. Thirteen years younger than Billy, he was named after his mother's brother, Reg Morley, who had "done a bit" himself and took his nephew in hand when he first laced up the gloves.

As well as local rings, Quinlan found himself a regular performer in the West Midlands, where he allied himself with promoter D.W. Davies, a Rhondda boy who had settled in Wolverhampton and was always ready to employ prospects from back home. There were four

Reg Quinlan

stoppage wins in consecutive visits to Walsall Town Hall as Reg stretched his unbeaten streak into double figures, but a trip to Liverpool brought a disastrous one-round defeat against Ulsterman Dan McAllister. Just two weeks afterwards – no mandatory suspensions in those days – he was back on Merseyside seeking revenge and gave the heavier Belfast battler a torrid eight rounds before losing a close decision.

Reg was already lined up for a Welsh lightweight eliminator at Judge's Hall, Trealaw, a mere eight days later and looked jaded, allowing Vernon Ball, from up the valley at Cwmparc, to dictate the pace. A late flurry had Quinlan's followers excited, but once that blew out Ball was able to stroll to a clear-cut verdict.

Next up was British ABA champion Eddie Thomas, having his second pro fight. The Ammanford product landed enough early on to bring blood from the Thomas nose and he might even have led going into the last round. But one moment's carelessness was costly: Eddie whipped over a right which knocked Reg through the ropes and on to the lap of top boxing writer Bert Allen. He still beat the count, but was floored twice more and was flat out when the final bell interrupted the count. Quinlan eventually came around to be told he had lost on points!

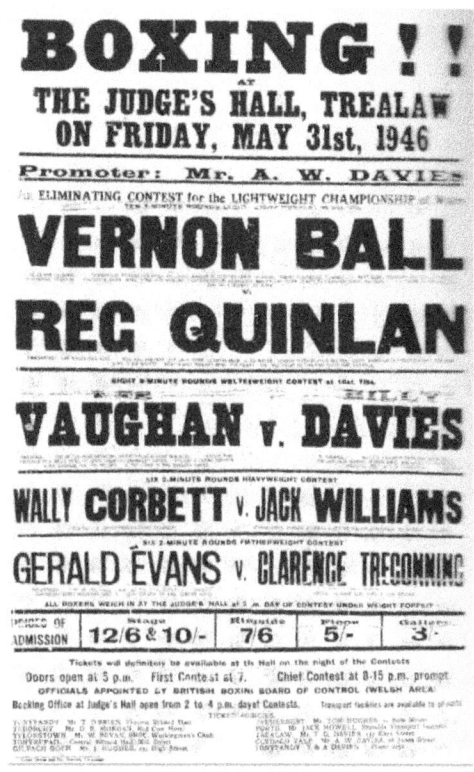

Poster advertising Reg's Welsh title eliminator

Four straight losses having derailed his progress, Reg crossed Offa's Dyke in search of better fortune: nine wins on the trot showed the wisdom of the choice and revived his title hopes, though he again lost two in a row before a second eliminator came his way.

Before he faced local Tommy Jones at Llanelli's Stebonheath football ground Reg had to deal with the loss of mentor D.W. Davies, who collapsed and died at a show in Hereford. Even Jones's home crowd applauded the decision in Quinlan's favour, so obvious that the most one-eyed 'Turk' could hardly object to it.

On occasion Reg had allowed himself to be drawn into slugging matches, but this time, with brother Billy in the corner, he exerted supreme self-control and boxed his way to victory in such style that he was promptly picked as favourite to unseat Kendall.

There was another hurdle to clear first, however, Skewen's Bryn Davies providing the opposition in a final eliminator at Ammanford, but he had little more than gameness to offer. That enabled him to survive the 12 rounds, but Reg's left won him the verdict with ease.

Before meeting Kendall, Quinlan suffered a cut-eye loss to Laurie Buxton, one of four boxing brothers appearing on the same bill in their native Watford. But the injury had healed by the time Reg went in with the champion – and, if it was at all fragile, his swift success meant we never found out.

Ammanford's new hero suggested the possibility of even greater things when he defied hand damage to earn a draw with highly touted Canadian Solly Cantor in Leeds, but the excellent Cliff Anderson, from British Guiana, a former Empire title challenger, exposed his limitations by flattening him in six at Porthcawl.

Quinlan put his belt on the line at Carmarthen's Market Hall on December 4, 1950, against a challenger from the Monmouthshire valleys, Ron Bruzas, a pro for barely a year. Bruzas, who had learned to box while in the RAF, was technically competent, but lacked the nous to keep Reg at bay. There were long periods of minimal action before the holder stirred himself and finally dropped his man in the 10th. Ron rose and immediately grabbed his tormentor; when the referee prized him away he realised that he was too dazed to continue.

There was only one further episode in the Quinlan career, a cuts stoppage of Yorkshireman Ronnie Latham. He was ordered to defend his Welsh honour against former victim Selwyn Evans, but instead announced his retirement from the ring.

TIM REDMAN
(1970-)

🥊 Welsh Cruiserweight Challenger 1999

On the face of it, there is little in common between boxing, a sport which demands strength and mobility, and rally driving, which takes place while sitting down. Yet anyone involved in motor sport will tell you that fitness is vital if you aspire to reach the top – or to stay there, like Gwyndaf Evans.

The ace from Dinas Mawddwy was around 40 when he began to frequent Royce Brown's gym and found himself sharing the ring with local pugilist Tim Redman, a decade younger. "I used to try and catch him when he was tired," recalls Gwyndaf, "but he still boxed my ears off. I held my own on the hill runs, though."

It was no surprise that Gwyndaf, whose world-class rallying heir, Elfyn, also uses boxing training as part of his routine, found things tough when it came to actual sparring. He was in with a former national amateur champion who had followed that triumph with a decent career in the paid ranks.

Timothy Patrician Redman – the full handle dates from World War II, when his grandfather palled up with an Irishman called Patrician and they agreed to give each other's name to their first-born sons – began boxing as a nine-year-old with Brown's Idris Sporting Club and picked up Welsh titles at schools and junior level before a spell in the Army.

Back in civvy street, he worked as a bricklayer for his father's construction firm, while focussing on the hunt for senior honours. But Cardiffian Richard Fenton stopped him in the semi-finals on his first attempt at the Welsh ABAs and knocked him out in the following year's final, although there was some joy for trainer Brown, whose son, also Tim, claimed the first of his two successes. After missing the 1994 tournament with injury, Redman finally finished top of Wales's amateur heavyweights and then signed pro forms with Hywel 'Cass' Davies, while still training with his amateur mentor.

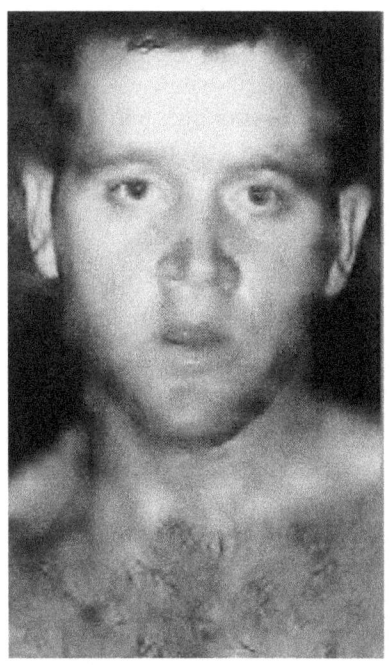

Tim Redman

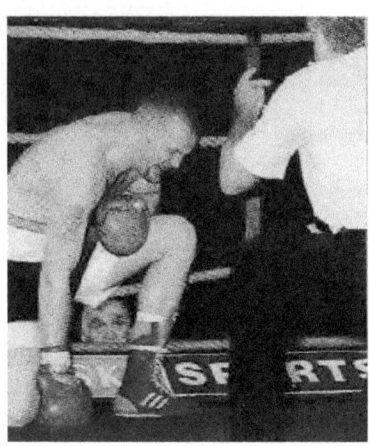
How it ended: Redman bows out against Sione Asipeli

Campaigning at cruiserweight, he started well enough, with a two-round dismissal of fellow first-timer Phill Day, from Swindon, on a Steve Robinson world title undercard at the Wales National Ice Rink in Cardiff. But a damaged shoulder forced the North Walian out after two sessions against future British and Commonwealth king Chris Oboh on a London dinner show and he then dropped a six-round decision to Gipsy Carmen that infuriated new manager Chris Sanigar.

Few would have expected much better when Redman came in as a late sub to face Jacklord Jacobs, a hulking Nigerian who boasted a silver medal at the world amateur championships. When Tim was dropped in the opener, the outcome seemed inevitable, but he recovered to fell Jacobs in the next, the first time the London-based African had ever found himself on the deck, and claim a meritorious draw.

Another managerial switch saw him link up with John Davies, who promptly employed him as the main attraction on his show in a Queensferry nightclub. The new recruit thrilled the fans when he floored John Pierre twice in the second, but faded dramatically to allow the Geordie to nick a deserved verdict.

Redman bounced back with three straight victories, but he bit off more than he could chew at the York Hall when he took on another full heavyweight in Reading's unbeaten Michael Sprott and was stopped in two; Sprott went on to wear British and Commmonwealth crowns. When Scot John Wilson and Irishman Cathal O'Grady repeated the treatment in three and two rounds respectively, Tim's path seemed to be heading downhill.

But the high point of his career, now guided by Dai Gardiner, was still to come. After a couple of wins, two defeats to touted Israel Ajose and a draw in Bristol – where repeated butts by hometown fighter Karl Andrews were ignored by referee Denzil Lewis, ironically a Welshman – the Dolgellau man was called up to dispute the Welsh cruiser throne, vacant for more than a decade, against Rhondda boy Darron Griffiths at Cardiff's Welsh Institute of Sport on February 23, 1999.

Southpaw Griffiths, already the super-middle ruler, seemed unsettled early on as Redman roughed him up inside, but briefly floored his rival in an ill-tempered second stanza. The man from Porth was gathering points with his more accurate work, but Tim was in no great difficulty until the seventh, when exhaustion suddenly set in. Wrestled over in a neutral corner, he was slow to rise; encouraged, Darron stormed in with a barrage which left the Northerner on the canvas in the centre of the ring, where he took the full count from referee Roddy Evans.

There was just one more entry in the ledger, when US-based Tongan Sione Asipeli, a future WBO title challenger, floored Redman four times in less than four minutes in Sheffield. Since then boxing has been firmly in the rear-view mirror as he moved to Barmouth and developed his own business.

ARCHIE RULE
(1902-1971)

🥊 European Amateur Bantamweight Gold Medallist 1925

The young man from the Amman Valley was one of the greatest amateur boxers Wales has ever produced. It is amazing that he achieved so much while having as many battles with the authorities as he fought inside the ropes. And yet, despite the obstacles placed in his path by the men in blazers, he rebuffed every attempt to persuade him to turn pro.

Archibald Leonard Rule first saw the light of day on the banks of the other River Aman, a tributary of the Cynon. Born at Cwmaman, a few miles from Aberdare, he moved west when miner father George took the family – mother Catherine, three sisters and baby brother Caradoc, who went on to box as 'Crad' – to Ystradgynlais and later to Penybanc. In due course, another seven children would join the tribe.

Young Archie first laced up the gloves in the booths that visited local fairgrounds, but with the emergence of the Amman Valley club, he appealed to the Welsh ABA to restore his amateur status. This was granted in January 1923, in time for him to enter the national championships. After losing the bantamweight final to Newport's George Thompson, he proceeded to gain his revenge, twice outpointing the champion, once on a show before disabled soldiers at Cardiff's Rookwood Hospital and then as part of a fund-raiser for Cardiff Royal Infirmary, staged in a marquee in Sophia Gardens.

After winning the Welsh title in 1924, the first of three successive triumphs, Rule entered the English competition – in effect, the British championships – and defeated future pro legend Nel Tarleton before being outpointed in the final by Coventry's Les Tarrant on the referee's casting vote after the two judges disagreed. Archie seemed unlucky, to say the least, having provided most of the positive work in a quiet encounter, and also being the recipient of two low rights without comment from the third man.

With the English ABA in sole control of Olympic selection and two representatives allowed in those days, they duly named the champion and runner-up at each weight – except bantamweight, the one division in which a non-English entrant reached the final. Instead, they invited Archie to take part in a box-off to see who would accompany Tarrant to Paris; he applied to the Welsh ABA for permission to box, but was refused.

Archie Rule

Rule (left) with Franz Dubbers, the German he beat to win gold

Welsh trawler owner Wilf Neale took Archie to the French capital to watch the finals, where the bantam gold was won by South African Willie Smith, later to defeat Londoner Teddy Baldock for a version of the professional world title. Rule was not impressed. "I could have beaten him six days a week and twice on Sundays," he said.

When Tarrant visited Cardiff as part of a Midlands select team, he again outpointed his rival, although the winner was said to be guilty of several actions "which would never have been tolerated in a professional bout in Wales". Tarrant then turned pro under the name Les Mack and disappeared from Archie's life.

Known as 'The Quiet Man' or, more imaginatively, 'The Boffin of Bash', Rule did not enter the 1925 English tournament, but he was invited by the English ABA – along with Cardiffian Fred Perry and Newport's Ben Marshall – to accompany the England boys to Stockholm, where 13 countries were contesting the European championships. The GB team was captained by the heavyweight rep, Lt Dudley Lister, whose army contacts provided the squad with a single trainer and a masseur.

Archie returned with a gold medal, his three victories culminating in a decision over German champion Franz Dübbers which was so convincing that the loser's countrymen – at war with Britain a decade earlier, remember – carried Archie from the ring on their shoulders. He was not unfamiliar to them, having been one of only two Welsh winners in an international meeting in Hamburg the previous year.

Rule was brought back to earth 10 days after his European triumph when three-time English flyweight champion Eddie Warwick outscored him at the annual fundraiser for Cardiff's Nazareth House orphanage.

After completing his Welsh triple crown, but falling at the first hurdle in the English event, Archie headed for pastures new. With Britain paralysed by the General Strike, he boarded the *Aquitania* and sailed to the US, earning a crust as a sparring partner, while also despatching a ringside report to the *South Wales Echo* on the world heavyweight collision between Jack Dempsey and Gene Tunney.

He was home in time for the 1927 Welsh ABAs, stepping up to featherweight, but after two wins had left him with several front teeth dislodged he had to withdraw from the decider against former European team-mate Perry, who had already eliminated kid brother Crad.

Having taken an office job with Westminster Borough Council, Archie began to wind down his boxing activities – though still active enough to have won a gold watch, a silver rose bowl and an expensive case of cutlery at various London occasions. As the twenties ended, however, Rule's focus turned more to the training side, passing on his wisdom to judo and athletics teams as well as those seeking tutelage in the fistic art.

Back home at Penybanc, he was employed for a while in insurance, before a spell making car seats in the recently opened Pullman factory. Now married to Gwyneth, he moved to Swansea, where he became a familiar figure as a commissionaire at the town's BBC studios.

But the fight game still dominated his life. He was part of a new promotional team in Ammanford, something of a fistic backwater since its guiding light, Johnny

ARCHIE RULE

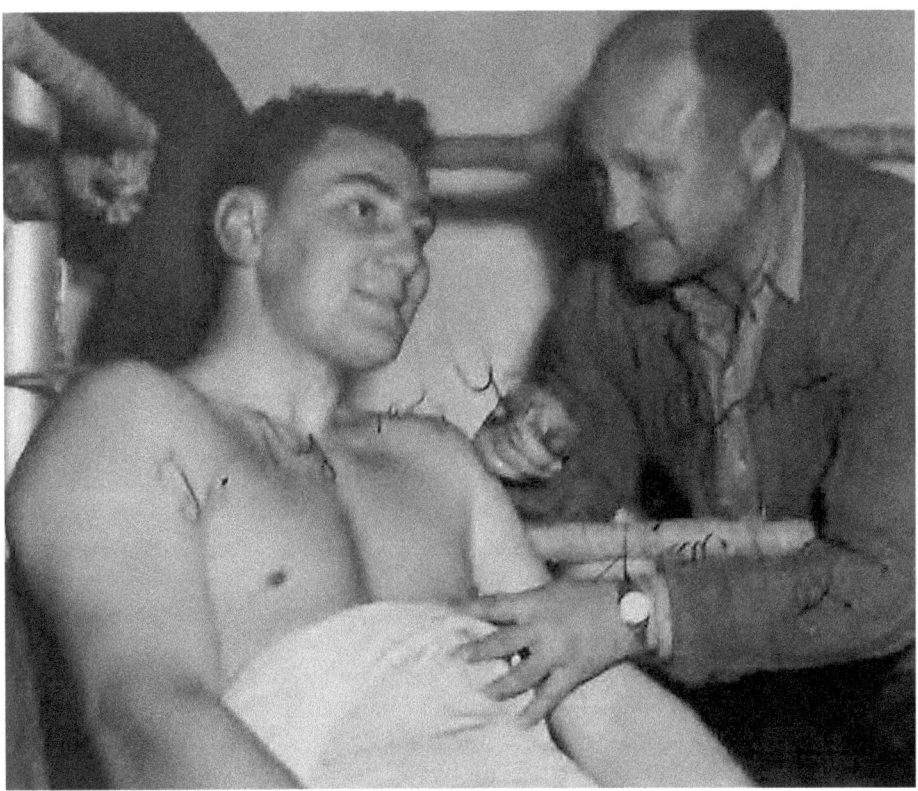

Trainer Archie with Joe Erskine, the man he guided to a Lonsdale Belt

Vaughan, had upped sticks and moved to Llanelli. After the new group's first venture, Johnny suggested that Archie's matchmaking was "too good for the small returns in that district".

His value as a cornerman saw him assist Eddie Thomas when Howard Winstone beat Mitsunori Seki to become world feather king and he also joined the Merthyr magus in helping Ken Buchanan, another to rule the globe. But Rule is principally recognised for his work with Cardiff heavyweight Joe Erskine, guiding him from novice to British and Empire champion.

In each of his contrasting roles as amateur boxer and professional trainer, Archie Rule left an indelible imprint on the sport in Wales.

NED TURNER

(1791-1826)

🥊 Bareknuckle Champion

Despite the suggestions that they should all have been drowned at birth, southpaws are a regular sight in our rings these days. Not so in the past. Just as left-handed schoolkids were forced to write with their other hand, boxers were invariably taught to adopt an orthodox stance.

But there have always been rebels. And one of the first was a Londoner born and bred, but whose parents came from the Newtown area. Edward Turner was always referred to as a Welshman. The land of his fathers was happy to claim him, the *North Wales Gazette* describing him as the "pugilistic prince of Wales".

As well as his wrong-way-round stance, Ned was an innovator in training methods, being one of the first boxers to use dumbbells to increase his arm strength, though he had plenty of skill to go with his physical prowess. Indeed, he was regarded as the most brilliant defensive boxer of his day.

Born at Crucifix Lane in Southwark, the teenage Turner found work in the tanneries, graduating to more specialised employment as a frizer, preparing sheepskin to be used for hat linings and the like. But when a foreman made disparaging remarks about his Welsh forebears, Ned handed out retribution in a manner which led to suggestions that his fists might become a source of income. His new career was officially launched when the 19-year-old saw off a rival named Balche in Bermondsey, the heart of the leather industry.

Ned Turner

But tragedy struck when he faced a groom called Jack Curtis at Moulsey Hurst in Surrey on October 22, 1816, in what was the first contest to take place in a ring limited to 20 feet square. After 68 rounds, spread over an hour and 25 minutes, Turner finally knocked his man out. Poor Jack never regained consciousness and died after a few hours at the nearby Red Lion. The inn was also the venue for the inquest three days later, which heard that Curtis's seconds had tried to persuade him to give in, only for their fighter to insist he would carry on as long as he could see his rival.

Turner was charged with wilful murder and appeared at the Old Bailey, where the judge, Baron Graham, accepted there was no malice involved. The jury returned after a short discussion to declare Ned guilty of manslaughter, with a recommendation that mercy be shown. The judge, obviously in agreement, sentenced him to two months in Newgate, where he was allowed unlimited visitors, including many titled patrons of the Noble Art.

Clearly there was no shadow over Turner's reputation when he returned to face stocky former sailor Jack Scroggins – real surname Palmer, he had been rebranded after a character in a comic song – and, with neither man having experienced defeat, the showdown caused much excitement among 'The Fancy', with an estimated 30,000 in attendance. Such a crowd proved unmanageable and those at the front were frequently forced into the ring, eventually leading to the bout being abandoned as a draw.

It was rearranged, with greater security, a few months later and Scroggins was confident enough to back himself at £120 to £80. It proved a rash decision. Ned, an accomplished technician, held his own before landing a blow to the neck which Jack later confessed had turned the fight against him. He was almost reprieved when a troop of yeomanry arrived on the scene, but they had come to watch the action rather than to stop it!

Scroggins was the better man at close-quarters – wrestling was allowed, of course – while Turner was the smarter boxer, enjoying particular success with the uppercut. After 33 rounds, Jack was exhausted and his second raised a handkerchief in token of surrender. He still believed he was the better man, however, and the pair met again on the banks of the Thames at Shepperton, where Ned repeated his previous triumph, this time leaving his victim draped across the ropes in the 39th round, after a battle lasting more than an hour and a half.

The emphatic victory led some to claim Turner – 'The Out-and-Outer', as he was now known – was the best in the country among the lighter men (he was usually around 10st 4lbs). Others preferred Jack Randall, a Londoner of Irish stock, whose speed and cleverness – he is credited with the invention of the "one-two", a straight left followed by a right hook – was recognised in his nickname, 'The Nonpareil'. They finally came head-to-head at Crawley Down on December 5, 1818.

Turner had met his match. Bleeding badly from the nose from the fourth, he was generally on the receiving end, though he did throw his foe out of the ring in the 17th round. Lacking the power to keep Randall at bay, he took tremendous punishment, with some calling for him to quit. He ignored them, only to be dropped for good by a right to the temple in the 34th. Awed by the Welshman's courage over two hours and 20 minutes – he was the only man to last that long with Randall – the winner brushed aside the congratulations of his friends to walk across and shake Ned's hand.

An unlikely observer at ringside was the poet John Keats, taken along in a bid to cheer him up after the death of his brother. The tussle was also the subject of a popular ballad penned by a lesser versifier, Bob Gregson.

Next up for Turner was a Bristolian butcher, Cyrus Davis, who was beaten in 52 minutes, Ned's greater experience being the decisive factor. At the same Surrey venue, the Welshman claimed another decent scalp in Jack Martin, a baker wittily dubbed 'The Master of the Rolls'. But he was to meet both again with different results.

Ned's lifestyle was partly responsible for the decline in his fortunes. His fondness for gin was widely known, one newspaper lamenting that his stamina had been affected "by copious libations of Seager and Evans's blue ruin".

Martin was the first to take advantage. The omens were against Turner from the start: on arrival he tossed his hat into the ring, according to custom, only for the wind to blow it back out, forcing him to repeat the gesture. The Welshman opened as favourite with the gamblers, but Martin gradually began to take command, the odds changing to reflect the fact. In the 43rd round, Ned seemed to find his second wind and blood poured down Jack's face, but the baker was once again kneading Turner's body in the ensuing sessions and the umpires called a halt after 60 rounds and 88 minutes.

A few days later Ned was struck by "an affliction of the eyes", dashing thoughts of a rubber match. Indeed, there was then a two-year gap before he was back for a second clash with Davis. A few weeks' training in the hills around the family home in Montgomeryshire did much to restore the veteran to full fitness for the showdown at Harpenden Common on February 23, 1823.

Early exchanges were even as the duo adapted to ground left slippery by heavy rain, but Cy, four years younger, more than a stone heavier and two inches taller, soon left his mark on the Welshman, who bled profusely from his left cheek with the adjacent eye soon closing completely.

Matters became so one-sided that Ned's main backer, James Soames, pleaded with him to concede, but was waved away by his brave protégé. Eventually, Soames ordered Turner's seconds, including the great former champion, Tom Cribb, to throw in the sponge. It was all over in 38 minutes.

Ironically, Davis, who celebrated by leaping over the ropes, never fought again. He had damaged his fist on Turner's teeth and the resultant infection meant the amputation of the index finger, ending his ring exploits. Ned's story had two further chapters, each involving a 21-year-old feather bed maker called Peace Inglis, and taking place at Colnbrook, just off the London-Bath road.

Their first encounter should have underlined the lesson provided by Davis: youth and strength will overcome an unfit and ageing rival, however talented. A somewhat flabby Turner controlled matters for more than an hour, but fatigue set in and by the time referee Harry Holt withdrew him from the fray after 47 rounds he could barely stand. Despite his victory, Inglis was reported in the *Morning Post* to have died of his injuries, with warrants apparently issued for the arrest of Ned and his seconds.

It proved to be fake news and the two met again seven months later. And this time Turner, two months shy of his 34th birthday, defied the calendar and went to war on Peace. Much trimmer after deserting the London taverns for the mountains of Mid Wales, "Ould Ned" demonstrated his greater science and ring generalship to such effect that Inglis, for all his courage, was given a hiding before being knocked out in the 15th round. But this triumph proved to be Turner's last stand, despite talk of a decider.

Early in April 1826, the legendary Tom Spring took the stage at a sparring exhibition to inform those present that Ned, long plagued by asthma, was "sinking into the grave" and that a benefit would be held a fortnight later. Alas, the Welshman breathed his last the night before the event. Several former opponents were among the mourners as he was buried in an Aldgate churchyard.

ALLAN WILKINS
(1926-2015)

- Welsh Welterweight Champion 1950-53

Allan Wilkins

The smiling southpaw from Ystradgynlais was a boxing cannibal. He feasted on his own kind. Of his 29 career victories, 27 came against Welshmen – and not once did he lose against a fellow-countryman.

Alan Edwin Owen Wilkins – his first name picked up an additional 'l' somewhere along the way – did not have to look far for his inspiration: opposite his home in Bryn Road lived the legendary Tiger Ellis. Indeed, on one occasion the ageing former champion was persuaded to spar with the young prodigy at manager Eddie Evans's gym. The experience confirmed the veteran's belief that he was right to stay retired.

Born in Swansea, young Wilkins knew early tragedy. His mother, Nancy, died of tuberculosis when he was only 12; his father, Tom, a fishmonger who had played rugby for Wales as a schoolboy, caught the disease while caring for his wife. When their home was damaged by German bombs, the remaining family moved to live with Nancy's widowed mother in the Breconshire mining town. Within a year Tom, too, was dead, followed five months later by his mother-in-law.

Granny Shaw's two children, Auntie Evelyn and Uncle Fred, became Allan's surrogate parents. He left school at 14 and worked down the pit throughout the war years. But peace brought new opportunities, with returning servicemen and their civilian neighbours flocking to watch football, rugby, cricket – and boxing. Despite minimal amateur experience, Allan joined the rush to cash in, making his pro bow three months before his 20th birthday.

He won, of course, and built a 14-bout unbeaten streak in rings across South Wales – two draws included – before venturing across Offa's Dyke for the first time. It was a step too far.

New champion Allan (right) is congratulated by colliery manager W.O. Jones, with Eddie Evans watching on

Londoner Alf Danahar may not have had the talent of big brother Arthur, whose British title showdown with Eric Boon remains one of the all-time great fights, but he was pretty decent himself and had lost only once when he met Wilkins at Leyton Baths. The Welshman was down no fewer than a dozen times before he was rescued in the sixth.

A return to home comforts saw him enjoy another successful run. But when he headed back to "foreign" parts – Plymouth, in this case – he lost on points to Cornish veteran Joe Perks, who proceeded to knock Allan out the next time he set foot in the West Country. And his first setback in a Welsh ring came against an Englishman, Slough's Pete Davis. By then, however, his successes against domestic rivals had put him in title contention.

Manager Evans had long been trumpeting the virtues of his amiable, opera-loving protégé and the Welsh authorities took notice, matching him in a welterweight eliminator with hot favourite Jack Coles, from Tiryberth. They met in Swansea and Wilkins, in his first 10-round bout, left-hooked his way to a decisive, if unexpected, verdict.

With Eddie Thomas relinquishing the belt, victory in Allan's clash with Barry's Bob Burniston at Neath would guarantee him a crack at the vacant throne. It proved straightforward, only Burniston's courage seeing him last the distance.

Former champion Gwyn Williams had opted out of the other eliminator in favour of a rematch with Cliff Curvis, so Cliff's older brother, Ken, awaited Wilkins on June 21, 1950 at Coney Beach Arena, Porthcawl. The Swansea man relied on the old adage that a right is the answer to a southpaw, throwing that fist from a variety of angles. It paid off in the third, when one such punch dropped Allan for a count of six.

But Curvis became more and more erratic and picked up warnings as his punches strayed south. Ken was also bleeding from the mouth and a cut by the left eye and the Ystradgynlais boxer was clearly on top when his foe swung a right to the body in the sixth. Once more his radar was faulty; this time the referee disqualified him. It marked the end of Ken's career.

For Wilkins, however, it meant he had a title and this boosted his marketability across the border. Unfortunately, it did not make him any more successful on his travels: his next six contests included trips to Scotland, Tees-side and the Midlands, but his only victory came when he outscored Merthyr's Ginger Ward in Carmarthen.

Realising that home was best, he stayed local for his remaining action. It paid dividends with a repeat win over Ward and a couple of eight-round decisions over Eddie Williams in Gwent, though the Tredegar fighter decked him twice in their second meeting.

Allan still had not defended his national honours, however, and was ordered to face Eric Davies, a Risca-born Midlander. It never happened. A newly acquired fiancée wanted him to give up both the ring and the mine. Eager to please, the lovesick champion joined Mid-Wales Police and announced that he would box no more. The relationship was not to last, but the retirement did.

PC Wilkins was posted to Brynmawr, where he met trainee teacher Cynthia Yates, marrying her in 1955. Daughter Angharad arrived a year later, before the family moved to Birmingham, with Allan serving in the city force for seven years.

The Wilkinses (there was now a second daughter, Bethan) returned to live at Cwmbran, later moving to Malpas. No longer a copper, Allan earned a crust as a security officer – and also as a private investigator. But Wales's answer to Sam Spade and Hercule Poirot was not entirely lost to boxing, sitting on the Welsh Area Council for several years. He died in the Royal Gwent Hospital, aged 88.

Trainee PC Wilkins

JOHNNY WILLIAMS
(1926-2007)

- Empire Heavyweight Champion 1952-1953
- British Heavyweight Champion 1952-1953

Johnny Williams

A youngster entering a village school in Northamptonshire knowing barely a word of English is likely to attract a degree of mockery, if not outright hostility, from his new classmates. But the curly-haired kid they called "Welshie" could look after himself, even at the age of five.

Two years earlier young John Jones Williams had been uprooted from Cell Fechan, the little farm in the hollow of the mountainside at Barmouth, where he was born on Christmas Day, 1926. But the warmth of a close, Welsh-speaking family eased the transition. And it was brother Robin, two years older, who taught him to use his fists. Not through fraternal love, particularly, more that Robin needed an opponent for sparring sessions on the lawn, but it gave Johnny an early, if bruising, introduction to the fight game. And while Robin lost interest in the sport once Johnny started getting the better of the exchanges, kid brother was in for life.

By the time he was 10, it was bringing Johnny some extra pocket money. Wearing long trousers to make him appear older (they were hidden under the bed, away from parental eyes), he called on the legendary Sam Minto, an opponent of Bill Beynon way back in 1912, but with a ring career destined to last another dozen years yet. And in Sam's booth, for shillings tossed through the ropes, "Young Taffy" learned his craft.

Johnny "went straight" at 19, joining the world of licensed boxing. George Biddles, the game's Godfather in the East Midlands, had just been demobbed and was looking for talent to feature on his first post-war promotion. The local colts were corralled in a cramped back room and invited: "Hands up those who want to fight." Every arm in the place shot aloft. A smiling Biddles began the intricate job of matchmaking: "You, you and you meet you, you and you." Johnny's selected foe had been sitting down; when he rose, he hit his head on the ceiling. Billy Rhodes's height proved no obstacle. After six rounds at the Railwaymen's Club in Leicester, the Welshman claimed the first win of his official career. And his first purse money: £1.

A year of victories later he had his first chance in London, outscoring Wally With over eight rounds. "They gave me the princely sum of £8, expenses included," he remembered. "By the time I'd made my way home, there was £2 left. So much for the big time."

Williams with manager Ted Broadribb

His return to the Smoke two months later proved more rewarding. Freddie Mills needed sparring partners and Williams, now a genuine light-heavyweight after starting out as a middle, was invited along. His performance earned Freddie's lifelong friendship. It also gained Johnny a manager – Ted Broadribb, the man who had steered Tommy Farr to a world title fight.

Progress was steady. Defeats at the hands of Southall southpaw Reg Spring and a teenage blacksmith from Battersea, Don Cockell, were both avenged in style, and the transplanted Welshman was now No 1 contender to stablemate Mills. But the wily Broadribb had no intention of letting one meal ticket devalue another. He had always visualised Johnny as a full heavyweight, and a trip to South Africa brought about the transformation. When he left the ration-book rule of 1948 Britain, the farmer's son weighed 12st 4lb. Six months, three victories and a lot of chocolate later, he scaled 13st 8lb.

He began to cut a swathe through the big men of Europe and the Empire, but the States boasted a higher class of heavyweight, and Johnny's first American opponent proved a tartar. The heavier Pat Comiskey bulled Williams out of his customary rhythm and gashed him beneath the left eye. Johnny staged a sixth-round recovery that briefly draped the giant over the White City ropes, but at the bell his face was covered in blood and his challenge was at an end.

Hardly the best way to prepare for the most important contest to date: a final eliminator for the British and Empire titles, at Leicester's Granby Halls against another

Johnny (right) does his roadwork with world champion stablemate Freddie Mills

Midlands farm boy, Jack Gardner. It proved an enthralling battle. Gardner moved in on his prey from the opening bell, and despite Johnny's defensive skills, the wound opened by Comiskey six weeks earlier was soon leaking again. The Market Harborough man, too, was cut in the second round and the blood flowed steadily from both combatants for the duration. Ignoring their wounds, they battled on in head-to-head exchanges which united the rival supporters in ecstasy.

Such commitment took its toll. As Gardner's hand was raised in triumph, Johnny lay back on his stool, white-faced and glassy-eyed, surrounded by medical men. After 10 minutes, he was carried to the dressing-room and then ferried to hospital, accompanied by wife Josie. His sense of humour, however, was undamaged. With morning came the discovery that alongside in the ward were two other battered victims of late-night fisticuffs. "At least," Johnny told them, "I got paid for it."

After a four-month rest, Williams took on young George Kaplan at Earls Court. Kaplan had the famous hypnotist, Jimmy Grippo, in his corner, but it was the American who was mesmerised by Williams's left hand on the way to seventh-round defeat. Grippo was so impressed he offered $25,000 for the Welshman's contract. Broadribb rejected it. And he gave the same reply to another prospective purchaser, film star Stewart Granger.

His manager's faith must have been shaken when Johnny had to retire against an ordinary American, Big Bill Weinberg, and an X-ray showed no fewer than nine vertebrae were out of alignment; Williams, who had been troubled by neck pains for months, now knew why. There was a gradual rehabilitation, physically and fistically, before March 11, 1952, at Earls Court, brought the opportunity Williams had been awaiting: not merely a shot at the British and Empire titles, but the chance of revenge over Gardner.

Hunting horns joined in the fanfares as the pair entered the ring, and although an all-action replay of their first meeting was too much to expect, it had its sanguinary similarities, both men being troubled by cuts from the opening rounds. Williams was timing his blows better, and Gardner, who had ended an illustrious career when he dethroned Bruce Woodcock, was frustrated by the Welshman's defence. The ex-Guardsman's famous black moustache was scarlet as he watched Jack Hart lift Williams's arm. Scattered boos could not diminish the Welshman's joy as the Lonsdale Belt was clipped about his waist.

A trip to the States brought a stoppage win over New Yorker Jimmy Rousse and interest in a future fight from no less than world heavy boss Jersey Joe Walcott, who suggested a defence against Williams might be more marketable than one against up-and-coming Rocky Marciano.

The Empire half of his domain was successfully defended against South African Olympic bronze medallist Johnny Arthur, while on the domestic scene, former light-heavy champion Cockell beat the ageing Tommy Farr in a final eliminator, robbing Johnny of the chance to face his boyhood idol. Instead, Williams entered Harringay Arena on May 12, 1953, to meet the barrel-shaped Cockney.

Williams (right) dethrones British titleholder Jack Gardner

Cockell forced the pace, with Williams, a hot favourite, seemingly content, relying on that educated left to keep him at bay. It had its effect, with Don's face soon showing signs of wear, but at least the expression beneath the blood was aggressive: Johnny looked apprehensive, perpetually giving ground as the eager challenger pressed forward. With only a fraction of Williams's skill, Cockell nevertheless landed firmly and often, taking the verdict after 15 repetitive and uninspiring rounds.

While the Londoner moved on towards his heroic challenge to Marciano, for Johnny bread and dripping had replaced the dreams of caviare. There was a little bratwurst in the diet as well, with two winning visits to Germany helping him re-establish his credentials. In June 1955, at Nottingham Ice Stadium, two former champions, Williams and Gardner, were matched to decide who should tackle the usurper Cockell. The Leicestershire man now weighed two stones more than Johnny, a decisive advantage. After repeated visits to the canvas, Williams was counted out on one knee, utterly exhausted. Just five rounds had apparently ended all hope of regaining his crowns.

Help arrived from an unexpected source – Tonga, a Pacific island known only for Queen Salote, a heavyweight herself, who had won British hearts as she smiled through London's rain at the Coronation two years earlier. Preacher's son Kitione Lave had run away to sea at the age of 10. Eleven years on, he reached Britain, plucking a guitar and proclaiming what he would do to Europe's finest. Alas, he walked straight on to Johnny's right and was stopped in a round. But colourful Kit's role in the Williams career was to embrace more than a mere restoration of confidence following the Gardner disaster.

A four-round defeat in Washington against Tommy "Hurricane" Jackson, the No 1 contender for Marciano's title, must have prompted thoughts of retirement, but they were dispelled a few weeks later on an amazing evening at Earls Court. Messrs Cockell and Gardner, preparing for their championship collision, were to flex their muscles against a couple of unconsidered sons of

Johnny (left) loses his crown to the unfancied Don Cockell

THE BOXERS OF WALES

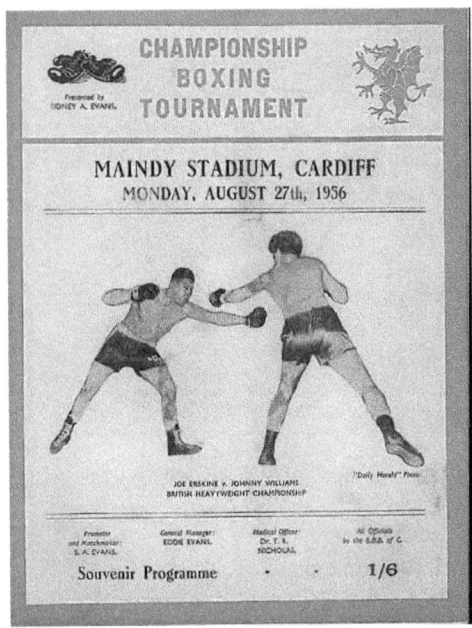

Youth v experience in the first British heavyweight title fight held in Wales

Empire. But our friend Lave knocked out Cockell in two rounds; Jamaica's Joe Bygraves demolished Gardner with equal speed. Neither loser ever fought again.

Williams was now a logical choice to contest the vacant title. Who better for the other stool at Cardiff's Maindy Stadium than Joe Erskine, a local 22-year-old unbeaten in 29 outings? They came together in a torrential downpour on August 27, 1956. The Cardiffian, fast, confident and seven years younger, predictably cut out the early work. More surprisingly, perhaps, Erskine was outjabbing the former champion, apparently unfazed by the defensive artistry which had disconcerted a galaxy of previous opponents. Only when Johnny opened cuts on both the hometown boy's cheeks did the tide ebb slightly and by the 10th Joe's right eye was a mere slit. But, conscious of his clear lead, Erskine was content to keep affairs at long range with his talented left hand. Rain and sweat mingling with the blood, Joe looked a mess. But his damage was superficial; Johnny's problems lay deeper and could be calculated on a calendar. The younger man was the new champion.

For the North Walian, the play was almost done. There was one remaining scene: a non-title encounter at Manchester's Belle Vue Stadium with Bygraves, by now king of the Empire. There were flashes of the old skill, but he could not keep the powerful West Indian away indefinitely, and after a savage sixth round, Johnny raised a glove in acknowledgement that the contest, and his career, were over.

He became a tutor in great demand to hone the rough edges on young prospects. But Whit Monday, 1959, almost ended everything. A horrific crash on the Coventry by-pass put him into a coma, with two broken legs as a bonus. It was several months before Johnny was back on the farm, thanking boxing for his survival. "When the crash came, I caught a glimpse of a lamp-post and my fighter's instinct made me duck," he said. "If I hadn't, my head would have been smashed. It's as simple as that."

So Johnny lived to guide Leicestershire's George Aldridge to the British middleweight title. When his champion retired in 1963, so did Williams, disillusioned at having to deal with some of the villains he found in the game. "I'd far rather spend my time buying and selling cattle," he said. It was a decision he never regretted.

CRAIG WINTER
(1971-)

- British Light-Middleweight Contender 1996
- Welsh Light-Middleweight Challenger 1998

For a few seconds the boy from the Vale of Clwyd stood on the brink of history. The most famous person to hail from Llandyrnog was Gwen ferch Ellis, the first woman in Wales known to have been executed as a witch. That was back in 1594. Four centuries later Craig David Winter was poised to become the first Welsh champion from his village.

Facing him across the ring on December 5, 1998, was Paul Samuels, an unbeaten banger from Newbridge, who had moved up from welterweight to contest the vacant Welsh throne at light-middle. And while the fans at Whitchurch Leisure Centre on the outskirts of Bristol, mostly there to cheer on local hero Glenn Catley, may have had little interest beforehand, they certainly paid attention once the bell had rung.

There was no feeling-out period. Both went at it hammer and tongs from the start, Winter bringing blood from Paul's mouth, but generally under pressure from the Gwent fighter's sharp, accurate shots. Then everything changed. A thumping straight right sent Samuels on to the seat of his pants.

He looked bewildered for a moment, before pulling himself upright to take the remainder of referee Wynford Jones's mandatory eight count. Craig, heart pounding, was on the verge of glory.

But he could not repeat the success before the end of the session. No matter; the plan had always been to wait for the fast-starting favourite to tire. But Winter, like his opponent,

Craig Winter

Winter, (left) faces Paul Samuels in a memorable up-and-downer

found it difficult to resist a tear-up and both were soon marked up, Samuels with a swelling near his right eye, Craig bleeding from the nose. And then the dream vanished.

Paul stood the North Walian up with a right and followed it with a thunderous left hook that sent his mouthpiece flying as its owner crashed forward on to his face. He tried bravely to rise, but was unable to beat the count and needed several minutes on his stool to recover fully.

The story had begun in Aylesbury, an ancient market town in Buckinghamshire more famous for ducks than boxers. Here Craig was born, but when he was eight his parents split up and he and his mother moved to Wales, soon to be joined by her parents. And his grandfather, who had boxed in the Army, introduced him to the sport.

When he was 12, his reluctant mother finally allowed him to join nearby Denbigh ABC. Three North Wales schools triumphs were followed by a national championship at youth level, but it took Winter three attempts to find success in the senior Welsh ABAs, first losing to Matthew Turner and then to a promising youngster named Joe Calzaghe. In 1993 he went all the way to the British final, only to be knocked out by a future two-time world title challenger in David Starie.

Just turned 23, Craig decided to turn pro under the stewardship of Richard Jones, a Welsh-born schoolteacher based at Warrington, where the new boy travelled to train with Jones and his son, Damian. After a successful debut in Glasgow, he kept busy around the north of England, building a 10-fight winning streak which caught the attention of the powers-that-be, who matched him in a British light-middleweight eliminator with Peter Waudby.

The Hull man was the Central Area champion and could point to the experience of tangling with the likes of future WBO ruler Paul Jones, Kevin Lueshing and Scottish ace Willie Quinn. He had lost to all three, but he did have home advantage at a Humberside hotel.

Not that it seemed to matter as Winter decked the local briefly in the second, only for Waudby to respond with attacks to the body. Craig was still ahead going into the fifth, but a moment's lapse in concentration cost him the fight. His left hand dropped momentarily, allowing Paul to land a right which sent the Welshman crashing. And that was not the worst of it: when he rose, blood was pouring from a gash above the left eye. Referee John Keane took one look and called a halt.

Waudby was given the chance to become Hull's first British champion, but was blitzed inside two minutes by Ryan Rhodes. Winter, on the other hand, became the figurehead of a North Wales boxing revival. His next five outings were all on Deeside, four on John Davies promotions at the Springfield Hotel in Pentre Halkyn and the other on a Frank Maloney bill at Queensferry. All five ended with Craig's arm being raised, with seasoned campaigners Jimmy Vincent, who floored him, and Jason Barker among his victims.

Winter, now living in Rhyl, had been patiently waiting for Welsh light-middle king Barry Thorogood to return from a lay-off and the Welsh Area Council, having allowed the Cardiffian a few warm-up fights, put the clash out to purse offers. Promoter Davies submitted the only bid, but Barry, unhappy with the money involved, pulled out. The authority, drained of patience, suspended him and stripped him of the belt.

By now Winter was being looked after by Bristol-based Chris Sanigar, who duly put on the up-and-downer with Samuels for the vacant title. But following that shattering defeat, Craig vanished from the scene for nearly four years.

He re-emerged in front of a Sunday afternoon full house at the Marina in Rhyl and almost found himself in the awkward situation of being refereed by his former manager. The show's designated official, Roddy Evans, was stuck in traffic on his way from Pontypool and Richard Jones, now secretary of the Central Area, took charge of the opening bout. Luckily, Mr Evans arrived in time to handle Winter's action and gave him all six rounds against Worcester traveller Harry Butler.

It was to be Craig's last action in the ring, at least under the auspices of the Board of Control. Out-of-the-ring problems and general disillusionment with the fight business, coupled by a decent income from a nightclub security business, led him to drift away.

The bug was still biting, however, and Winter returned on the unlicensed scene, campaigning into his early forties, and then training youngsters and promoting the occasional show. Now the wheel has turned full circle. Not only has Craig moved back to the Denbigh area, but he has taken out a Board licence as a trainer. Covid has, inevitably, interfered with his plans, but he hopes to see a few of his pupils turning pro before long.

SUPPORTING CAST

The champions and challengers who feature in the preceding pages are far from the only people to make noteworthy contributions to our fistic history. As ever in these books, here we take the opportunity to namecheck a few others.

One of the biggest names in British boxing in the 1960s was Alan Rudkin, who took on three all-time greats on three different continents for the world bantamweight crown. Rudkin, who faced Japan's Fighting Harada and Aussie Lionel Rose in their homelands and Mexican legend Rubén Olivares in the US, was as Scouse as they come. Yet he was born in Corwen.

His mother was among many to be evacuated from Merseyside to avoid the Blitz and young Alan first saw the light of day in 1941 in the shadow of the Berwyn mountains. Ironically, he was to return 21 years later for his last contest as an amateur, representing England against Wales at the town's Pavilion. Rudkin had already signed a pro contract and made his debut at Liverpool Stadium just 12 days later.

There were others who found fame over the border, but had Welsh connections. Les McAteer, the Birkenhead man who won British and Commonwealth middleweight honours in 1969, had worn the vest of Buckley ABC to the Welsh ABA title six years earlier while working at Gresford Colliery.

Another to win British and Commonwealth belts, this time at super-feather, was Burnley-born, Carlisle-based Charlie Shepherd. His father once ran a chippy at Penygroes and 15-year-old Charlie joined Bangor ABC to shed a few pounds acquired by over-enthusiastic consumption of the shop's wares. Within a year he was a Welsh schools champion and actually represented his temporary homeland against the country of his birth.

Some would-be boxers found sporting fame in other arenas. Ian Woosnam, the little giant from Llanymynech, dreamed of being a star of the ring, but was persuaded that he was too small. So he turned to golf and went on to win the US Masters in 1991 – the first Welshman to succeed at one of the "majors".

When 11-year-old Michael Owen, from Hawarden, had a couple of amateur bouts in the vest of Shotton ABC, nobody took much notice. Each time he outpointed a future pro from Llanrug, Kenny Griffith, but suffered a broken nose which prompted him to focus on football. Just seven years later he scored an outstanding individual goal for England against

Three-time world title challenger Alan Rudkin was born at Corwen

Argentina at the World Cup and was chosen as the BBC Sports Personality of the Year.

Rugby was to benefit when Bancyfelin boy Mike Phillips decided to take sparring sessions with big brother Mark no further. While Mark went on to have 69 fights as a pro, scrum-half Mike represented both Wales and the British and Irish Lions. As with Woosnam and Owen, nobody could say he made the wrong choice.

Others attempted to mix their sports. One notable example was Brecon-born Welsh international centre-forward Tom Hoddinott, whose many clubs included Chelsea. He confined most of his pugilistic activity to charity shows, but usually proved the winner; perhaps if he had taken the ring seriously, he might have beaten former Sheffield United footballer Curtis Woodhouse to a Lonsdale Belt by 80-odd years.

Boxing has often been a family affair, but few could boast the achievements of the Pritchard brothers of Ynys Môn. Ned won no fewer than eight Welsh ABA titles in three weight classes – the last as part of a comeback after breaking both legs in a show-jumping accident. Eifion reached an incredible 10 finals, all at lightweight, winning four of them. Throw in the middleweight success of another sibling, John, and you have a tally to be proud of.

There are also those family connections which cross boundaries. Tenby-born painter Augustus John was a regular ringsider in the heyday of the National Sporting Club and his son Edwin fought professionally as a middleweight. Himself a dab hand with brush and easel, Edwin attracted sizeable crowds to Croydon Stadium in the early 1930s, his Bohemian followers providing a colourful contrast to the usual ringside roughnecks.

Aaron Thomas, son of Wrexham football legend Mickey, boxed for Wales at the Commonwealth Games and had a brief four-win pro career before outside events brought it to a premature close.

Alternatively, former fighters have spawned sons who attained success beyond the sporting world, a trend that seems particularly prevalent in the Amman Valley. Rhys Davies was a useful amateur heavyweight in the 1930s; his son, John Rhys Davies, appeared in *Indiana Jones* and the *Lord of the Rings* movies. Don Chiswell, whose pro career spanned World War II, is the father of Welsh-language singer-songwriter Huw, one of whose best-loved works, *Cân Joe*, is about an ex-boxer suffering the mental scars of his former profession.

In politics we have Plaid Cymru leader Adam Price, whose old man, Rufus, took two Welsh ABA titles back to Ammanford before enjoying a brief pro career as Gary Price (He was managed by Dickie Maxwell, the father of singer Dickie Valentine). In fact, Adam is not the only Senedd member who can point to some paternal pugilism. Tim Davies, father of the former head of the Welsh Conservatives,

Michael Owen boxed for Shotton as a schoolboy

Ten-time Welsh ABA finalist Eifion Pritchard, from a famous fighting family

Edwin John, son of painter Augustus

Paul, was a regular on Ron Taylor's booth and held a Board licence in the 1950s.

Those left inside the ropes when the bell rings rightly attract the bulk of public praise, but there are others whose roles are essential to the sport's existence. Managers, for example.

The outstanding figure was Johnny Vaughan, whose own career as a featherweight – he was a Welsh title claimant in the unregulated years before World War I – was ended by ill-health. He became a trainer and ended up as something of a one-man fight industry on his own patch, where he produced a string of champions from his gym in an outbuilding at the Cross Inn, on the square at Ammanford, also staging shows in the courtyard outside. In 1929 he spent a princely £80 to erect a pavilion on the site.

At one time, he had four reigning Welsh titleholders in his stable. In fact, it could have been five had Randy Jones not been dethroned just eight days before Bobby Morgan won the flyweight crown. Johnny died in 1964, a year that also saw the demolition of the old Cross Inn.

Vaughan's record was matched in 1952 by Eddie Evans, a collier from Ystradgynlais, although Johnny always pointed out that he had trained his boys from scratch, whereas three of Evans's men had been contenders before signing with him.

Referees may not always be popular, but they are essential to the proceedings. The north has produced a couple of note. Billy Jones, from Connah's Quay, handled a string of British and Commonwealth title fights in the 1960s, while Phil Edwards went a step further in 2017: when Anthony Joshua defended his world heavyweight belts against Carlos Takam at the Principality Stadium, the third man was announced as from Preston, where he lives. In fact, Edwards was born and bred in Bangor and was particularly proud to be selected for the bout in his nation's capital.

Bangor-born referee Phil Edwards keeps an eye on Joshua and Takam

Others have contributed less directly to the sport. The Dennie Mancini Trophy, presented at the Board awards dinner each year, was designed by Pembrokeshire-based Tanya Petersen, whose husband, Gideon, is a grandson of former British heavyweight king Jack. Tanya was also responsible for the panels that adorn the Howard Winstone statue in Merthyr.

Llangefni was at one time home to a renowned boxing museum, where local butcher Glyn Jones displayed his collection of memorabilia, including signed gloves and shorts from Britain and the US. Glyn described it as "the finest collection of its kind in the world" and he probably wasn't far wrong.

A North Wales beauty spot played its part in one of the greatest upsets in British boxing history. Gwrych Castle, at Abergele, is now known as the venue for TV extravaganza *I'm a Celebrity ... Get Me Out of Here!* But it first attracted attention in 1951 when Randy Turpin trained there before his earth-shaking world middleweight title win over the incomparable Sugar Ray Robinson. The castle belonged to his business partner, Leslie Salts, who also owned a complex at the summit of the Great Orme, along the coast at Llandudno, which included Randy's Bar, dedicated to the champion.

Randy Turpin trains at Gwrych Castle before fighting Sugar Ray Robinson

A small West Wales club had its moment in the sun, too. When the powers-that-be recognised female amateur boxers, the first show in Britain to involve them, in 1997, was promoted by Whitland ABC, with television cameras in attendance as Marie Leafe outpointed Marie Davies in a contest between 16-year-old friends.

Keeping Faith actress Eve Myles is a keen fight fan and once fancied taking an active part herself. But she abandoned the idea after breaking a knuckle punching a wet sandbag. One who went in the opposite direction was Rhyl heavyweight Spencer Wilding, a former martial artist who had a brief – and unbeaten – pro career in 2002. He went on to appear in films, although few would have recognised him. The 6ft 7in Welshman's CV included, among others, roles as the monster in *Victor Frankenstein*, with Daniel Radcliffe, and behind the mask of Darth Vader in *Star Wars: Rogue One*.

Actress Eve Myles had ambitions to box

Boxing has always attracted fans from all ranks of society. One of the keenest supporters of the 19th-century prizefighting scene was Robert Ricketts Evans, who grew up at Fern Hill, the farm immortalised by Dylan Thomas. He was better known throughout the area as "Evans the Hangman" and sent many a man – and woman – to meet their maker, including one might assume, some of the bare-knuckle brawlers he had cheered in the ring.

BIBLIOGRAPHY

The following are among many publications consulted during the writing of this book:

Sporting Life, Mirror of Life, Boxing, Boxing News, Boxing Monthly, Western Mail, South Wales Echo, South Wales Daily News, South Wales Evening Post, South Wales Guardian, Western Telegraph, Liverpool Daily Post.

Wales and its Boxers, ed. Peter Stead and Gareth Williams (University of Wales)

All in my Corner, by Tony Lee (TL Associates)

Born to Box: The Extraordinary Story of Nipper Pat Daly, by Alex Daley (Pitch Publishing)

Sweet Fighting Man, Vol II, by Melanie Lloyd (Sweet Touch)

The following websites and their contributors were also useful sources of information:

Boxrec.com, Welsh Warriors, www.boxinghistory.org.uk, Amateur Boxing Results, Ancestry, Find My Past, Facebook.

St David's Press

THE BOXERS OF WALES
CARDIFF

'Some of the greatest boxers in Britain have come out of Cardiff and this book is a must read for fight fans, whether you're Welsh or not.'
Colin Hart, The Sun

'This book is not just about the famous fighters, it's about the forgotten heroes.'
Steve Bunce, Boxing Broadcaster & Journalist

'A compelling and fascinating study.'
Claude Abrams, Editor, Boxing News

'Boxing fans in and out of Wales will love this collection of mini biographies profiling no less than 50 classic boxers from the Cardiff area...An indispensable guide to Cardiff boxers and a great resource for compiling those pub quizzes!'
South Wales Argus

'...a long overdue reminder of how much Cardiff has given to boxing. The verdict? A knockout.
Dan O'Neill, South Wales Echo

978-1-902719-26-9   160pp   £14.99 PB

THE BOXERS OF WALES
MERTHYR
ABERDARE & PONTYPRIDD

'masterpiece... a must-read for any boxing fan...Compelling stuff.'
Steve Lillis, News of the World

'The Valleys of South Wales have produced many fighters known worldwide ... but this book reminds us that there were others who lit up the ring in their day.'
Gareth A. Davies, Daily Telegraph

'For generations of Merthyr's youth, boxing has been as much a means of self-expression as a way out of grinding poverty. This book does full justice to a sporting tradition that has shaped the town's character and given the world some unforgettable champions.'
Mario Basini

978-1-902719-29-0   160pp   £14.99 PB

THE BOXERS OF WALES
RHONDDA
Second Edition

'When Boxing News marked its centenary in 2009 by choosing the best British boxer of the previous 100 years, we opted for the one and only Jimmy Wilde. But the Rhondda produced many other outstanding fighters, as this book reminds us.'
Tris Dixon, Editor, Boxing News

'When it comes to in-depth research, they don't come much better than Gareth Jones - as his latest tome perfectly illustrates, with a trawl through the Rhondda's staggering boxing history. The likes of the great Tommy Farr and Jimmy Wilde get the Jones treatment, along with a host of tales surrounding so many boxers from this mining area that produced such a rich seam of boxing greats.'
Kevin Francis, Boxing Correspondent, Daily Star

978-1-902719-95-5   172pp   £19.99 PB
978-1-902719-96-2   172pp   £19.99 EBK

St David's Press

THE BOXERS OF WALES
SWANSEA & LLANELLI

'My co-commentator, Enzo Maccarinelli, keeps telling me what a great fight town Swansea is. And here's the evidence. It's not just about the big names, like Colin Jones, Ronnie James and the Curvises - here you can learn of the only Welsh-speaker ever to win a Scottish title and the Llanelli girl who took on Germany's boxing queen. A great read!'
John Rawling, Commentator, BoxNation

'Wales has a rich boxing history and there is no one better than Gareth Jones at bringing vividly to life the exploits of the many fine Welsh fighters, from the famous to the largely forgotten. This book is a must for all serious boxing fans.'
Graham Houston, Editor, Boxing Monthly

978-1-902719-450   176pp   £14.99 PB

THE BOXERS OF WALES
NEWPORT
THE GWENT VALLEYS AND MONMOUTHSHIRE

'If you want to learn more about some of the finest fighters to appear on Sky Sports - Regan, Rees, Cleverly and the man I consider Britain's best boxer since the war, Joe Calzaghe - this book has the answers. And it's not just the stars. There is also plenty about fighters you may have forgotten - or never knew existed.'
Adam Smith, Head of Boxing, Sky Sports

'Gareth Jones is THE authority on Welsh boxing, and always a joy to read. His exhaustive research uncovers wonderful stories that should not be missed.'
Matt Christie, Editor, Boxing News

'Nobody knows Welsh boxing with quite the depth, understanding and empathy of Gareth Jones. This time he profiles not merely the area's four world champions and the likes of Dick Richardson, Steve Sims and the gloriously named Johnny Basham. This engaging volume also stretches back to the bare-knuckle era to chronicle the deeds of Morgan Crowther, who drank and gambled around Newport, fought enthusiastically, and after several visits to police cells in the vicinity, became that rare beast, a respected bookmaker.'
Kevin Mitchell, The Observer

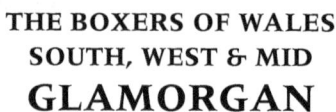

978-1-902719-634   192pp   £14.99 PB

THE BOXERS OF WALES
SOUTH, WEST & MID
GLAMORGAN

'The Selby boys are here. Amateur glory, world title, so much talent. But once again it is a fighter that only the purest of fans can recall who catches the eye. This time it is Wee Willie Davies, a world-class flyweight, born near Maesteg, who moved to America as a child and met nine world champions. Welsh boxing, British boxing and even world boxing owes Gareth a great debt.'
Steve Bunce

978-1-902719-801   176pp   £16.99 PB

Lightning Source UK Ltd.
Milton Keynes UK
UKHW032248311021
393171UK00008B/133